ZITA

ZITA

Empress of Austria and Queen of Hungary

CHARLES A. COULOMBE

TAN Books
Gastonia, North Carolina

Cover design by Jordan Avery

Front cover image: *Zita of Bourbon Parma (1892–1989) wife of austrian emperor Charles of Habsburg official portrait the day of her wedding in 1911*. Collection Gregoire / Bridgeman Images

Back cover image: *Charles of Austria-Este and Zita of Bourbon-Parma*, Carl Pietzner (1853–1927), 1911, Photograph. Wikimedia Commons.

ISBN: 978-1-5051-2730-0
Kindle ISBN: 978-1-5051-2731-7
ePUB ISBN: 978-1-5051-2732-4

Published in the United States by
TAN Books
PO Box 269
Gastonia, NC 28053

www.TANBooks.com

Printed in the United States of America

To His Imperial and Royal Highness the Archduke Karl and all the living members of the House of Habsburg, in whom reside the hopes that Zita so deeply cherished.

"Charles Coulombe has written a new biography of my grandmother, Empress Zita. This is very appropriate, as through the opening of her cause of Canonization the interest in her will grow in the next years. It seems that there is much love for Blessed Emperor Karl in the English-speaking world, and it is to be hoped that this erudite, well written biography of Zita will enable many to get to know better the long, moving, and moved life of Karl's wife, the last Empress of Austria."

—Karl von Habsburg

CONTENTS

ACKNOWLEDGEMENTS

This writer is indebted to the contributions of many other authors and speakers who have dedicated their work to the goal of preserving and promoting the rich Austro-Hungarian history, especially as it relates to the last royal couple, Charles and Zita. Of particular note is the work of Elisabeth Kovács, an Austrian historian, who wrote two volumes on Charles's life. These volumes were originally published in German as *Untergang oder Rettung der Donaumonarchie?* Her work is used, in varying degrees, to fill in many of the details of chapters 7 through 10 within this manuscript. For example, chapter 24 of Kovács's first volume is heavily relied upon for content of chapter 9 within this manuscript. Kovács's books were also a great source for quotes from the likes of Zita, Charles, and many other prominent historical figures. This writer is indebted to the Order of the Golden Fleece, which has been generous in granting permission to use Kovács's work for this purpose.

INTRODUCTION

Once more, this writer finds himself with his readers in the half-enchanted, half-doomed land of Austria-Hungary at the end of the nineteenth century. The last time we visited this legend-haunted time and place of Strauss waltzes, picturesque folklore, Ruritanian intrigue, and—most important for our purposes—deep and age-old piety, it was to explore the life and times of Blessed Charles of the House of Habsburg. Emperor of Austria, Apostolic King of Hungary, King of Bohemia, Dalmatia, Croatia, Slavonia, Galicia and Lodomeria, Illyria, Jerusalem, Grand Prince of Transylvania, Grand Voivode of Serbia, and duke or count of dozens of other places—forty-two titles in all. In the last book, *Blessed Charles of Austria*, we explored the venerable tradition that Blessed Charles inherited from his fathers, bound up with the very roots of our Western civilization: Greek philosophy, Roman legal and imperial tradition (the latter going back in some ways to the Persians), and the Catholic Faith. We saw his birth to a younger member of the family, his becoming heir to the throne through a series of unlikely (and occasionally tragic) events, his marriage to Zita and the start of their family, and his ascension to the throne at the direst point in his family's dramatic history—World War I. At the same time, we witnessed the growth of his deep Catholic Faith, shared by his wife, which would sustain them both through the loss of his beloved uncle and mentor, Franz Ferdinand, their ascension to power, and the betrayal on all sides that would hound them until his untimely death in Madeira in 1922. To some degree, we then followed Zita's adventures and those of her children, culminating in her death in 1989, Charles's beatification in 2004, the passing of their oldest son, Otto, in 2012, and their religious and political legacy since.

In an age when westerners have seen an almost total failure of leadership, the story of a couple who combined their aspiration for holiness with heroism cannot help but inspire fascination in a public who hungers for such traits in those who govern them. As of this writing, there are now twenty-five shrines to Bl. Charles in the United States—ironically, the country most responsible for his fall (a terrible tragedy not just for him, his family, and his people, but for all of us, if we accept Winston Churchill's attribution of the cause of Hitler's rise to Bl. Charles's deposition). Thus, this writer was happy to oblige when asked to write a companion biography of Zita, Bl. Charles's helpmate in good times and bad.

But it is, in several ways, a rather more challenging assignment. While her husband has been beatified—and the second miracle through his intercession required for canonization has been approved by the requisite authorities—Zita is, at present, a servant of God. This means that her cause has been introduced, material about her is being gathered, and miracles wrought through her intercession are being sought. But there is no assurance by the Church of anything, save that a sufficient number of people believe in her sanctity to warrant an investigation into the possibility. In a word, the book is open, and Catholics are free to believe or not in her current Heavenly position. It is not up to this writer to make that determination but to provide enough facts for his readers to look into the case further and decide for themselves, while awaiting the final decision by Rome.

The second factor is that she lived a lot longer than her husband and entirely without the support and counsel he would have given her had he lived. She found herself alone in the world, not only with eight children to provide for but a cause she considered greater than herself to keep afloat—that of the House of Habsburg. It was a daunting task and required a great deal of fortitude on her part—toward herself and those around her. Thus, she left behind a great many memories, both positive and negative, among those who knew her. Not having had that privilege himself, this writer must make sense of the sometimes contradictory impressions that Zita left on those who did know her.

Being fallen creatures, the personal, familial, and national histories of human beings are filled with these sorts of paradoxes. While those of us who are outside these occurrences may have some insights that the actual participants lacked, it is also true that we cannot know the actual circumstances as well as those who were there to experience them. This truth must haunt every historian in every case; it certainly haunts this writer now. All one can try to do is to present the truth as well as he can, and so it falls to us in this particular case.

On a minor level, having written a book about Bl. Charles, which also subsequently dealt with Zita's life, it will be impossible not to repeat certain things already written. However, while reading *Blessed Charles of Austria* would be a good preparation for this book, we shall endeavor to tell a story that shall stand alone.

There is one last point to make. On April 1, 2022, this writer had the immense privilege of being present at Madeira for the centennial of Bl. Charles's death. It was a wonderful occasion that shall last forever in his memory. But the site of the Blessed Emperor's shrine church itself, as it would have been a century before, was chilly, foggy, and wet—a huge contrast to the warm and sunny town of Funchal directly below. Remembering how weak Bl. Charles's lungs had been (he had survived the pandemic of 1918 but was left with severe respiratory damage), I had a sudden rush of horrified sympathy for the poor woman who had struggled so hard to keep her husband alive in such a terrible situation.

With all of this in mind, we shall do our best to unlock the story of Servant of God Zita, Empress of Austria, Queen of Hungary, and consort to each of her husband's other titles. We shall begin by exploring her Bourbon and Braganza inheritance and then tell a tale starting in the Belle Epoque, when, as the 1937 film *The Prisoner of Zenda* assures us, "History still wore a rose, and Politics had not yet outgrown the Waltz," down through the various unfolding horrors unleashed by modernity, and finally, to our own time. It nevertheless will show us that while all else may change, loyalty, family, the aspiration to holiness, and all the contradictions and conflicts these may involve among us poor mortals do not.

Charles A. Coulombe
Trumau, Austria
July 4, 2022
Feast of St. Elizabeth of Portugal

Chapter 1

MANY NATIONS, ONE FAMILY

"Regardless of his personal imperfections, a monarch represents the majesty of history. He is an heir—a link in a chain that leads to the Middle Ages that in turn connects to antiquity and beyond, to the beginning of measured time when the first hero slew the dragon of disorder and established the rule of law."

—Charles Fenyvesi[1]

To truly understand the extraordinary woman born as Zita, Princess of Bourbon-Parma, we have to understand the history that, on the one hand, produced her and, on the other, that she strove ever to be worthy of, even before she married into her future husband's equally venerable Habsburg dynasty. Both the Bourbons (Zita's paternal family) and the Braganzas (her maternal family) boasted lineages and chronicles at least as complex as the Habsburgs could offer. As with her husband's clan, both of these family lines boasted of saints and sinners, peacemakers and warriors, even as all three virtually created the nations over which they ruled. Each of these three Houses is worthy of long volumes on their own, and many such have been produced, but

[1] Charles Fenyvesi, *Splendour in Exile* (New York: New Republic Books 1979), pp. 278–79.

we will give our readers just what is essential to understand Zita. Even so, we must start on her father's side, going very far back in time to a man named Robert the Strong (AD 830–866).

In the chaotic days after Charlemagne's empire was divided among his grandsons, each of their three realms suffered further fragmentation. After the bright, brief promise of the Carolingian Renaissance, when learning, political, and, above all, religious life reached a height unseen in the West for centuries, the greed for more power by the already powerful and the external attacks of the Vikings against the West altered the scene. But all the while, various nobles—some principled and some not—pursued their various aims, peacefully and otherwise, the monasteries and parishes continued to pray, scholars to learn, and farmers to farm. In the midst of this tumult, Count Robert the Strong—at times opposed to, and at other times allied with, Charlemagne's grandson, Charles the Bald, first King of West Francia—made a place for his family and their followers in what is now central France. His son Odo (AD 857–898) succeeded his father at age nine.

Odo grew up under Charles the Bald, who, in turn, later became emperor of the briefly reunited empire. In 882, the same year that Charles died and was succeeded by his sons, Odo was appointed Count of Paris, an originally military title that became hereditary in his descendants. Two years later, when Carloman II of Bavaria (who succeeded Charles the Bald as king of Italy and was the childless son of Louis the Stammerer) died, his cousin, Emperor Charles the Fat, inherited his throne, resulting in the Frankish Empire being reunited for the last time. In 885, as both emperor and count, Charles the Fat would have his mettle supremely tested by the Vikings, who besieged the future French capital of Paris. Starting in late November of that year, Norsemen sailed up the Seine and demanded tribute. Count Odo refused, and thus began—after the repulse of several attempts to storm the walls—a siege that lasted almost a year. When the emperor and his troops finally arrived, Charles bought the Vikings off rather than fight them. This was a huge blow to his prestige, which was crumbling in East Francia and Italy as well as the West; he would be deposed in separate rebellions in 887. The following year, the French nobility took Odo as their king, and from that day to this, France has been independent. However, when Odo died in 898, he was succeeded by another Carolingian, Charles the Simple. The new king, having unwittingly set the stage for innumerable future dramas by allowing the Norse to settle in and rule Normandy, initially got on well with Odo's brother, Robert. Nonetheless, in 922, believing Charles had favored his enemies, Robert led another coalition of nobles against the king. Robert was crowned king at Rheims, but he would fall in battle in 923. Thereafter, the throne went back and forth between his relatives and the Carolingians until 987, when the last of these died, and Hugh Capet, grandson of Robert, became king. His descendants would rule France after him without interruption until 1792 and again from 1814 to 1848, and they would continue to have loyal adherents until today.

It is important to remember that those descendants quite literally made France. First, the direct line produced such luminaries as Robert II, the Pious (whose older son, Henry I, would succeed him and whose younger son, Robert, would be the ancestor of the Dukes of Burgundy and the kings of Portugal), Philip Augustus, and St. Louis IX. The latter two went on crusade, and the last named is commemorated all over the world for combining strength with sanctity. Philip III, the son of St. Louis IX, would have, in turn, several sons: the eldest, Philip IV, would become famous for attacking Pope Boniface VIII and destroying the Knights Templars, and his second son, John Tristan, would found the House of Valois. John Tristan's son would then succeed Philip IV's childless heir.

The Valois, having succeeded the extinct main line of the House of Capet, would go on to produce some great luminaries of their own. When the son of Charles the Bald became King Philip VI of France in 1328, he started the French eastward expansion by securing the heirship of the Province of Dauphine (named after its ruler's title) for his own eldest son and future king. From that time on, the successor to the French was the Dauphin, just as the heir to the British throne is the Prince of Wales. Intermarriage with the kings of England eventually led to the inheritance struggle between the French and English monarchs called the Hundred Years' War, conclusively resolved in favor of the Valois by heavenly intervention under St. Joan of Arc. The sixteenth century saw disasters fall upon the royal house. Francis I, king during the French Renaissance, unsuccessfully struggled against both England's Henry VIII and the Habsburg Charles V for the position of Holy Roman Emperor. This began a series of conflicts between Francis I and the victorious Charles V, which did not do them any good, and which saw Francis I ally Catholic France with the Muslim Turks against fellow Christians. Francis I's son, Henry II, would die as a result of a jousting accident, and all three of Henry II's sons would succeed him in turn, each dying childless. The eldest, Francis II, who was the first husband of Mary Queen of Scots, died early. Following his death, Mary returned to her homeland, where terrible events awaited her. His brother, Charles IX, who also died young, was under the thumb of their mother, Catherine de' Medici. The youngest then succeeded the throne, having already been briefly King of Poland, as Henry III.

The Protestant revolt's local version in France had already unleashed the terrible Wars of Religion; the last of these would be called the War of the Three Henries, as its protagonists were King Henry III; his distant cousin, Henry de Bourbon, leader of the Huguenot or Protestant party; and Henry Duke of Guise. The third was murdered by bodyguards of the first in 1588, and King Henry III was himself murdered by one of Guise's followers a year later. Henry de Bourbon abjured the Protestant religion and became king of a ruined country in 1589.

The House of Bourbon, as we know it, dates back to 1270, when St. Louis IX's sixth son, Robert, Count of Clermont, married the heiress Beatrix of Bourbon. Her family, rulers of the province of Bourbonnais, date back to 913. After a little over three centuries, this obscure branch of the Capets had outlasted all the others—save their distant cousins in Portugal, who had already had one break in their legitimate line and would shortly suffer another one (as we shall see). Along the way, the Bourbons had acquired the Kingdom of Navarre but, shortly after, lost most of it to the newly united Kingdoms of Castile and Aragon. But despite the terrible damage done to France by the wars of religion and the immense amount of rebuilding that would be required, the monarchy inherited by Henry IV, King of France and Navarre (as we must now call him), was the second greatest in Europe.

As with the other Catholic monarchies, the kings of France had important spiritual duties. If the Holy Roman Emperor was made a canon of St. Peter's at his coronation, the King of France was, in his turn, by right, a canon of St. John Lateran. While the Holy Roman Emperor could serve as a deacon at papal Masses in St. Peter's, the King of France could serve as a subdeacon at papal Masses in St. John Lateran. While the Holy Roman Emperor's subjects might suspect their sovereign of having some sort of control over the weather—and so dubbed a pleasant day *Kaiserswetter* (emperor's weather)—the French kings, at least since the time of St. Louis IX, were believed to have the ability to cure the disease of scrofula—for this reason called "king's evil"—by touching the infected. Both the Holy Roman Emperor and the kings of France were successors of Charlemagne, and for this reason, the lists of both sovereigns began with Charles I. As a token of this, when the kings of France died, their funeral shrouds would be sent to Aachen for a second funeral to be conducted by the canons of the cathedral, who had custody of Charlemagne's shrine. Both monarchs were girded with swords believed to have been owned by the great emperor at their respective coronations. In truth, the Holy Roman Emperor was crowned at Rome by the pope with the crown of Charlemagne, but when crowned at Rheims, the King of France was anointed with the Sacred Chrism, which was supposedly brought by the Holy Ghost from heaven for the baptism of Clovis in 496—an event seen as the beginning of the Christian Frankish realm. Since France claimed the Franks—who were the first barbarian tribe to convert to orthodox Catholicism (as opposed to the Arian beliefs of the Goths and Vandals)—as its forebears, the country became known as the oldest daughter of the Church, and her king as that communion's oldest son. Moreover, the saintly Frankish queens—such as Sts. Clotilde, Radegonde, Bathilde, and the rest, each of whom founded monasteries and nurtured the Church while their husbands were often too busy to do so—were held to have passed on some of their deep but combative holiness to their French successors. The Habsburgs had their renowned and venerable *Pietas Austriaca* (Austrian piety) as their own unique method of practicing Catholicism, but the Bourbons inherited from their Capet and Valois ancestors the *religion royale* (the royal religion). Henry and his successors would use it both to try to save their own souls and to inspire their subjects to help them rebuild and expand the shattered nation their ancestors had built together.

So it was that Henry was crowned at Rheims with all the pomp of his forebears. Also like them, he was anointed with the Sacred Chrism of Clovis, supposedly granting him the ability to cure the king's evil in all whom he touched. With his minister, Sully, he began a program of reconstruction for his devastated country, ranging from improving roads to conserving forests. The Edict of Nantes allowed his erstwhile Huguenot co-religionists to basically rule themselves in fortified cities around the kingdom. Henry also promoted France's trade with the rest of the world and supported Samuel de Champlain's expeditions to the New World. In many ways, he was the father of French Canada, the city of Quebec being founded in his reign. Unfortunately, he continued the alliance with the Turks against the Habsburgs that the Valois had initiated. Despite this, Henry's queen, Marie de' Medici, was Habsburg on her mother's side and a very strong woman. When her husband was assassinated in 1610, she was left as regent for her son, the nine-year-old Louis XIII.

Although he was declared of age in 1614, Louis XIII's mother continued to rule the kingdom until, at age seventeen, the young king took power from his mother, sending her away from court and executing her most unpopular assistants. Despite the enmity between the Habsburgs and the French, Louis XIII married the daughter of Philip III of Spain, Anne of Austria—truly one of the most remarkable women of the seventeenth century, although this was not evident at that time, not least because of her mother-in-law's antipathy. When Marie's influence was removed, Anne could breathe a little more freely.

In the meantime, skillfully dealing with various plots against the throne, Louis XIII made use of various able men—most notably Cardinal Richelieu—to form and carry out policy. Huguenot plotting required military repression of their armed fortress-cities, although they retained toleration. But all of this meant that Louis had little time for his queen. Four miscarriages over twenty years did not help, neither did the rift that developed between her and Cardinal Richelieu over both personal issues and the cardinal's opposition to the

Catholic side in the German Thirty Years' War. The latter tension started with support for the Swedes and culminated in outright French intervention. Worse yet, in 1635, war broke out between Spain and France, putting the queen in an almost impossible position. Two years later, Richelieu made her a virtual prisoner, but heaven came to her rescue.

Anne was extremely devout, receiving this by way of her parents, to whom she had been quite close. This piety stood her well during the various ups and downs of her married life. After two barren decades, Louis XIII vowed to the Blessed Virgin that he would consecrate his kingdom to her if only she would give him an heir, and his dutiful queen most certainly added her prayers to his. Louis XIII was as good as his word. Dom Gueranger describes the event in his coverage of the feast of the Assumption in his *Liturgical Year*:

> In all the churches of France there takes place today the solemn procession which was instituted in memory of the vow whereby Louis XIII dedicated the most Christian Kingdom to the Blessed Virgin.
>
> By letters given at Saint-Germain-en-Laye, February 10, 1638, the pious king consecrated to Mary his person, his kingdom, his crown, and his people. Then he continued: "We command the Archbishop of Paris to make a commemoration every year, on the Feast of the Assumption, of this decree at the High Mass in his cathedral; and after Vespers on the said day let there be a procession in the said church, at which the royal associations and the corporation shall assist, with the same ceremonies as in the most solemn processions. We wish

the same to be done also in all churches, whether parochial or monastic, in the said town and its suburbs, and in all the towns, hamlets, and villages of the said diocese of Paris. Moreover, we exhort and command all the archbishops and bishops of our kingdom to have Mass solemnly celebrated in their cathedrals and in all churches in their dioceses; and we wish the Parliaments and other royal associations and the principal municipal officers to be present at the ceremony. We exhort the said archbishops and bishops to admonish all our people to have a special devotion to the holy Virgin, and on this day to implore her protection, so that our Kingdom may be guarded by so powerful a patroness from all attacks of its enemies, and may enjoy good and lasting peace; and that God may be so well served and honoured therein, that both we and our subjects may be enabled happily to attain the end for which we were created; for such is our pleasure!"

Thus was France again proclaimed Mary's kingdom. Within a month after the first celebration of the feast, according to the royal prescriptions, the Queen, after twenty years' barrenness, gave birth on September 5, 1638, to Louis XIV. This prince also consecrated his crown and sceptre to Mary. The Assumption, then, will always be the national feast of France, except for those of her sons who celebrate the anniversaries of revolutions and assassinations.[2]

---

[2] Prosper Gueranger, *The Liturgical Year*, vol. 4, *Time after Pentecost* (1901), pp. 418–19.

The birth of Louis XIV was followed two years later by a brother, Philippe d'Orleans, who is the progenitor of today's House of Bourbon-Orleans. This custom of consecrating their country to the Blessed Virgin Mary has continued to this day and is why the French, French Canadians, and French Acadians in Louisiana celebrate the Assumption as a holiday.

In 1643, Louis XIII died, and Anne became regent for their four-year-old son, whom she had crowned at Rheims almost immediately, with all the customary pomp. Appointing Cardinal Mazarin—a one-time protégé of Richelieu's who had switched sides—she would be faced with a rebellion of the higher nobility, called the *Fronde*, which she and her minister would successfully repress. They then turned their attention to improving the kingdom and its daughter in Canada.

Anne bears comparison with her descendant Zita. Both were strong women of deep piety, who were nevertheless forced by historical events to take difficult stands and whose toughness was wondered at by contemporaries and descendants alike. Anne's piety was shown in many ways during her regency. Already, with her husband, she had founded the great Royal Abbey of Val-de-Grace in Paris, which survives today as a hospital. She took her son on tours of their realm, visiting innumerable shrines and abbeys, among which were Sainte Anne d'Apt in Provence, where St. Anne's body is venerated to this day; Notre Dame de Cotignac, also in Provence (where an apparition of St. Joseph in 1660 would lead Louis XIV to consecrate his kingdom to Our Lord's foster father); Sainte Anne d'Auray in Brittany; Notre Dame de Rochefort du Gard in Languedoc; and many others. So devoted was the queen to her name saint that she supported the first shrine at Sainte-Anne-de-Beaupre in Quebec. This, together with her interest in the colony in general, led to the great devotion to St. Anne that characterized Quebec until the Quiet Revolution in the 1960s.

Although her regency ended in 1651, she continued to wield a great deal of influence with her son. The war with Spain ended in 1659, and peace was sealed with a wedding between her niece, Marie-Therese, and her son. Two years later, a son—another Louis—was born to the royal couple, and Anne retired to Val-de-Grace to live a life of monastic piety. Although her son's infidelity from practically the beginning of his marriage caused Anne great pain, she suffered in silence until breast cancer claimed her life five years later. But she had the satisfaction of knowing that she had left her son a strong kingdom.

Louis XIV would reign for seventy-two years and one-hundred-and-one days—thus far, the longest reign of any monarch in recorded history (although Elizabeth II, Queen of the United Kingdom, nearly caught up with him). On the positive side, Louis XIV continued the great program of domestic growth that his grandfather and father had initiated. He built a number of impressive buildings, the greatest of which remains his Palace of Versailles, which would remain the center of the court until the French Revolution. In many ways, Louis XIV was the prototypical Bourbon. For good and ill, his image would hover over his and his brother's descendants until the present day. In his own time, he was the monarch against whom all others set the standard.

The "Sun King's" centralizing internal policy created the foundation of the modern French state (although the Revolution would carry this to its logical extreme by destroying the provinces). His expulsion of those Huguenots who would not immediately convert eliminated a potential fifth column, while chasing away a number of talented individuals to Protestant Europe and the English colonies in America. His foreign policy continued the enmity between France and the Habsburgs; while gaining large territories for France, it also plunged the country into a series of wars that cost far more in blood and treasure than they brought.

One of these wars was the War of Spanish Succession (1701–1714). Louis XIV's brother-in-law, Carlos II of Spain, was somewhat enfeebled mentally and physically (although not nearly so much as later legend would have it) and produced no heirs. Carlos II's older sister, Marie-Therese, had married Louis XIV and produced two boys: Louis, the Grand Dauphin and presumed heir to his father as King of France, and Phillip, whom his father proposed to Carlos II as his heir. But Carlos II's younger sister, Margaret Theresa, had married the Holy Roman Emperor, Leopold I, who had his own two sons—the heir, the future Emperor Joseph I, and his younger son, Archduke Charles. Moreover, the archduke was a Habsburg. Although Carlos II would recognize Philip as his heir, after his death in 1700, war broke out between France and Spain on the one hand and Austria and its allies on the other. When the smoke cleared, Philip was indeed king of Spain and its American and Asian colonies, but Austria retained Spain's Belgian and Italian possessions. Louis XIV lived only another year. As his son and grandson predeceased him, his five-year-old great-grandson became Louis XV.

Philip V, who had married in 1701, became the unquestioned king of Spain in 1714 on the proviso that neither he nor his descendants could sit on both the Spanish and French thrones. By his first wife, Maria Luisa of Savoy, Philip V had one son, Ferdinand, who would survive him. His wife died in February of 1714, but so anxious was Philip V to secure the succession that he remarried in December of that year to Elizabeth Farnese, heiress to the Italian Duchy of Parma. A little over a year later, she presented her new husband with the first of six children: the Infante Carlos. Ever since renouncing Spain's Italian territories in 1714, Philip V had schemed to get them back, and Carlos would be a big part of those schemes.

When Philip V's brother-in-law, the Duke of Parma, died in 1731, the fifteen-year-old Carlos succeeded him. Four years later, when war broke out between Spain and the Habsburgs, Carlos commanded the Spanish troops in Italy and reconquered Naples and Sicily. He was crowned king, becoming the first Bourbon King of the Two Sicilies, as he was already the first Bourbon Duke of Parma. But just as treaties prevented one man from becoming King of both France and Spain, so too with being king of Spain, king of the Two Sicilies, and duke of Parma. Although Parma was temporarily returned to the Habsburgs, the foundation was set for the creation of four separate Bourbon dynasties, descending from Louis XIV, and five in total, if counting the House of Orleans.

In 1744, as part of the War of Austrian Succession, Carlos reconquered Parma, which he gave to his younger brother, Felipe. He, in turn, became the progenitor of the House of Bourbon-Parma and Zita's direct male ancestor. Carlos, meanwhile, as Carlos VII, ruled happily in the Two Sicilies. His father, Philip V of Spain, died in 1746 and was succeeded by Carlos's older half-brother, Ferdinand VI. However, the new king of Spain remained childless, and when he died in 1759, Carlos succeeded him, taking the title of Carlos III of Spain. By the terms of the treaty, his oldest son (also Carlos) became heir to the Spanish throne, while his next son—yet another Ferdinand—was left behind in Naples as king. In time, he would become the father of the House of Bourbon-Two Sicilies. So it is that, when Louis XV died in 1774, the branches of the House of Bourbon were Bourbon-France, Bourbon-Spain, Bourbon-Parma, Bourbon-Two Sicilies, and Bourbon-Orleans (listed in order of seniority).

Louis XV's son had predeceased him, so it was his grandson who succeeded him as Louis XVI. Unlike his grandfather, Louis XVI was extremely moral and devout, and he was deeply in love with his wife, Marie Antoinette. She was, as the Archduchess Maria Antonia, the daughter of the Holy Roman Emperor, Francis I of Lorraine, and his wife, the last Habsburg heiress, Maria Theresa.

It was the failure of the male line of the Habsburgs that led to the War of Austrian Succession, wherein Carlos III had reconquered Parma. But the marriage of Louis XVI and Marie Antoinette in 1756 had signified a diplomatic revolution; henceforth, France, Spain, the Two Sicilies, Parma, and Sardinia were to be allied with the Holy Roman Empire. France's former ally Prussia allied with the Habsburg's once-close British friends. Had this alliance occurred two centuries earlier, the history of the world would have been quite different. But, in any case, this realliance set the stage for the Seven Years' War, which would see France lose her empire in North America and prepare the way for rebellion in Britain's American colonies.

In the meantime, Carlos III, in many ways an able ruler, had imposed the sort of centralizing policies that his great-grandfather Louis XIV had used with France on Spain and its colonies. He had also joined with Louis XV and the other Catholic sovereigns of Europe in forcing the pope to abolish the Jesuits, whom he summarily expelled from his dominions. Both of these moves would bear bad fruit in Spanish America after his time because they ensured an ongoing lack of clerical personnel, and so weakened the missionary Church in the Americas. However, as a personally devout Catholic, Carlos required all of his civil servants to swear belief in the Immaculate Conception of the Blessed Virgin (a hotly debated topic at that time). Moreover, to replace the Jesuits, he financed various other orders and sent St. Junipero Serra and the Franciscans to evangelize California. Carlos is, in fact, the founder of the city of Los Angeles, which boasts a statue of him in its downtown plaza.

By that time, the British colonies in America were engulfed in civil war between the Loyalists, loyal to the Crown and supported by British troops, and the rebels, who were fighting for independence. Louis XVI, having put his country through a crash course of administrative and economic reform, entered the conflict in 1778. His cousin, Carlos III, joined him the following year, thus ensuring the rebels' eventual victory—American Independence. Although this decisive intervention by two Catholic kings eventually forced the newly independent states to end their laws against Catholics (ironic, given the rebels' opposition to the British grant of religious freedom to Catholics in French Canada and the role this played in sparking the American Revolution), it turned George III, who felt deeply betrayed by Louis's and Carlos's actions, against Catholic emancipation in his remaining colonies, as well as in Great Britain and Ireland.

Moreover, their intervention did neither Bourbon cousin much good. Spain had Florida returned to her, having lost it to Britain in 1763, and France got nothing but bankruptcy out of her contribution. When, five years after the war, an Icelandic volcano erupted and destroyed many of the crops in France, there was neither money nor credit to aid the starving. The stage was set for the French Revolution, which would break out in 1789, with horrific consequences for every branch of the House of Bourbon (even the Orleans, who initially supported it in hopes of taking the throne), every other European dynasty, and of course, thousands upon thousands of Europeans.

Louis XVI and his queen would be judicially murdered in 1793; Louis's sister, Elizabeth, would be martyred the following year; their son, Louis XVII, would die of neglect in 1797; Carlos IV, who had succeeded his father in 1788, would be forced by the invading French to abdicate in 1808; and so it went. The rise of Napoleon Bonaparte brought order out of chaos and peace to the Church for a while—and then despotism. It took all of Europe acting in concert to defeat him. The result was the Congress of Vienna and the period called Restoration.

The long road that led the House of Bourbon from the time of Charlemagne to the Congress of Vienna—that storied gathering in the Habsburg capital—was, if anything, even more convoluted for the Portuguese dynasty, the House of Braganza. In the beginning, it was the same path because the Braganzas also descend from Robert II, the Pious, whose younger son, likewise named Robert, was made Duke of Burgundy in 1032. In a sense, they, too, are Capets. Robert's younger grandson, Henry, born in 1066, had two older brothers and, therefore, no prospects in Burgundy. He did, however, have relatives among various Spanish noble houses. When he was twenty years old, his kinsman, Alfonso VI, King of Leon and Castile, sent out a call for volunteer warriors after his army was decimated by the Moors in battle. It turned out to be a fateful trip.

Arriving with a group of French knights in 1087, Henry soon made a name for himself in the never-ending fight with the Moors. Iberia was in the throes of the *Reconquista* that began with Christian resistance after the Muslims conquered most of the Iberian Peninsula in 711. What would later become the major kingdoms of Iberia—Asturias, Leon, Castile, Aragon, Navarre, etc.—emerged from those first small refuges in the north, including Covodonga, where King Pelayo, founder of the Christian Kingdom of Asturias, won a decisive battle against the Moors in 722. Given a strong boost by Charlemagne, the Christian armies had pushed the Moors back considerably when Henry of Burgundy arrived, but much remained to be done. To reward his prowess, Alfonso VI gave him control of the territories between the Minho and Tagus Rivers, an area that would be called the County of Portugal. In 1109, after Alfonso VI's death, Henry declared himself independent. He fixed his residence at the Castle of Guimaraes and started the building of Braga Cathedral, where he would be entombed when he died in 1112, leaving his three-year-old son, Alfonso, to succeed him.

In time, Alfonso proved himself the worthy son of his father—overcoming various difficulties culminating in the battle of San Manuel in 1128, whereby he secured his country's independence, and on July 25, 1139, he delivered a crushing defeat to the Moors at the Battle of Ourique. From that time on, his subjects acclaimed him as the first king of Portugal, a title confirmed by a treaty with the mother state of Leon in 1142. So important is this battle in Portuguese consciousness that the country's coat of arms bears five small cross-shaped shields that represent the five Moorish kings defeated by Alfonso.

Alfonso I of Portugal died in 1185 and was succeeded by his son, Sancho I, who kept pushing ever southward against the Moors, eventually setting up a capital, Coimbra. His troops eventually reached the Algarve, now the southernmost province of the country. His grandson Alfonso III would complete the liberation of the country from the Moors in 1249. As with France, Spain, and most of Europe, Portugal's kings would literally assemble their country.

One king would succeed another in Portugal until King Ferdinand I died in 1383. His widow, who was regent for their young daughter, was Castilian and very unpopular. The result was an uprising that drove out mother and daughter and placed Ferdinand's illegitimate half-brother, Juan, on the throne. As Juan had been Grand Master of the Knightly Order of Aviz when he officially assumed the kingship in 1385, his new dynasty was called the House of Aviz. His son, Duarte I began the Portuguese conquests in Africa when he seized Ceuta in Morocco from the Moors. Duarte I's younger brother, Prince Henry the Navigator, founded the famous school that, in time, would produce such explorers as Vasco da Gama. This continued as the fifteenth century progressed, and more exploration gave way to more colonies and markets along the African coast. Under Manuel I, the characteristic *Manueline* architecture developed, and Brazil was discovered. The reign of John III (1521–1557) saw Portugal become a world power, controlling lands from the East Indies to the Caribbean. But John III's son predeceased him, and so his grandson succeeded him as Sebastian I.

Many of the kings of Portugal had been heroic, and some were literary, but Sebastian I was both. Like Arthur, like Charlemagne, and like Barbarossa, his reign cast a giant shadow in Portuguese history and literature. Extremely devout, the young and handsome king was determined to renew the Crusades, deciding to attack Morocco as being not only close to Portugal but also the headquarters of the slave trade. The result, however, was a disaster. Although the Muslims were severely mauled in battle and both of their senior commanders were killed, so too was Sebastian I and a large part of the Portuguese nobility. Sebastian I passed into legend as one of those sleeping monarchs who shall return when his country needs him. His nearest heir was his great uncle, Cardinal

Henry, who duly became king. Elderly and unable to marry, his death two years later found him and Portugal without heirs. After a short fight with an illegitimate relation, Antonio, Prior of Crato, Philip II of Spain—the Habsburg son of Charles V—became king as the nearest heir.

So it was that, from 1580 to 1640, the Habsburgs, in the persons of Philp II, Philip III, and Philip IV, ruled Portugal as well as their numerous territories. Being ruled by Spain made the Portuguese overseas colonies in the East Indies targets of the rebellious Dutch; nevertheless, under Philip II, there was little resentment toward Habsburg rule. However, under his successors, taxes rose, and there appeared to be little attempt to defend Portugal's own empire. At last, in 1640, the nobility began a revolt and selected the Duke of Braganza, a descendant of an illegitimate son of Alfonso I, to be their king. Nicknamed the Restorer by his subjects, the new king took the name of John IV and ushered in the latest dynasty, the House of Braganza. After he and his allies defeated the Spanish, the new monarch set about reasserting Portugal's independence. Although he lost Malacca and Ceylon to the Dutch, John IV's troops pushed them out of Brazil and Angola. When he died in 1656, he left his son a kingdom that, while still sporadically attacked by the Spanish, was fairly secure.

That son, Alfonso VI, would at last secure Spain's recognition of his realm's independence in 1668. Unfortunately, in that same year of triumph, Alfonso VI was somewhat enfeebled mentally and physically, and he found himself imprisoned by his brother, Peter, who proclaimed himself regent. Alfonso VI's queen, who had her marriage with him annulled, married his brother. When Alfonso VI died at last in 1683, Peter succeeded him as Peter II. Peter II then renewed Portugal's old alliance with England as a counter to Spain.

When Peter II died in 1706, he was succeeded by his son, John V. An extremely devout ruler, John V cultivated a close relationship with the papacy, despite some ups and downs. As marks of favor, different popes had granted various titles to some of Europe's kings: as king of Hungary, the Habsburg Emperor was given the title Apostolic Majesty, while the king of Poland was Orthodox Majesty, and the sovereigns of France and Spain were the Most Christian King and Most Catholic King respectively. The kings of Portugal joined the elevated company when, in 1748, Pope Benedict XIV declared John V and his heirs the title of Most Faithful King. Patron of the arts and builder of palaces, keen diplomat, and skillful colonial administrator, John V's reign is considered an apogee in Portuguese history.

By contrast, his son Joseph's reign saw a great many problems. In 1755, five years after Joseph's accession, Lisbon was hit by a major earthquake that devastated a good piece of the country. Real power fell into the hands of his chief minister, Pombal. A child of the nascent Enlightenment, Pombal was anticlerical—and particularly hated the Jesuits, whom he expelled from the country in 1759. The other major Catholic monarchs of Europe joined in this crusade, which would culminate in the Order's wholesale suppression in 1773.

As Joseph had no sons, his oldest daughter, Maria, succeeded him as Portugal's first reigning queen in 1777. Although she married her uncle—who took the name Peter III—she was queen in her own right. As such, and sharing her grandfather's piety, her first act was to dismiss Pombal. Particularly devoted to the Sacred Heart of Jesus, she had that divine image put on the insignia of the Portuguese Orders of Knighthood and built the first church in the world dedicated to the Sacred Heart—Lisbon's Estrela Basilica. The economy boomed under her careful management, and the first years of her reign were happy. But under the strain produced by the successive deaths of her husband, eldest son, and beloved confessor, the queen's mind gave way; in 1792, she was declared incapable, and her second son, John, became regent for the remainder of her life.

This year, which saw the final overthrow of Louis XVI, was a fateful one for Portugal and all of Europe. When Spain fell under the domination of Napoleonic France in 1800, it would only be a matter of time until Portugal's turn came. In 1807, the Franco-Spanish forces invaded. While the British committed themselves to defend Lisbon and its surrounding hinterland (a defense that would prove successful and spell the beginning of the end for Napoleon in the Iberian peninsula), they could not guarantee their victory. At Britain's advice, the regent, queen, royal family, and court fled to Rio de Janeiro to start a government-in-exile in Brazil. In the year of Napoleon's final defeat, 1815, the regent declared Brazil to be equal in status with the mother country, and he proclaimed his mother to be Queen of the United Kingdom of Portugal, Brazil, and the Algarves. Despite Napoleon's defeat, the Braganzas remained in Brazil for the moment and sent emissaries to represent them at the congress gathered in Vienna.

Chapter 2

MONARCHY, YES–BUT WHAT KIND?

"We have a great work to do together. I am ready, quite ready to undertake it when we want it, from tomorrow, from this evening, from this moment. This is why I want to remain entirely what I am. Reduced today, I will be powerless tomorrow.

It is a matter of nothing less than constituting a deeply troubled society on its new foundations, of ensuring with energy the reign of law, of reviving prosperity within, of contracting lasting alliances abroad, and above all of not being afraid to use force in the service of order and justice."

—Henry V of France[3]

The victors of 1815—Austria, Russia, Prussia, Great Britain, a renewed Bourbon-France, and the other European monarchies—had a daunting task ahead of them: How to repair a continent shattered by over two decades

[3] *L'Union* no. 304, Friday, October 31, 1873, letter from the Count of Chambord to Charles Chesnelong dated "Salzburg, October 27, 1873," p. 1, col. 1.

of war, revolution, class conflict, and militant irreligiosity? Given the innumerable changes in boundaries and countries put in place by Bonaparte and his predecessors ruling Revolutionary France—and the varying amounts of complicity that certain rulers had with him—the great question was how to establish a just and lasting peace that would be social as well as political. How could this restoration, as it was called, be made durable?

There were countless issues facing the congress, from the status of Saxony to the independence (or lack thereof) of the Republic of Genoa. But above all, for both the congress and the thinking members of the European population, there was an overarching issue. Having shed oceans of blood and spent enormous amounts of treasure to put the revolutionary genie back in the bottle, how would Europe and its monarchs keep it there? How did it arise in the first place? Then, and in subsequent decades, various writers and thinkers would ask these two questions. For some, such as Chateaubriand, de Maistre, de Bonald, Haller, Gentz, Cobbett, and Adam Müller, the answer lay in the decay of religious belief that had characterized the eighteenth century and in the centralizing tendencies of the Enlightened despots, which broke down both provincial liberties and the autonomy of mediating institutions in society; an example of which is the guilds that had paradoxically also helped to bring the populace together. For these thinkers, a return to a modern version of the medieval synthesis required a type of monarchy in which the sovereign would simultaneously be free to determine military and foreign policy as he chose, and in domestic affairs, he would respect the rights and privileges of the provinces, guilds, Church, etc. He would rule as well as reign, but limitations on his power would come from traditional institutions rather than the never-ending attempts by a political class to take as much power for themselves as they could. Adherents of these beliefs went by a number of names, but in France and elsewhere, they were called Ultra-Royalists or just Ultras.

These ideas were sanctioned by the sovereigns of Austria, Russia, Prussia, and France. As a result, when Tsar Alexander I convinced Emperor Franz I of Austria and King Frederick William III of Prussia to join him in a Holy Alliance, the first article read,

> Conformably to the words of the Holy Scriptures, which command all men to consider each other as brethren, the Three contracting Monarchs will remain united by the bonds of a true and indissoluble fraternity, and considering each other as fellow countrymen, they will, on all occasions and in all places, lend each other aid and assistance; and, regarding themselves towards their subjects and armies as fathers of families, they will lead them, in the same spirit of fraternity with which they are animated, to protect Religion, Peace, and Justice.[4]

These ideas were even congenial, in spirit anyway, to the Prince Regent of Great Britain (the later George IV), who was a fan of Sir Walter Scott and, on that account, eventually beloved by his Welsh, Scots, and Irish subjects. When

---

4 *Encyclopædia Britannica* (1911),s.v. "Holy Alliance, The."

membership to the Alliance was opened up to all the other rulers of Europe, George gleefully joined as Prince-Regent of Hanover; he could not, however, join as Prince-Regent of Great Britain.

Therein lay a tremendous difficulty. The British monarchy had been, ever since 1688, subjected to Parliament, itself dominated by the same sort of wealthy folk who had stirred up the poor against the monarchy in France back in 1789. As regent in Hanover, the future George IV could form his own foreign policy; however, in Great Britain, he had to follow the dictates of his ministers. Although his foreign minister in 1815, Lord Castlereagh, was sympathetic to the "Congress System," there was simply no way in which Castlereagh and the government he served would accede to the Holy Alliance. As might be expected, for the wealthy bourgeois on the continent, the British monarchy seemed an ideal model: the picturesque forms and ceremonial, as well as the essential social cohesion brought by a monarchical structure, were retained, and so the danger of revolution by the lower classes lessened. But the real power in the state lay with such as themselves.

At this point, we might well mention an institution that played an important if hard to define role in the era we are discussing: Freemasonry. Leaving aside whatever their secret teachings may be, Freemasonry has almost always been antithetical to the Catholic Church. The reason is that the order holds to natural religion, if any, and to "conduct over creed," as the old Masonic saying has it; it doesn't matter what one believes, so long as he is *nice*. As a result, it has little use for revealed religion in the Catholic sense or for the social order developed from it. In Protestant countries, there was little opposition to Masonic ideas on the part of the establishment, to which it was quickly assimilated, such that it became a basic pillar of society in such areas as Scandinavia, the British Empire, Protestant Germany, and the United States. As a result, in the latter, Masonry prides itself on being a major force behind the American Revolution, whereas in Canada and Britain, it is equally able to boast of its loyalty to the Crown in that and all subsequent conflicts. But in countries where Catholicism was the essential binding force of society, Masonry, of necessity, became a subversive influence, hoping to break the monopoly of the Church on religion and to reduce the role of the monarch to the status of the King of Great Britain or else to eliminate him altogether. On the one hand, these ideas would attract many of the wealthiest and most influential men, especially of the would-be oligarchical variety. On the other hand, the Ultras and their allies throughout Europe and Latin America would see Freemasonry as their ultimate foe, which in the light of subsequent results, does not seem unreasonable. Certainly, Zita would come to see it that way.

During this era, Romanticism was dominant. This poetic and artistic reaction to the bloodshed caused by the Age of Reason had benefits and dangers for both types of monarchy. As to the benefits, neomedievalism played a big role in the Romantic Revolt. Also, it is no coincidence that the counterrevolutionary writers earlier mentioned were all, more or less, to be considered members, and the Holy Alliance was considered an expression of it. This element of the movement called for a return to the Faith that once had bound society and the entirety of Europe together. However, by the same token, another element called for a revival of the various nationalities. To a point, Romantic Nationalism was constructive and inspired scholars to delve into the forgotten folklore of the European peoples. Alternatively, it could also arouse hatred of the other in the breasts of those who imbibed it—a danger for the independence of the various Italian and German monarchs, as well as a recipe for disaster for multinational states. Yet a third current within Romanticism exalted the individual to the point of exalting the rebel purely for his rebellion, regardless of what it might be about.

In the immediate, these two kinds of monarchism—conservative and liberal (or British)—could cooperate so long as memories of the Revolution and Bonaparte were fresh. Regardless, the struggle between them would grow to engulf all of western and much of central Europe. It would also create the milieu that produced the future Empress Zita and, in many ways, affected her political outlook. This background would not only define her worldview, but it would also contribute heavily to making her the perfect spouse for her future husband.

Initially, the Congress System, which featured the representatives of the major powers gathering every few years to ensure the continued repression of revolutionary movements, worked well. However, the gulf between Britain and the other powers was growing. In 1820, a revolution broke out in the Bourbon-ruled Kingdom of the Two Sicilies, and the following year, the powers authorized its suppression at the Congress of Laibach. In the meantime, however, the revolutions that had swept Latin America as a result of the occupation of Spain by the French were supported by the British. Although two-thirds of the "Spanish" troops then employed in fighting the revolutionaries were born in the American viceroyalties, Britain opposed Spanish America's government troops being reinforced.

The attempt by Spain's king, Ferdinand VII, to reinforce his American soldiers led to a revolution in 1821 in which he was forced to grant a constitution by the liberals—who in Spain owed their origins as a party to being one of the groups fighting Bonaparte's occupation. At the Congress of Verona the following year, Austria, Russia, and Prussia backed France in sending an army of one hundred thousand into Spain to suppress the revolt, which it did successfully. However, the British refused their consent, which destroyed their alliance with the conservative powers. From this time on, the British government would support liberal revolutionaries throughout Europe, although sometimes they would grant refuge to their victims.

In France, the newly restored Louis XVIII, brother of the martyred (in the opinion of Pope Pius VI) Louis XVI, attempted to balance the appearance of a restored monarchy with the reality that the Revolution and Napoleon had aided the ongoing creation of a very wealthy oligarchical class who wished to transform the country into something like Britain with a *democratic* system that they would control. Louis XVIII managed this feat successfully, but following his death in 1824, he was succeeded by his younger brother Charles X, who did not have the same aptitude as him.

Charles X, the youngest of the three grandsons of Louis XV, had lived a scandalous younger life. But with the experiences of his brother and sister-in-law's murder, his own exile, and the utter humiliation of France, he changed. For one thing, as with many who shared his views, the new king had become much more devout—and indeed, penitential. He required the same sort of coronation at Rheims as his predecessors—the same ceremony that St. Joan of Arc sought for Charles VIII, who saw his coronation as a sealing of his royal vocation with God, the Church, and his country. This attitude would not be lost on his great-great-great niece Zita. So, too, with her forebear's views on the right relationship between the king and his subjects. This was summed up by Chateaubriand, who said,

> To them, the king represents the ideas of legitimate authority and order, of peace, and of equal and monarchical liberty. The memories of the old France, of religion, of our ancient ways and family customs, of the habits of our childhood, of our cradles and tombs, all of these are attached to the sacred word 'king'. The king, the judge, the father: for a Frenchman they are all one. . . . It is a ruler whose paternal power is regulated by institutions, tempered by customs, softened and made excellent by time, like a generous wine born of the soil of the fatherland and ripened by the French sun. Let us no longer hide this truth from ourselves.[5]

This was, as well, the view of like-minded people of their own monarchs throughout Europe. However, trouble

---

[5] François-René de Chateaubriand, "De Buonaparte, des Bourbons," *Grands écrits politiques* (Paris: Imprimerie Nationale, 1993), tome I, p. 92.

was already brewing for the current son of St. Louis IX, as Charles X was called. His distant cousin, the Duke of Orleans, whose father had voted for the decapitation of Louis XVI and then lost his own, was in contact with men who wished to see him on the throne. For the *haute bourgeoisie* (the upper middle class), wealth without power was like a straitjacket. They wanted a king who, in return for the semblance of rule, would allow them to direct the state as they pleased.

In the meantime, Zita's grandfather, Dom Miguel of Portugal, was facing major problems in his own country. His father, Zita's great-grandfather, King John VI of Portugal, would die the year following Charles X's coronation. His reign had been long and turbulent. It began when he was forced to become regent in 1799 for his mother, Queen Maria, because personal misfortunes and the strains of dealing with the fallout from the Revolution rendered her incapable of ruling. At the end of 1807, in order to avoid what appeared to be the impending fall of Lisbon to the French, Prince John evacuated the royal family and government to Brazil. Arriving in 1808, Prince John raised Brazil's status, proclaiming "the United Kingdom of Portugal, Brazil, and the Algarves." He and his family initially remained in Brazil after the defeat of Napoleon. In 1816, when his mother died, Prince John became King John VI. But a revolution broke out in Portugal in 1820, and it became necessary for him to return. John's departure made his eldest son, Pedro, regent in Brazil. John then returned to Portugal, where he found himself forced to swear allegiance to a liberal constitution, the nature of which established a parliament that he had to be subject to. Meanwhile, inspired by the increasingly successful revolutions in Spanish America, a similar movement arose in Brazil. John urged his son to put himself at the head of it; and so, in 1822, Pedro I was proclaimed Emperor of the independent Empire of Brazil. As far as John's second son, Miguel (as noted, Zita's grandfather), was concerned, this removed from Pedro and his children any right to the throne of Portugal, but his father felt differently.

At any rate, a popular uprising in 1823, spearheaded by Miguel, ended the liberal regime and restored the king to his proper place. His proclamation gives a good example of what the believers in traditional monarchy throughout western Europe stood for:

> Men of Portugal: It is time to break the iron yoke in which we live. . . . The strength of national ills, already without limits, leaves me no choice. . . .
>
> In place of the long-established national rights which they promised you would recover on August 24, 1820, they gave you ruin and the King has been reduced to a mere ghost . . . that to which you owe your glory in the lands of Africa and the seas of Asia, has been reduced to baseness and stripped of the brilliance that [it] had once possessed from royal recognition; religion and its ministers, mocked and scorned . . . .
>
> I find myself in the midst of valiant and brave Portuguese, determined as I am to die or to restore to His Majesty his freedom and authority.

> Do not hesitate, churchmen and citizens of all classes. Come and help the cause of religion, royalty and of you all, and swear not to kiss the royal hand again, until after His Majesty is restored to his authority.[6]

However, Miguel felt that his father, Pedro I, had left far too many liberals in place in government and feared that they would accomplish by stealth, under his father's aegis, what they failed to do by violence against him. So, the following year, he attempted a coup, which he claimed was precipitated by a Masonic plot against his father. Miguel took command of the capital, but a British officer brought King John to a British warship in the harbor. Miguel's troops surrendered, and Miguel went to the ship to make his submission. He was ordered to Vienna by the king. He was there when his father died in 1826, and during the time that his older brother was proclaimed King Pedro IV in Brazil. But the new king was committed to staying on as Emperor of Brazil and instituted a regency under their sister with a constitutional charter. After two months, he abdicated the throne in favor of his seven-year-old daughter, Maria II. Due to the increasing political instability of the regency, the Brazilian emperor proposed that Miguel would become regent and marry his niece when she came of age. In 1828, Dom Miguel returned from Vienna to Lisbon.

Dom Miguel set foot in Lisbon on January 13, 1828. He found himself in a deeply, if familiarly, divided

---

6 Father Amaro, *Father Amaro, or, Sovéla, politics, history and literature* (London: R. Greenlaw, 1823), p. 248.

country—familiarly because it was a pattern to be seen throughout Europe. The liberals—those desiring a limited monarchy and a less influential role for the Church—were primarily the *haute bourgeoisie* (the middle-class business owners and merchants), the intellectuals, and a number of the "advanced" nobles. Their opponents were found among the more devout, the more traditional, and the poorer. These latter began to demonstrate in favor of Miguel assuming the throne directly. On March 13, 1828, he dissolved the *cortes*, and in May, a traditional Cortes of the Three Estates proclaimed Miguel as King Miguel I and abolished Pedro IV's constitutional charter.

The liberals did not take this measure lightly. Almost immediately, attempted mutinies and selected murders of Miguel's supporters began, and his supporters responded in kind. Thus was set in motion a cycle of violence that, in time, would explode into full-blown rebellion. Both sides had foreign allies: Great Britain and Brazil favored the liberal party, while the Holy See, Austria, Russia, Prussia, Spain, and France were in favor of Miguel.

But while Zita's grandfather was holding on in Portugal, her great-great-grandfather, King Charles X, was encountering ever greater difficulties in France. In 1820, before his ascension to the throne, his younger son, the Duke de Berry, was assassinated; the duke's pregnant wife, Marie-Caroline of Bourbon-Two Sicilies, gave birth afterward to Henry, Count de Chambord—the king's only male heir after his childless older son, Louis, Duke d'Angouleme. Henry's older sister, Louise, would become Zita's maternal grandmother. As we shall see, both were determined women who did not allow wreck and ruin to derail their chosen paths. It is not too much to see in Louise's adventures a foreshadowing of what lay ahead for the as-yet-unborn Zita.

France operated under a constitutional charter, which despite its being couched by Louis XVIII as a gracious grant, retained the organs of the Napoleonic state in a number of key ways. Among these were the retention of the artificial departments created by the revolutionaries rather than the revival of the historic provinces, the establishment of a House of Commons-style Chamber of Deputies—many of whose members wanted to have the government and its ministries responsible to them rather than to the king, and Napoleon's concordat with the Holy See, which despite regaining some lost ground for the Church, still kept her in a legally subordinate position while denying that Catholicism was the official state religion—rather it was "the religion of the great majority of the French."[7] Many of the king's political allies were eager to address these and other issues, while his enemies wished to use them as a jumping-off point for further alterations.

Although Charles X's longtime prime minister, the Count de Villele, was good at quieting controversy, the discontent of the liberal opposition of its wealthy backers in Parliament steadily rose, leading Charles X to appoint the Viscount de Martignac, who was a more conciliatory figure. At the time, the ministry of war was given to an interesting figure who might be taken as a symbol of many Europeans in

---

[7] "Documents upon Napoleon and the Reorganization of Religion," The Napoleon Series, https://www.napoleon-series.org/research/government/diplomatic/c_concordat.html.

this era: Louis, Count de Bourmont. During the period of 1789–1800, Bourmont fought with the *Chouans* in western France against the Revolution and intrigued constantly to return the Bourbons to the throne. When the exiled Louis XVIII seemed uninterested in regaining the throne, Bourmont joined the army under Bonaparte, returning again to the royal service as soon as it was possible to do so. When Napoleon returned in 1815, Louis XVIII told Bourmont that he did not intend to resist but would rely on foreign arms. At first, this led Bourmont to return to Bonaparte's service, but on the eve of Waterloo, an action of Napoleon against the Bourbons led him to defect without revealing any deep secrets, as he promised his commanding general in a letter upon departure. He was a commander of the French in Spain during the 1821 intervention, held various high military posts afterward, and was named minister of war in 1829. When the Algerian War broke out in early 1830, Bourmont was placed in command of the invasion forces. Highly successful, the French troops seized Algiers, Oran, Bone, and elsewhere in rapid succession.

If tension was brewing in Portugal and France in early 1830, Spain was not to be spared either. Ferdinand VII had been married three times and had not produced a male heir, and his third wife died on May 27, 1829. According to the Salic Law followed by the Bourbons, the king's heir was his brother, Don Carlos. But on December 12, Ferdinand married for the fourth and last time. The bride was the Duchess de Berry's sister, Maria Cristina of the Two Sicilies. The liberals at the Spanish court began to see her as their champion, even as the traditionalists, or *Apostolicos*, looked to Don Carlos. Under the new (and now pregnant) queen's influence, on March 29, 1830, Ferdinand announced the Pragmatic Sanction, whereby his firstborn child would be heir, regardless of sex, and his brother was excluded from the succession entirely. Don Carlos refused to accept the new measure; in this, he had the sympathy of Dom Miguel, whose embattled crown was in a similar state.

The events unfolding in France were to have an enormous effect upon both Spain and Portugal. Charles X was ever more concerned for the future of his country by what he saw as the sharpening political differences between the parties, the increasing clamor of the press, and the radicalization (and secularization) of the *haute bourgeoisie*. One might see parallels here to events in the United States in our own time, where the political parties, media, and corporations all appear to push in a single direction, which many might feel is detrimental to the nation and society. There is nothing really to oppose them in the here and now, but in the France of July 1830, Charles X believed it to be his God-given duty to try. The result was the July Ordinances, promulgated by Charles X (who was out of the city at St. Cloud) and his prime minister, Polignac. These, amongst other things, suppressed "freedom of the press" and deprived the commercial *haute bourgeoisie* of its voting rights, as well as dissolved the Chamber of Deputies.

In response, the liberal politicians incited the Parisian mob to revolt. The commander of the Paris garrison, himself a liberal, refused to act without orders from the king. Charles, remembering all too well the horrors of the Revolution, was not keen on slaughtering his subjects, rebels though they might be. The result was that in three days, the capital was in the hands of the rebels, and the liberal politicians formed a provisional government. Shaken, Charles named his cousin, Louis Philippe, the Duke of Orleans, as Lieutenant General of the Realm. He then abdicated and prevailed upon his eldest son to do the same in favor of Charles's grandson, Henry—now *de jure* Henry V. Legally, he was Louis XIX for twenty minutes—surely the shortest reign in history. The Duke of Orleans faithfully promised that he would negotiate with the rebels on behalf of young Henry, and the royal family, the new king in tow, departed for Scotland, where they took up residence in Mary Queen of Scots's old palace of Holyrood. As soon as they were out of the way, the duke made a deal with the regnant politicos and was proclaimed "Louis Philippe, King of the French." It was intended that he should reign over a British-style monarchy.

Indeed, Louis Philippe, the so-called "Citizen King," imitated the bourgeois as much as he could, cutting down severely on royal ritual. He encouraged the middle classes with the snappy slogan *enrichissez vous*, or "enrich yourselves!" However, what is most important for our story is that he replaced Bourmont (who refused to recognize him) in Algeria and withdrew from the Holy Alliance. Thus, the Alliance was reduced to the three eastern powers, the German and Italian states, and Spain and Portugal. Sardinia would essentially leave the Alliance in 1831 after the extinction of the main line of the ruling House of Savoy and the accession of a distant and liberal cousin. Louis Philippe also allied with Britain and joined them in supporting Maria II's exiled government against Dom Miguel.

The following year, Maria II's father, Dom Pedro, abdicated as Emperor of Brazil in favor of his son, Pedro II, and sailed for Britain to get assistance. With that accomplished, he went to Terceira in the Azores—which had held out for Maria II—to start a government in exile on her behalf. Miguel's navy initially blockaded the island, but the blockade was broken by Louis Philippe's fleet. Thanks to Dom Miguel's friendship with Don Carlos, Ferdinand VII also switched alliances, quietly backing Pedro and Maria II's partisans and giving them sanctuary in Spain.

In the meantime, the Duchess of Berry had found exile with the French royal family in Edinburgh little to her liking. Marshal Bourmont and several others had joined them there, but a difference of opinion developed between Maria Carolina and her father-in-law. He believed that diplomacy might somehow regain the throne for Henry, whereas she believed that only military action could do so. Leaving her children with their grandparents, she returned to her family in sunny Naples and immediately began planning a counterrevolution in France in favor of her son. She was joined there by Bourmont and several others. Unbeknownst to them, however, while in her parental home, she secretly married an Italian nobleman, Count Hector Charles Lucchesi Palli. In April of 1832, she landed at Marseilles and began secretly crisscrossing northwestern France, raising troops for an insurrection from among the peasantry and veterans and descendants of the wars in the Vendee.

The rising began on May 26. Poorly organized, it was defeated by June 6, and the duchess made her way to Nantes, where she would hide among the populace, avoiding capture for several months. The following month, Dom Pedro, having taken over all of the Azores with British and French naval support, launched a successful attack on the city of Porto in northern Portugal. But a year-long siege began with Dom Miguel's forces stiffened by the addition of Bourmont as their commander (having escaped the wreck of the Duchess's abortive rebellion). In November of 1832, she was discovered and arrested at last and kept as a prisoner of state in the Chateau de Blaye. During her captivity, it became apparent that she was pregnant, and so she was forced to reveal her marriage. Her French nationality and legal right to act as regent for her son were based upon her marriage to the Duke of Berry, which was voided by her second marriage. This removed her as a threat to Louis Philippe's government, and so, after giving birth, she was deported to Italy in June of 1833, bereft of influence among French legitimists. Charles X, then living with the royal family temporarily at Prague Castle, initially refused to allow her to see her children until proof was produced that her second marriage was valid and recognized by the Vatican.

That same month, Dom Miguel's cause in Portugal suffered an enormous setback. While Dom Pedro's forces were still besieged, a liberal force with British naval support landed at Faro in the far southern province of Algarve and marched steadily northward, and they took Lisbon on July 24. Dom Pedro marched south to link up with his southern forces. A stalemate then began that would last for nine months. As is usually the case in civil wars, the two sides fought bitterly, often asking for no quarter and giving none. This would also be the case in Spain, where in 1833, there began a series of civil wars that would last over a century.

On September 29, 1833, Ferdinand VII breathed his last. According to the Pragmatic Sanction, his young daughter became Queen Isabella II, with the Duchess of Berry's sister, Maria Cristina, as regent. Her government, which was liberal and included a number of Freemasons, worked with the House of Rothschild to finance the government and immediately went to work to weaken provincial autonomy and the rights of the Church. The rebellion would begin in the Basque country, whose ancient institutions were the first the new government would attack. Don Carlos's supporters, the Carlists, responded with a relatively simple program: *Dios, Patria, Rey, y Fueros*: "God [the rights of the Church], Fatherland [the traditional governance of Spain], King [a monarch untrammeled by politicians], and *Fueros* [traditional local liberties]." As Bradley Smith put it, "The first Carlist war was fought not so much on the basis of the legal claim of Don Carlos, but because a passionate, dedicated section of the Spanish people favored a return to a kind of absolute monarchy that they felt would protect their individual freedoms (*fueros*), their regional individuality and their religious conservatism."[8] Dismayed at the stalemate in Portugal, Bourmont crossed the border to fight for Don Carlos.

Early the next year, however, fighting in Portugal began in earnest. Supported with money and arms by the governments of Great Britain, France, and Spain, Dom Pedro's

---

8 Bradley Smith, *Spain: A History in Art* (New York: Gemini-Smith, 1979), p. 259.

forces, despite some setbacks, pushed ever forward. On April 24, they signed the Quadruple Alliance for the precise purpose of driving Dom Miguel out of Portugal. The flow of aid to the liberal army could not really be countered by this point, and the Battle of Asseiceira, fought on May 16, 1834, was the last major engagement in the conflict. Ten days later, Dom Miguel signed the Concession of Evoramonte, in which he agreed to go into permanent exile. He then denounced this agreement once he reached Genoa, as it had been extracted by force from him thanks to the Quadruple Alliance. Because of this, he was denied the pension that had been part of the agreement. Later in the year, the new liberal government suppressed five hundred monasteries in Portugal and seized their property to punish the Church for its support of Dom Miguel. Initially, the pope hosted the impoverished Miguel in Rome. But, in 1851, he moved to Kloster Bronnbach in Baden, having married Princess Adelaide of Löwenstein, whose family owned it. The following year, their oldest daughter, Maria das Neves, was born. A decade later, their sixth daughter and seventh child, Maria Antonia, was born. She would, in time, become the mother of Empress Zita.

In Spain, the First Carlist War went on until 1840, when the defeated Don Carlos retired to the Austrian City of Trieste. From 1835 to 1837, the Spanish government suppressed the monasteries, claiming they had all been praying for Don Carlos. Successive heirs would return to Spain for the Second and Third Carlist Wars over the course of the nineteenth century—and with each successive defeat, they returned to the welcome of Austria, where the Bourbons of

France were already ensconced. Charles X had died in Goriza and was entombed in the nearby Franciscan friary. His crypt would become a mini-Saint Denis for the French Bourbons, even as the Castle of Frohsdorf in Lower Austria became a sort of mini-Versailles. Henry V held court there after 1846, while the year before, Henry's sister married Charles III, the future Duke of Parma. In time, she would bear him a son, Robert of Bourbon-Parma, who would become the father of Empress Zita.

So it was that the quintessence of western European legitimism came to Austria, the last major representative of traditional Catholic monarchy—France, Spain, Sardinia, and Portugal all having embraced liberalism. Legitimism was still dominant in the German and Italian states, and Prussia and Russia remained her partners in the Holy Alliance. But those relationships were somewhat strained, and over all three loomed the issue of a partitioned Poland with only Austria trying to maintain a shred of Polish autonomy. Austria's wartime Prussian ally, King Frederick William III, after arranging a forced marriage between the Lutheran and Calvinist churches of his realm, got into a dispute with the Catholic Church over mixed marriages, going so far as to throw the Archbishop of Cologne in prison. That particular fight ended with the king's death in 1840. His son Frederick William IV, "the Romantic upon the Throne," immediately ordered the archbishop's release.

However, things were not as rosy in Russia. The year of revolts (1830–1831) had seen successful revolutions, as in Belgium, and unsuccessful, as in Poland. Primarily directed against Russia, the Polish revolt not only failed to gain more loyalty than it lost and, thereby, end Russian interference in Poland's autonomy, but it had another unintended consequence. The last two tsars, Paul I and Alexander I, had been quite friendly with the Catholic Church—indeed, this was why the latter could conceive of the Holy Alliance in the first place. Unfortunately, Nicholas I, who succeeded Alexander in 1825, was a Slavophile and suspicious of Catholicism in general and of Polish Catholicism in particular. As a result of the partitions of Poland, Russia had inherited a great many Ruthenian (Belarusian and Ukrainian) Greek Catholics, which were grouped under the Archeparchy (Archdiocese) of Polotsk. In a delayed response to the Polish rebellion, Nicholas I forced the bishops, priests, and laity of the archeparchy to join the Russian Orthodox Church in 1839. Given the ongoing Habsburg concern and sponsorship of eastern Catholicism, it was a slap in the face for Austria. But the two empires would once again grow close, thanks to unexpected revolutionary activity that threatened them both and all Europe. This activity would also, in crucial ways, determine the future of the as-yet-unborn Zita.

The revolutionary year of 1848 began in January in Sicily with a revolt against the Bourbon King, Ferdinand II, who was the brother of Marie-Caroline, Duchess of Berry, and Maria Cristina, Queen-Regent of Spain, whose adventures we have just seen. In the end, it was a complicated affair, affecting over fifty countries and involving a relatively new social class, which was the product of the Industrial Revolution that had been spreading throughout Europe and North America since 1815. The industrial proletariat, who lived and worked in the most miserable of conditions, were disaffected from the traditions of their countries and primarily concerned with a way out of their misery—a concern often not shared by the primarily liberal holders of capital, who were more interested in strengthening their own oligarchical hold on the state while minimizing or eliminating altogether the monarchical and aristocratic control over the same. There was also the influence of Romantic Nationalism, especially among the re-emergent ethnicities in central and eastern Europe. Ultimately unsuccessful, its last embers were not put out until 1851.

While Dom Miguel, the French Bourbons, and the Spanish Carlist claimants watched the events unfold from relative security, the same could not be said for their Habsburg hosts, or for that matter, their cousins in Parma. In Italy, Charles Albert, the earlier referenced cousin who inherited the Sardinian throne when the far more tradition-oriented male line died out, aimed to unite the peninsula in a centralized liberal kingdom over which he would preside. As the various revolutions toppled the other Italian princes, he took command of the movement and invaded the Austrian-held areas of Lombardy. The German states, which since the Congress of Vienna had included the non-Hungarian, non-Galician parts of Austria in the Germanic Confederation as a sort of replacement for the Holy Roman Empire, were shaken with a number of small revolts. The rebels wished to impose liberal constitutions on each of the constituent monarchies and unite them into a single reich. Two major issues of contention were whether or not this would include the Austrian parts of the Confederation, and what role the Habsburgs might play. There were also revolts and provisional governments in Vienna and Prague and, most distressing of all, in Budapest.

The sitting emperor, Ferdinand I, although a very pleasant man and a genius at personal finances, was not up to dealing with all of these challenges, especially after Metternich resigned. He was prevailed upon by the rest of the family to abdicate and was replaced with his nineteen-year-old nephew, Franz Joseph. A dashing young man, the new emperor was decades away from the omnipresent elderly figure still to be seen in pictures on walls and as statues in public places throughout his old dominions from Tyrol to Transylvania and from Czechia to Croatia. The tragedies of losing successively his brother, son, wife, and nephew lay far in the future at this point. What fell to him at present was the unenviable task of putting back together a humpty-dumpty of an empire divided by ethnic hatreds. That he was able to do so was due to his own talents and those of his loyal lieutenants, most notably Field Marshal Radetzky, after whom the eponymous march by Strauss was named.

The greatest challenge, after Vienna and Prague were tamed and Italy quieted by the field marshal, was Hungary. Here Lajos Kossuth, in defiance of such wise heads as Istvan Széchenyi, ended the eight-hundred-year-old Kingdom of the Holy Crown and declared a liberal Republic of Hungary. While Széchenyi looked empathetically at the aspirations of the nationalities living in the territory of the Kingdom of Hungary, Kossuth openly stated, "I will never, ever, under the Hungarian holy crown, recognize any nation or nationality other than Hungarian."[9] Apart from the obvious contradiction of invoking that sacred emblem for a republic, Kossuth ignored an important fact. While the Magyars had been deeply stirred by the fires of Romantic Nationalism, so too had the Slovaks, Romanians, Croats, and Serbs with whom they had lived more or less peacefully in the Apostolic Kingdom—the last realm in Europe where Latin was the official language until Kossuth replaced it with Magyar in testament to the country's ethnic diversity. The result was predictable; alongside loyal Magyars, the subject nationalities rallied to the Habsburgs and the Holy Crown as well as their own national aspirations. Nevertheless, it took Russian intervention to end the Hungarian Revolution. The bitterness on all sides would continue to poison relations between the Magyars and their neighbors, leading directly to the trauma of Trianon, and it even now impedes efforts to bring central Europe together in the face of challenges from both West and East.

In any case, even the German situation was solved. The whole idea of a resurgent German Empire foundered on two rocks. The first was the inability to resolve the question of Greater Germany (including some or all of largely non-German Austria) versus Lesser Germany (without Austria). The second was the refusal of Prussian King Frederick William IV, a devotee of traditional, albeit Protestant, monarchy, to accept the emperorship thereof. His pithy remark

---

[9] László Katus, "Nationality Question and Policy Towards National Minorities in 1848–1849," *Minorities Research* 5 (2005): p. 156. https://epa.oszk.hu/00400/00463/00005/pdf/.

was, "I will not pick up a crown from the gutter."[10] But the Frankfurt Assembly, which had acted as the putative legislature for the abortive empire, introduced to public life a Prussian liberal who was to make his mark on the nineteenth century: Otto von Bismarck. Despite all of the fighting and deaths, it did indeed seem as though Humpty Dumpty had been repaired. Yet the fissures remained within and between the European states.

In the meantime, the House of Bourbon-Parma, which at the Congress of Vienna had been temporarily deprived of the duchy for which it was named (it was assigned to Marie Louise, Franz I's daughter and Napoleon's empress, for the term of her remaining years), had undergone some changes of its own. Given the Duchy of Lucca on an equally temporary basis, Charles II of Parma and his Duchess Maria Teresa of Savoy (daughter of Sardinian King Victor Emmanuel I of the soon-to-expire elder line of Savoy) made a number of improvements to their small realm. Amongst other things, they built the Villa Borbone in a town on the coast called Pianore. When Marie Louise at last died in 1847, Charles II and his wife took control of their proper country, and Lucca reverted to the Grand Duchy of Tuscany, but they retained Pianore and some other properties as private landholders. The next year, as we have seen, the cataclysm of 1848 hit the Italian States, and Parma was not spared. Ousted by the revolutionaries, Charles II was restored by Austrian troops the following year. Exhausted by the situation, he abdicated

---

[10] Christopher Clark, *Iron Kingdom: The Rise and Downfall of Prussia, 1600–1947* (Massachusetts: Belknap Press of Harvard University Press, 2006), p. 494.

on March 13, 1849, in favor of his son, Charles III. In 1845, the new duke had married the Count de Chambord's sister, Louise, at Frohsdorf. They would have four children, of whom the second and the oldest son, Robert (born in 1848), was both heir to the duchy and future father of Empress Zita.

In the meantime, events within France—which would have as great or greater effects on the Habsburgs, Bourbons, and Europe as a whole—were moving into the larger world. In 1852, Prince-President Louis Napoleon Bonaparte of France's Second Republic overthrew the government and ushered in the Second Empire with himself as Emperor Napoleon III. The following year, desirous of securing the well-being of Orthodox Christians within the Ottoman Empire and realizing the long-held desire of Russia to occupy Constantinople and the straits, Tsar Nicholas I declared war on Turkey and occupied the Principalities of Moldavia and Wallachia. Great Britain and Imperial France, fearful of the results of a Turkish defeat, declared war on Russia in 1854. Seeing a chance to benefit later, the wily Count Cavour, Prime Minister of Sardinia, joined them. The result was the Crimean War, famous forever for the bloody Charge of the Light Brigade.

At this juncture, Nicholas I turned to Franz Joseph for support, citing his essential assistance to Austria in suppressing the Hungarian revolt. Field Marshal Radetsky advised his emperor to do so, declaring that dispatching himself and a few squadrons of cavalry would fulfill the debt of honor. But here, Franz Joseph made what—we can now see in hindsight—was perhaps the biggest mistake of his entire sixty-seven-year-long reign. Rather than going to Russia's aid, he made a neutrality pact with Russia and backed Turkey diplomatically. The bitterness this engendered in Russia's ruling circles would have enormous effects.

Although not connected, Charles III was assassinated during the Crimean War, leaving his wife as regent for young Duke Robert. For a scant few more years, she and her little boy ruled their small duchy peacefully. However, circumstances beyond their control were about to overwhelm them and their fellow Italian princes.

In joining the British and French against Russia, Camillo Benso, Count Cavour correctly predicted that this alliance would build alliances for his main project—the construction of a liberal Italian kingdom with the Sardinian king, Victor Emmanuel II, as nominal head. He was able to prevail upon Napoleon III to declare war on Austria in return for promising the cession of Nice and Savoy to France. Still smarting from the Crimean debacle, Russia had no interest in supporting Austria, and so Franz Joseph faced the French alone. Austria was defeated and duly ceded Lombardy to Napoleon III. He, in turn, passed it on to Sardinia and received the promised French-speaking sections of Victor Emmanuel II's realm. As Cavour had instituted heavy taxation and conscription years before—so strengthening their military, the Sardinians rapidly occupied Parma,[11] Modena, Tuscany, and the Papal Province of Romagna. Sardinia called upon Bl. Pope Pius IX to surrender the entirety of the Papal States,

[11] The Sardinian occupation of Parma forced Louise and Robert to flee to her family in Austria.

but the pontiff dug in his heels and called upon the young men of the entire Catholic world to defend their pope. The result was the formation of that gallant army called the Papal Zouaves.

They received their baptism of fire the following year when the Sardinians invaded what remained of the pope's territories and, after a sharp series of battles, subjugated the Marches and Umbria. Things changed when Napoleon III, hoping to placate the now outraged Catholics of France, sent an army to Rome to secure Lazio for the pope. In the meantime, Garibaldi conquered the Kingdom of the Two Sicilies and gave it to Sardinia. The following year, Frederick Wilhelm IV died and was succeeded by his brother Wilhelm I, who would play Victor Emmanuel II to Bismarck's Cavour. But, in his exile in Baden, Dom Miguel and his wife Adelaide of Löwenstein-Wertheim-Rosenberg welcomed their seventh and last child, Princess Maria Antonia. She would be Zita's mother.

Six years later, Austria was maneuvered into war with Prussia by Bismarck. Again without a Russian ally, Austria and most of the German States went into the disastrous Seven Weeks' War. The Habsburgs were expelled from Germany, and their allies—the Kingdom of Hanover, the Electorate of Hesse-Kassel,[12] the Duchy of Nassau, and the Free City of Frankfurt[13]—were annexed by Prussia. The now enlarged kingdom forced the minor northern German states and the defeated Austrian ally Saxony into the North German

[12] The Electorate of Hesse-Kassel (famed as a source of mercenaries for the British during the American Revolution).

[13] Heretofore capital of the now defunct Germanic Confederation.

Confederation. Austria's remaining co-combatants—Bavaria, Wuertemmberg, Baden, and Hesse Darmstadt—were allowed to retain their independence for the moment. Sardinia, having entered the war on Prussia's side, received Venetia despite her navy being defeated by the Austrian fleet at the Battle of Lissa.

This debacle forced Franz Joseph to come to an accommodation with the liberal Hungarian leadership, who considered themselves Kossuth's heirs; they would be dominated by the Tisza clan. This compromise was the *Ausgleich* of 1867, which replaced the more or less unitary Empire of Austria with the Dual Monarchy of Austria-Hungary. Franz Joseph would be crowned at Budapest, and his Austrian lands would retain their various rights and privileges. Hungary was to be a unitary kingdom, albeit with Croatia as a kingdom on its own linked to Hungary as Hungary was to Austria. In coming decades, despite the efforts and opinions of the opposing Catholic Party in Parliament—led by the Zichys—the liberals' Magyarisation policies would be keenly resented by the minorities, many of whom felt betrayed by the dynasty after standing by the emperor in 1848. Even as the Magyars' sense of nationality had been revived by Romanticism, the same wind swept through the Slovaks, Croats, Romanians, and Serbs, rendering each of them intent on reviving their cultures, and righting ancient or current wrongs—real or imagined. The result was a mix of fear and resentment on the part of both rulers and ruled toward each other.

While all of this was happening, Robert of Bourbon-Parma grew into manhood under the watchful eyes of his uncle,

Henry V, Count of Chambord, in the "Little Versailles" of Frohsdorf. The *de jure* King of France had no children of his own, and so his nephew was as much a surrogate son as Henry V was a surrogate father. He passed on to him his theories regarding monarchy and politics in general, even though Robert might not have had a chance to put them into practice. Yet when the time came for Robert to have a family of his own, these ideas would be in the air in his household. In 1869, young Robert married Princess Maria Pia of Bourbon-Two Sicilies. It was a happy marriage, and they would have twelve children in all.

In the meantime, events were again brewing in the greater world. Having dealt with Austria, Bismarck now set his eyes on France. There, Napoleon III, still smarting over the Mexican debacle and the murder in that country of Franz Joseph's brother, Emperor Maximilian, was looking for a way to restore his military reputation. Spain, having undergone yet another revolution, offered Bismarck a chance. He indicated that the Prussian Hohenzollerns would be happy to provide a prince for that country's momentarily empty throne. Napoleon III fell for the bait and withdrew his troops from Rome, thus allowing the Sardinians to occupy the remaining papal territories and proclaim the Kingdom of Italy. It is interesting to note that while few Italians left the peninsula prior to 1860, millions of Italians did leave after 1870; they emigrated for the United States, Argentina, Canada, Australia, and elsewhere to escape the taxation and conscription that were Cavour's legacy.

In any case, Napoleon III was defeated at Sedan and abdicated. The Prussians and other German troops pushed the

French back and besieged Paris. While the siege continued, Bismarck proclaimed Wilhelm I as the German Emperor at the Hall of Mirrors in the Palace of Versailles on January 18, 1871. But as all of this was happening, the parliamentary elections of 1870, held in the wake of Napoleon III's fall, ushered in a solid majority of monarchists, who were of course divided between the Legitimist supporters of Henry V and the Orleanist adherents of Louis Philippe's grandson, Philippe, Count of Paris. The two sides were able to cooperate because—not having sons—it was presumed by many that Henry V would accept the count as his heir. When negotiations began with Henry V, however, he made it apparent that he would not accept the tricolor as the flag of his kingdom, as had Louis Philippe, but would insist upon the white flag of the Bourbons. Henry V then returned to France. After the stalled negotiations in Paris, he stayed a few nights at the Chateau of Chambord on the Loire, which had been bought for him by a national subscription when he was a child and left to him when he and his family were exiled. After an exile of forty-one years, he returned briefly. Resolving to return to Austria, he delivered a speech outlining his reasons for refusing the terms under which the throne was offered.[14]

Implicit in this was not simply the matter of the flag but of what kind of monarchy Henry V would preside over. His cousins in France and Spain and his grandfather had braved exile and death rather than submit to being a figurehead for oligarchs. This is precisely what Henry refused to become. In

[14] For full text of the speech, see Appendix I.

a manifesto written in 1872, the king declared, "I am asked today to sacrifice my honor. What can I answer? except that I take nothing from my previous statements. The pretensions of the day before give me the measure of the demands of tomorrow, and I cannot consent to inaugurate a restorative and strong reign by an act of weakness."[15] He would return in 1873 but found the conditions of the offer much the same. Furthermore, Marshal MacMahon, President of the nascent Third Republic, refused to meet him. Henry V returned to Frohsdorf mournful but convinced he had done his duty, giving both example and precept to his nephew from Parma.

On September 22, 1882, Robert's wife died in childbirth with their twelfth child, a boy. This was a crushing blow to the father of eleven—a number of whom had learning disabilities. On August 24, 1883, his beloved uncle Henry V died at Frohsdorf. Although many of Henry V's followers accepted the Count of Paris as Philippe VII, his wife and a number of others refused. Instead, they acclaimed the Carlist heir, Don Juan, as Jean II. Henry V had left Frohsdorf itself to Don Jaime, Jean's younger son. The Chateau of Chambord was left to Robert, who was already wealthy in his own right. Oddly enough, while his property in Parma had been seized by the Italian government, what Robert owned in Lucca, including the Villa Borbone in Pianore, remained in his hands as private property rather than as an estate of the Duke of Parma.

---

[15] *L'Union*, n 166, du samedi 8 juillet 1871, [p. 1, col. 1 & 2].

On October 14 of the following year, Robert married again, this time to Maria Antonia, the youngest daughter of Dom Miguel and Princess Adelaide. They, too, would have twelve children, the fifth of whom, born on May 9, 1892 at Pianore, would be named Zita. Robert bought a castle in Austria, Schwarzau, near Frohsdorf in 1886. And so, the large Bourbon-Parma clan—eventually numbering twenty-five in all—would move several times a year between Chambord, Schwarzau, Pianore, and several other properties. As we shall see in the next chapter, it would be a unique upbringing—and all the history that we have seen in this chapter was a part of it, as family stories are in every upbringing. Without understanding how much this history influenced Zita's background, we cannot understand her.

Chapter 3

THE RAISING OF A PRINCESS

"Do not think, Monseigneur, that it is only because of your mistakes in grammar that we correct you so severely at your lessons. No doubt a prince, who ought to be accurate in all things, should be ashamed to make such mistakes, but our indignation has higher grounds. For it is not so much the mistake that we blame as the lack of attention that is the cause of it. If you put words in their wrong places now you will misdirect affairs in time to come; you will reward when you should punish, and punish when you should reward; everything, in short, that you do will be disordered if you do not in childhood train your mind to be attentive and to give serious thought to whatever you have in hand."

—Jacques-Benigne Bossuet to his student, the Dauphin, son of Louis XIV[16]

The birth of Princess Zita of Bourbon-Parma at Pianore on May 9, 1892, was a source of great joy to her parents. After all the excitement of the events described in the last chapter, the 1890s would be a period of relative calm

[16] Jacques-Benigne Bossuet, *Œuvres de Bossuet* (Paris: Firmin Didot, 1860), tome 1, p.13–16.

in European history. Despite Robert's forcible ejection from his duchy back in 1859, he and his family were far from sidelined. Austria-Hungary, thanks to Franz Joseph's dedication to legitimist principles, offered refuge to most of the sovereign families dispossessed by the preceding conflicts. Moreover, at a time when both reigning and exiled dynasties were very strict about maintaining their marriage laws, the growing number of Bourbon-Parma children was a distinct factor in the marriage diplomacy of the era.

An irony, however, was that around the time of Zita's birth, Robert—a staunch partisan of his uncle, the now deceased Henry V of France—began negotiating the marriage of his oldest daughter, Marie Louise (Zita's half-sister), with the son of his cousin, Princess Clementine of Orleans. Princess Clementine was the youngest daughter of Louis Philippe, who had dispossessed Henry V. Nevertheless, they were friends, and the princess's husband, Prince August of Saxe-Coburg and Gotha—although a cousin of Prince Albert who married Queen Victoria—was a member of the Catholic branch of the family, long settled in Austria. Their son, Ferdinand, had been elected Prince of Autonomous Bulgaria in 1886—that autonomy from Turkey having been granted by the Congress of Berlin in 1878. It fell to his mother to find a suitable spouse for her son. She and Robert came to an agreement, and the engagement was celebrated at Schwarzau Castle, where Zita would later be married. It was the first time that the young couple had met—Ferdinand being nine years older than his twenty-three-year-old fiancée. On April 20, 1893, they were married at Pianore.

Nine months and ten days later, the first of their four children, the future King Boris III, was born and baptized Catholic. Marie Louise was a dutiful wife despite how little her husband may have cared for her. Yet her heart was broken when, in the summer of 1895, in response to both the demands of their Bulgarian subjects and to please the Russian tsar upon whom their long-term prospects depended, Ferdinand had their son converted to Bulgarian Orthodoxy. Marie Louise, supported by both Robert and his wife, argued against it. Nevertheless, the ceremony was performed. When her second son, Kirill, was born in November of that year, she insisted once more upon a Catholic baptism, and that day, she took her children with her to France. Marie Louise brought them back to Bulgaria in May of 1896 and took up her duties, both marital and public. That summer, she accompanied Ferdinand to London to celebrate Queen Victoria's Diamond Jubilee. In January of 1898, Princess Eudoxia was born, and in July, Marie Louise visited St. Petersburg with her husband, thus gaining the all-important approval of Tsar Nicholas II. On January 30, 1899, she gave birth to her last child and died of pneumonia twenty-four hours later.

Of course, because of this union, Boris III would be Zita's half-nephew, and his son, the present-day *de jure* King of Bulgaria, Simeon II, would be her half-great-nephew. One cannot help but suspect that the episode had a great effect on the Bourbon-Parmas. On the one hand, finding a spouse of the same belief and fervor would appear to have become an important issue for the children. On the other, the question of finding a spouse with a like temperament would also have emerged.

The scenes of Zita's childhood that we have mentioned were also of importance to her upbringing. Castle Schwarzau was originally built in the baroque style by the Wurmbrand-Stuppach family around 1720, and it was greatly expanded two centuries later. After buying it, Robert increased the size and added a new courtyard, housing his famous collection of early liturgical prints here. The extensive park was redesigned and fitted with new structures, such as magnificent stables and outbuildings, and it was surrounded by game. The chapel, where Zita would later be married, had an organ upon which the young princess would learn to play. The liturgical vestments in the sacristy were very fine, in keeping with Duke Robert's interest in such things, and the stained-glass windows bore the Bourbon lilies. This was not the only familial connection with the area, however. Henry V's wife, born Archduchess Maria Theresa of Austria-Este, had subsidized the expansion of the parish church at Schwarzau in 1865.

Just as Schwarzau had to be adapted to the needs of Robert's expanding family, so too with Pianore. In 1826, Robert's grandmother, Maria Theresa of Savoy, had built the Villa Maria Theresa on the property. However, Robert needed something rather larger for his expanding family. So, in 1888, he built a much larger three-story villa.

Every six months, the entire household would pack up and move by way of a specially commissioned train from one of these two places to the other, spending the colder months in Italy and the warmer in Austria. The family still held two other properties, although they were far less used at the time. One of these properties, however, would become vital to their very survival later on.

The first of these, and by far the most famous, was the Chateau of Chambord—the largest of the many chateaux in France's Loire Valley. It had been built by King Francis I in 1516 but was confiscated from the royal family by revolutionaries. During the reign of Charles X, a popular subscription across the country raised the funds to buy the place for the very young future Henry V, whose grandfather gave him the title Count of Chambord after the chateau. Although he was forbidden by law to return to France after 1830, the chateau was not reconfiscated by the various regimes that followed, and so Henry, as we saw, stayed there a few nights in 1871. Henry had made some attempts to keep it up, but it was in a rather dilapidated state when Robert inherited it. He did his best to maintain what he could of the majestic structure.

The other property was Schloss Wartegg on Switzerland's Bodensee. Robert's mother had bought the castle in 1859 as a place of exile. In the period that followed, the palace building was expanded to include the south wing and a typical English park. During his first marriage, Robert used it a great deal, and two of his children by Maria Pia—Henry and Maria Immacolata—were born there, as were Adelaide and Sixtus, his two eldest by Maria Antonia. Robert had refurbished the existing Loretto Chapel in neo-Romanesque style in 1873, and to this day, the gold lilies on the wall of the sanctuary around the altar are reminders of the Bourbon-Parma tenancy.

Zita's early memories of life in this milieu were very happy and carefree. Although some of her half-brothers and half-sisters were in their mid-teens, and some of those had what we would call learning disabilities, the duke and duchess made a point of treating both sets the same—as one family. She recalled her father as being very genial, never using corporal punishment. Usually, wrongdoing brought a long and stern lecture, and the worst offenses brought the miscreant exclusion from a family outing or else being denied dessert when all the others at dinner was enjoying theirs.

There was another result of all the history that we looked at in the last chapter. The empress recalled many years later,

> I think this sense of all belonging together came to us naturally, as part of the times we lived in. We were international in our background in any case, for all the royal and princely families of Europe—at least all the Catholic ones—were related to some degree by marriage. Thus, though my father was French, there were Italians and Austrians among others in his ancestry, and while my maternal grandfather was [of] the line of Portugal, his mother had been Spanish and his wife a German, the Princess Adelhaid Loewenstein. So apart from half-brothers and half-sisters, the world seemed full of cousins and second cousins. One result of this was that we were brought up to hear around us and learn several languages as a matter of course: in my case French, which was our main language, but also Italian which my father often used, and German

> because of our roots in Austria. English too, although that was mainly with visitors.[17]

This was, of course, very much par for the course for the young royals of all European countries of that era, as much for the Protestant and Orthodox dynasties as the Catholic ones. Two European monarchs at that time, Christian IX of Denmark (1818–1906) and Nicholas I of Montenegro (1841–1921) shared the nickname Father-in-law of Europe. The Danish king's offspring included King Frederick VIII of Denmark (1843–1912), Queen Alexandra of the United Kingdom (1844–1925), who was queen consort of King Edward VII, King George I of Greece (1845–1913), Empress Maria Feodorovna of Russia (1847–1928), who was empress consort of Emperor Alexander III, and Crown Princess Thyra of Hanover (1853–1933), who married Crown Prince Ernest Augustus. Among his grandchildren were numbered King George V of the United Kingdom, Emperor Nicholas II of Russia, King Constantine I of Greece, and both King Haakon VII and his consort, Queen Maud of Norway. Nicholas's daughters were Zorka of Montenegro, who married King Peter I of Serbia, Elena of Montenegro, who married King Victor Emmanuel III of Italy, and Anna of Montenegro, who married Prince Francis Joseph of Battenberg. Queen Victoria's sobriquet was Grandmother of Europe. Both Britain's George V and Germany's Wilhelm II (in whose arms she died) were her grandsons, and they were both first cousins of Russia's Nicholas II, who was often

---

[17] Gordon Brook-Shepherd, *The Last Empress* (London: HarperCollins, 1991), pp. 6–7.

taken for George V. Wilhelm II and Nicholas II were particularly good friends.

One might have hoped that this interrelationship of all the continent's ruling houses might have staved off a major war indefinitely. Such presumptions would be false because France was a republic after all, and in the liberal monarchies of western Europe, the political establishments decided policy regardless of the wishes of their nominal crowned heads. Even in the "conservative" monarchies of Russia and Germany, where the popular imagination believed the tsar and kaiser were primarily in charge, it was not really the case. This was proved by the events following Nicholas II and William II's attempts at signing the Treaty of Björkö on July 24, 1905. The two cousins, both enjoying sea voyages on their respective yachts, were anchored side by side in the Russian Björkö islands near St. Petersburg. Russia was then engaged in the Russo-Japanese War, and both sovereigns were fearful for the future of peace in Europe. After discussing their worries, pen was put to paper, and they co-wrote a treaty that began, "Their Majesties the Emperors of all the Russias and Germany, in order to ensure the continuance of peace in Europe have decreed the following Articles of a Defensive Alliance Treaty."[18] It bound them to defend each other in case of attack by a third party and ended by declaring that "The Emperor of all the Russias, after the entry into force of this treaty, will take the necessary steps to initiate France to this agreement and engage it to join as an ally."[19] Upon their

[18] Lujo Brentano, *Die Urheber des Weltkriegs* (Munich: Drei Masken Verlag, 1922), p. 48.

[19] Brentano, *Die Urheber des Weltkriegs*, p. 48.

returns to their respective capitals, "their" governments each refused to ratify the treaty, thus helping to pave the way to future conflict. That same year, Franz Joseph, when asked by former president Theodore Roosevelt what he conceived his role as a modern monarch to be, responded, "Protecting my people from their politicians!"[20] While certainly laudable (and much needed), this was not the response of an "absolute emperor." As we shall see, royal consanguinity would prove little match for the power wielded by politicians on behalf of their wealthy backers. The fears of such as Henry V, Dom Miguel, and Don Carlos were to be proved correct.

The aforementioned events, however, did not affect the semi-nomadic Bourbon-Parma clan where Zita was spending her first happy years. The upbringing of the children was not lavish; it was, in some ways, spartan and simple. But it was literate. Robert loved his books; he had large libraries in each of his houses and loved reading to the children, regardless of how well they could read themselves. Their upbringing was also devout. We have seen the care Robert gave to each of his chapels and how Zita played the organ for Mass. Her name was derived from a request by the Bishop of Lucca that, if the child was a girl, she be named after St. Zita, patroness of servants and much venerated in the area. The duke kept his promise.

Religion was part and parcel of the upbringing Zita and her siblings received. They were lovingly taught the doctrines of the Catholic Church and participated in all the

---

[20] Eduard von Habsburg, *The Habsburg Way: Seven Rules for Turbulent Times* (Bedford, NH: Sophia Institute, 2023), p. 102.

family Masses and devotions. They were also taught that the Faith meant helping those less fortunate. Zita and her sisters would join their mother in making clothes for the poor while at Schwarzau and bringing food packages to them at Pianore. From an early age, Zita had close contact with the Abbey of Saint Cecilia of Solesmes. She first visited in 1899 to see her grandmother, Queen Adelheid of Portugal, who had entered the Order two years earlier under the name of Mother Adelheid of Braganza. Brought up in the wake of all the excitement we have examined, if there was one thing of which Robert and Maria Antonia were sure, it was that the Faith survives when all about it is tossed and broken. They were a couple for whom the distinction between perishable earthly and imperishable heavenly crowns was manifest in their own lives. But at the same time, they were only too aware that the fleeting nature of the former did not lessen the responsibility of those born to them. It may be assumed that the travails and triumphs of various family members were observed and discussed by the parents with their children.

She would certainly have heard of her grandfather's travails in attempting to keep the Portuguese throne, of her great-uncle refusing to sacrifice his honor for the crown of France, and of her Carlist cousins' thrilling exploits, sharing their triumphs and miseries in attempting to retake their place as kings of Spain. One cannot help but wonder, in the light of later events, if the story of Zita's great-grandmother, the Princess Marie Caroline of the Two Sicilies, Duchess of Berry, did not make a particular impact upon young Zita. There certainly are parallels between the two. Both were married to men they loved deeply and, when widowed, were left with the responsibility of trying to keep the flag of the family they had married into flying and to regain a lost throne for their sons. Yet, by pursuing her own happiness in the end, the duchess destroyed her ability to help either her adopted country or her son—with catastrophic results for France. Did this example haunt the young girl? Certainly, when the time came to choose either her own happiness or the hard path toward what she thought might lead to the triumph of the Habsburgs, Zita did not choose the former. Of course, those who are hard on themselves can notoriously be hard on others.

All of that lay far in the future, however, when the princess received her First Communion on the feast of the Sacred Heart on Friday, June 6, 1902, in the chapel of Pianore. The following year, Zita was sent to school at the Visitation Sister's Convent of St. Joseph in Zangberg, Bavaria. A school for elite young ladies, it sat in a seventeenth-century castle, bought by the sisters and turned into a convent and school in 1862. Preceding Zita was her first cousin, Elizabeth of Bavaria, daughter of her mother's older sister, Maria Jose. In 1900, she had married Prince Albert of the Belgians; he would become king, and she queen, in 1909. In some ways, the school would be considered rather strict today. Water for washing up was brought to the girls' rooms in jugs, usually cold. Make-up, even powder, was strictly forbidden, and the girls changed under their big nightgowns. The girls were allowed to speak only French for three days, English for two days, and German for the remaining days—a fitting preparation for female members of a multinational aristocracy. Zita perfected her German there, and as empress, she was later to have a perfect command of the language, both spoken and written. Moreover, mathematics, geography, history, natural history, music, sewing, and darning were also on the curriculum.

The chapel, dedicated to the Sacred Heart, was the location of the daily early Mass. Given the dedication of the entire Order to the Sacred Heart,[21] her time there must have deepened Zita's dedication to this devotion. The girls had a great many enjoyable customs—the Epiphany always featured a King Cake with a bean baked in it. Whoever received the piece with the bean played queen for the day, and costumes were issued to "courtiers" for the day's festivities. Zita said of her time there, "The very caring nuns applied their educational principles very strictly and rigorously, but always fairly and with an eye for balance. If I had later been able to freely choose who to entrust my daughters to, I would have sent them to Zangberg."[22]

It was while enjoying her happy school days at Zangberg that two things occurred—one happy, if surprising, the other very sad. The first was that her eldest sister, Adelaide, a very strong and remarkable lady, decided to follow their grandmother into the convent and become a nun of St. Cécile at Solesmes, which had had to move to Ryde on the Isle of Wight in England because of the anticlerical laws. The second was the death of her father in November. This

---

[21] St. Margaret Mary Alacoque, to whom Jesus's revelations about the devotion were given, was a member of the Order.

[22] "Spiritual Connections," Association Pour la Béatification de L'Impératrice Zita, https://associationimperatricezita.com/zita/liens-spirituels/.

event, apart from the deep sadness felt on all sides of the family, required some legal work with unpleasant elements. Her half-brother Elias, the youngest of Robert's sons by his first wife, was the only one of the first twelve children who was not mentally disabled in one way or another. So, less than four months later, the Grand Marshal of the Austrian court declared Henry, the eldest and current *de jure* Duke of Parma, and five of his siblings legally incompetent. Elias became regent for Henry and guardian for his disabled siblings. Zita's older fully biological brothers would eventually agree to split the estate in half with Elias, but they would revisit the issue after World War I, and an unsuccessful dispute would ensue. This matter, however, lies in the future.

In February of 1909, Zita was sent to the Benedictine monastery-in-exile in England, where her grandmother and sister resided. The former supervised her final classes in Latin, history, philosophy, and music. While there, Zita witnessed the death of Mother Cécile Bruyère, the founding abbess and collaborator in reviving French Benedictine life with the great Dom Prosper Gueranger. This holy death made a great impression on the seventeen-year-old girl. However, as her own health began to suffer, she was called back to Austria. It was decided that she would recover at the Hotel Imperial in the spa town of Franzenbad (now Františkovy Lázně) in Bohemia. There, she would act as a companion to her first cousin, Maria Annunziata.

This relationship requires a little explanation. One of Zita's mother's older sisters was Maria Theresa. By virtue of marrying Emperor Franz Joseph's next younger brother (after the murdered Emperor Maximilian of Mexico), Karl Ludwig in

1873, she became an Archduchess of Austria. Her husband had been married and widowed twice before, so with her new status came four stepchildren: Franz Ferdinand, Otto, Ferdinand Karl, and Margarete Sophie. In 1889, Franz Joseph's son, Crown Prince Rudolph, died under mysterious circumstances, and Karl Ludwig became heir to the throne. Maria Theresa's sister-in-law, Empress Elisabeth—in some ways the Princess Diana of the nineteenth century—spent increasingly long periods in travel, even more so after Prince Rudolph's death. Maria Theresa acted as her substitute as Franz Joseph's hostess. As well as becoming very close to her stepchildren, Maria Theresa had two daughters of her own with her husband: Maria Annunziata and Elisabeth Amalie. It was the former who would now look after Zita in the summer of 1909.

In 1894, Maria Annunziata became Abbess of the Order of Noble Ladies of the Hradschin at Prague. This was a unique institution. Although the members lived a quasi-religious life, they were not bound by perpetual vows and could leave to get married—although, of course, that meant leaving the Order. Called *canonesses*, they did have to observe certain rules, wear a unique habit, and attend the daily office and Mass. As their abbess, Maria Annunziata had the right to crown the Queen of Bohemia at the country's coronation when the Archbishop of Prague would crown the king, although this had not happened since 1836 for Emperor Ferdinand I, Ferdinand V for Bohemians. She could wear a miter and ring (which her canonesses would kiss) and wield a crozier.

She might well have been content with this arrangement, but in 1902, love in the form of Prince Siegfried of Bavaria came into her life. She met him at her half-brother Franz Ferdinand's castle in Bohemia. He was dashing, handsome, and a great horseman, while she was brilliant and lovely herself. They made a handsome couple and were soon engaged. Unfortunately, Siegfried had been thrown from his horse and landed on his head back in 1899, after which his mental acuity and behavior began to decay. Admitting this to his intended, they mutually agreed to break off the engagement, and he, in due course, descended entirely into insanity. Maria Annunziata was broken-hearted and resolved to follow her grandmother into the Benedictine Order. Despite her desires, the emperor refused her permission, pointing out that she was already an abbess and suggesting that she rededicate herself to that. This she did and pursued the religious vocation of the canonesses quite seriously; she would never marry. She also began to share the duties of Imperial hostess that had fallen to her mother and had grown even more onerous after the empress's murder in 1898.

Both mother and daughter were very popular among the disparate members of the Habsburg dynasty. Both extended a great deal of goodwill to all the members of the clan and provided a source of common sense, something that had been tested already. Karl Ludwig had gone on a pilgrimage to the Holy Land and caught typhoid from drinking the waters of the River Jordan. Upon his death, his oldest son, Franz Ferdinand, became heir to the throne. It was expected that he would marry a royal, but instead, he fell in love with Countess Sophie Chotek, a Bohemian noblewoman who was both bright and beautiful. In fact, she had every quality save royal birth. Franz Joseph was dead set against the match, but Franz Ferdinand would not be gainsaid. Fortunately, the mother and daughter, who loved them both, helped to smooth things out. Franz Ferdinand would, in the end, marry the woman he loved, but it would be a morganatic marriage; Sophie would never be empress, and their children could not inherit the throne. A high price to pay for love, perhaps, but one that the heir to the throne was willing to pay.

Because of this, Franz Ferdinand's heir—and ultimately Franz Joseph's heir—was his younger brother, Otto. "Handsome Otto," as the Viennese referred to him in his younger days, was very much unlike his devout father and older brother. He was a playboy in his youth, and his marriage to Princess Maria Josepha of Saxony did little to slow him down. After an initial period of contentment, which produced two sons, he went back to his old ways. His wife was not only as devout as Karl Ludwig and Franz Ferdinand but she was also a bit dour. When Otto fell victim to syphilis, the palace became a sort of hospice, and his only visitors were his stepmother and his oldest son, Charles. When Otto finally succumbed to the disease in 1906, Charles became heir to Franz Ferdinand and to Franz Joseph.

Both Maria Theresa and Maria Annunziata thought that Zita and Charles would be a good match. Since, by 1909, Charles was stationed with his cavalry unit in Bohemia, it was a simple thing to invite him to Maria Annunziata's lodgings in Franzenbad. Although they had been playmates in childhood, Charles was five years older than Zita, and when he had visited Schwarzau years before, he was more interested in seeing her older brothers, Sixtus and Xavier. Yet much had changed in the intervening period, and they continued to see each other intermittently at Franzenbad.

Zita had grown into a witty, charming, lovely young lady with a keen eye and sharp judgment. Charles, on the other hand, was a dashing cavalryman, affable, and light-hearted, but also high-minded and devout. Zita's upbringing had given her a strong sense of duty as well as an awareness that she must share the fate of and take on the responsibilities of whomever she might marry. Had she married her cousin and neighbor at Frohsdorf, Don Jaime, the Duke of Madrid, there can be no doubt that she would have made his restoration to the Spanish throne and the triumph of the Carlist cause her second major interest in life after her own salvation and that of her husband and children. Sources vary considerably as to how serious Don Jaime's suit was on the one hand or how receptive Zita was on the other. But either way, it played a role in Charles's finally asking for her hand after a two-year-long unofficial courtship. Charles's mother requested that Maria Theresa take a hand in the matter as the general confidante on romantic matters to the younger Habsburgs and Charles's step-grandmother. As Zita remembered it,

> We were glad to meet again and become close friends. On my side, feelings developed gradually over the next two years. He seemed to have made up his mind much more quickly, however, and even became more keen when, in the autumn of 1910, a rumour spread about

> that I had got engaged to a distant Spanish relative, Don Jaime, the Duke of Madrid.
>
> On hearing this, the Archduke came down post-haste from his regiment at Brandeis and sought out his grandmother, the Archduchess Maria Theresa (who was also my great-aunt) and the natural "confidante" in such matters. He asked her whether the rumour was true and when told it was not, replied: "Well, I had better hurry or else she really will get engaged to someone else."[23]

The following spring, Maria Theresa invited both young people to her hunting lodge at Sankt Jakob in Walde in Styria to hunt the *caipercailzie*, or "wood grouse." In their long walks through the beautiful forests, the young couple revealed their inmost thoughts to each other, and at length, Charles proposed and was accepted. To commemorate the occasion, Zita donated a carpet to the parish church, which is still to be seen there. On June 13 of that year, an official announcement and engagement party was held at the Villa Borbone in Pianore; auspiciously, it was the feast of St. Anthony of Padua and the birthday of Zita's mother.

Unlike other Habsburg betrothal parties over the past century, there were no apparent shadows. The couple were very obviously in love, and all of their relations were very much approving of the match. Most importantly, and particularly, this included the approval of the old emperor. For a man who had suffered so much in terms of personal

---

[23] Gordon Brook-Shepherd, *The Last Habsburg* (New York: Weybright and Talley, 1968), p. 18.

family loss, the gloom lifted with a match that both the most effusive romantic and the most exacting genealogist could accept happily. Beyond being in love, the couple had similar interests and outlooks on life.

Even the one person who might have been thought to harbor a touch of bitterness over the whole thing, Charles's uncle, Franz Ferdinand—who had entered into a morganatic marriage and whose wife, whom he adored, was constantly slighted—did not object. Far from it, he insisted on being the best man at the forthcoming wedding. It is in his relationship with his nephew that the true greatness of Franz Ferdinand can be noticed: a lesser man would have resented his nephew as the supplanter of his own children and husband of a wife whom everyone treated with respect. Yet he did not, and their shared affection for Charles, and now his fiancée, was one of the few things on which Franz Ferdinand and his uncle, the emperor, saw eye to eye.

Before the happy couple could be married, however, there were a few official duties to be dealt with. Charles would head over to London to represent Franz Joseph at the Coronation of King George V at Westminster Abbey. While he was thus employed, Zita and her mother would make a pilgrimage to Rome to seek Pope St. Pius X's blessings upon the upcoming wedding. During Charles's stay in London, it was noted that, out of deference to his fiancée, he did not dance at any of the many balls he attended. But for Zita, a surprise of sorts was in order.

On June 24, 1910, St. Pius X received Zita and unwittingly made her a prophecy: "You are going to marry the heir to the throne. I wish you all the blessings then."[24] In response, Zita dared timidly to point out that the heir was Franz Ferdinand, but the saintly pope insisted, "And I am infinitely delighted, because Charles is the reward that God has reserved for Austria, for all that she has done for the Church."[25] Zita left the private audience troubled and told her mother, "Thank God, the pope is not infallible in matters of politics."[26] Sadly, he was to be proved right.

When the happy couple returned from their last official duties as single folk, they threw themselves into preparing for the wedding, which was to be on October 21 at the castle chapel at Schwarzau. The town itself was absolutely enthralled to be at the center of the wedding, which the newspapers in Vienna, Budapest, and Prague, and monarchies from all over the world, greeted with delight:

> The house colours of bride and groom, blue-red for Parma and black-yellow for Habsburg, hung in streamers from all the low-roofed houses; flags stuck out of the narrow windows; the walls were plastered with royal portraits and coats-of-arms. The night before the ceremony, the villagers, their ranks swollen by groups of firemen and war veterans from all over the district, joined in a torchlight march of homage along the paths of the castle park. Fireworks blazed into the sky which had made its own contribution to

---

[24] Leo J. Hammerschmid, *Zita: The Last Empress of Austria* (Montreal: Meridian Press, 1989), pp. 42–43.

[25] James Bogle and Joanna Bogle, *A Heart for Europe* (Leominster: Gracewing, 2004), p. 32.

[26] Hammerschmid, *Zita*, pp. 42–43.

> the scores of wedding gifts (headed by the diamond tiara given by the emperor) spread out in two large rooms inside. The Viennese astronomer Dr. Palisa had just discovered a small new body in the heavens which he had named "Zita" and "presented" to the bride.[27]

The wedding itself was quite literally a glittering affair. Msgr. Gaetano Bisletti—only a little over a month away from being named a cardinal who would crown the future Pius XI with the papal tiara—performed the marriage ceremony as the personal representative of the pope. Franz Ferdinand served as Charles's best man, and Don Jaime, as senior member of the House of Bourbon, gave Zita away. Charles's maternal uncle, King Frederick Augustus III of Saxony, and of course, his great uncle, Franz Joseph, were present and offered toasts at the celebration afterward. Indeed, as may be seen in pictures of the event afterwards, Franz Joseph was exceedingly jolly—far more than most people ever saw him. Part of the bride's wedding gown would later be turned into a chasuble and is still used for Mass at the chapel, even though the castle is under radically different management than it was in 1911.

Indeed, for everyone involved, the wedding day was a high point. No one could have predicted the horrors that awaited the Habsburgs, Bourbons, Braganzas, Wittelsbachs, and Wettins—and indeed, all of Europe and much of the world—in the coming decade. Whether the date would be fondly (even if sadly) looked back on by the surviving

---

[27] Gordon Brook-Shepherd, *The Last Empress* (London: HarperCollins, 1991), pp. 18–19.

participants as their years passed, it definitely has importance for those of us living today. When Charles was beatified, it was decided by Pope St. John Paul II that his feast would not be the day of his death, April 1, but the day of his wedding, October 21. Thus, if Zita is beatified, she shall undoubtedly share the date with him.

This would be fitting, for when they left on their honeymoon, their first stop was the great shrine of Mariazell, beloved under the names of *Magna Mater Austriae*, *Magna Domina Hungarorum*, and *Magna Mater Gentium Slavorum* by all the Catholic peoples of the monarchy. On each of their wedding rings, Charles had inscribed "Karl von Österreich—Zita von Bourbon-Parma. *Sub tuum præsidium confugimus sancta Dei Genitrix* (Under thy protection we seek refuge, O Holy Mother of God)," the words of an ancient prayer to Our Lady. At Mariazell, Charles said to his new wife, "Now we must begin to help each other get to Heaven."[28] If Zita is indeed beatified, we shall know that Charles achieved his wish.

In any case, their honeymoon would take them to Trieste, Dalmatia, Kotor (in what is now Montenegro), and then Bosnia. They would then proceed by way of Vienna to Bradeis in Bohemia, where Charles's regiment was stationed. But before we join them, we need to take a closer look at Zita's new husband.

---

[28] Bogle, *A Heart for Europe*, p. 35.

CHAPTER 4

THE MAN SHE MARRIED

"Very exacting is the education of Princes. Scholastic, religious and military discipline converge to grip the boy. Teachers, bishops, and generals stand over every hour of the youthful life. All inculcate the sense of majesty; all emphasize the idea of duty; all ingeminate decorum. Real Kings have a unique point of view. Not even the most eminent of their subjects has the same association with the life of the whole people. Lifted far above party and faction, they personify the spirit of the State. But that anyone so reared and trained, so surfeited with honour, should grow up to be a practical, genial man of the world with a noble air, but without a scrap of conceit, proves that he was endowed at birth with an attractive nature."

—WINSTON CHURCHILL[29]

The man whom Zita married had already had a rather eventful life. His father, Archduke Otto Franz (1865–1906), younger son of Franz Joseph's second brother, Karl Ludwig, had been the toast of Vienna society—both respectable and otherwise. "Handsome Otto's" good looks and

[29] Winston Churchill, *Great Contemporaries* (London: Reprint Society, 1941), p. 172.

ready charm made up for a multitude of vices in his youth, at least in the eyes of courtiers, the press, and the public. Partly to settle him down and partly to mend fences with Saxony over two rejected marriages, he was wed to Princess Maria Josepha, daughter of King George, on October 2, 1886. As was her father, the new archduchess was extremely devout and particularly devoted to the Sacred Heart of Jesus. As a wedding gift, Karl Ludwig gave the newlyweds the Castle of Persenbeug.

There, on August 17, 1887, Archduke Charles was born and baptized two days later in the palace chapel. His uncle, Franz Ferdinand, was present at the baptism, and he would play a huge role in the formation of Charles, giving him an example of a true man, father, and husband, of which his father was incapable of doing. Moreover, his religious and political guidance was key in forming young Charles's views. But the Franz Ferdinand who appeared at the baptism that day was quite different from the confident *paterfamilias* (or "father of a family") who would leave such a mark on the young man.

Of course, it was highly unlikely that either the baby boy, his father, his uncle, or his grandfather would ever be heirs to the throne. Franz Joseph's son, Crown Prince Rudolph, was married and had a daughter already. He and his wife were young, and there was no reason to suppose that they would not produce an heir. However, in the same year as Otto and Maria Josepha's wedding, Rudolph had bought a hunting lodge that would one day be notorious around the world—Mayerling. On January 30, 1889, Rudolph and his young mistress, Maria Vetsera, would be found dead in the bedroom of the lodge. The Mayerling affair was truly the Kennedy assassination of the nineteenth century. Was it a suicide pact? A murder-suicide? Murder alone? Although most evidence would point to the first named, in later years, Zita would maintain that it was murder, a claim backed up by the oral tradition of the monks of Heiligenkreuz Abbey, who received the body of the prince and maintained that his fingers were all broken.

Whatever the truth of the matter, Rudolph's untimely death made Karl Ludwig and his two sons heirs to the throne. Of course, Franz Ferdinand was unmarried, but it was likely that he would marry at some point in the near future. In the meantime, Charles's life was fairly idyllic. His family revolved between Persenbeug, the Villa Wartholz in Reichenau-an-der-Rax, and his father's military billets, successively in Prague, Brno, and Sopron. He had an Irish nanny from whom he began to pick up English early on. In 1895, the family was joined by a new baby son, Charles's younger brother Maximilian Eugen. Charles dutifully looked after him. Indeed, as a child, one of the things that impressed Zita about her future spouse was his conscientious care for his little brother.

It was that sort of care—not just for little Max but for servants and even random people whom the young archduke chanced to meet—that was noticed quite early on. When, in 1895, the family moved to Sopron, it was decided that Charles's formal schooling should begin. A local Dominican priest, Fr. Norbert Geggerle, was hired as his first teacher. Much impressed with his new charge's intelligence and good-heartedness, the priest bragged about him to the local Ursuline Mother Superior, Vincentia Fauland. Unbeknownst to the reverend gentleman, Mother Vincentia was a stigmatic and had come to have a reputation as something of a prophetess. She warned Charles's tutor that the little boy would be emperor one day and "would be a special target of hell."[30] Mother Vincentia counseled him to gather as many people as he could to pray for young Charles. The priest complied, and this was the beginning of the Gebetsliga (the League of Prayer), which would pray for Charles throughout the various episodes of his life and, after his death, become the promoters of his cause for beatification and present cause for canonization. This is certainly unusual, as most such organizations originate after a possible saint's death when people begin to look into his holiness. On November 19, 1898, Karl received his First Holy Communion from the hand of Auxiliary Bishop Marschall in the chapel of Villa Wartholz.

The following year, Charles's grandfather, as we noted earlier, died of typhoid contracted from drinking polluted water from the River Jordan while on a pilgrimage to the Holy Land. Now, the still unmarried Franz Ferdinand was heir to the throne, and Otto was his heir presumptive. Franz Ferdinand was given the Belvedere as his Vienna residence, and Otto and his family the Augarten. In the meantime, Franz Ferdinand had fallen in love with Countess Sophie Chotek, as earlier recounted. After all of the difficulty, he was united at last with his beloved Sophie in 1899, after

---

[30] Emperor Karl League of Prayers for Peace Among Nations—Official Website, Gebetsliga, https://www.gebetsliga.com/home/die-gebetsliga/geschichte/.

agreeing to the emperor's conditions regarding a morganatic marriage. But this meant that Otto was now his older brother's heir—and Charles was his. That year, Fr. Norbert Geggerle presented Charles with the brown scapular of Mount Carmel and, in his speech, urged Charles to "carry it undefiled and pure until in death you can give it back to the heavenly Mother!"[31]

Consulting with Franz Joseph, it was decided to send Charles to a regular school—the Schottengymnasium in Vienna—from August 1899 to June 1901. The monastery to which it was attached had been founded in 1155 when Irish ("Scots") monks from Regensburg came to Vienna at the invitation of the Babenberg ruler, Henry II. The monks and their charges were—and still are—very proud of the school, and Charles fit in very well. His classmates gave him the nickname of *Erzkarl* (ArchCharles) in joking reference to his exalted status.

As he grew into a teenager, there were many witnesses to his genuine piety as well as his good nature. The summer before Charles started at the Schottengymnasium, on June 11, 1899, Pope Leo XIII consecrated the entire world to the Sacred Heart of Jesus. Emperor Franz Joseph and the imperial family joined him in doing so by reciting the appointed prayer of consecration at the Stephansdom at the precise hour when the pope did so in Rome. But Charles, being sick with whooping cough, was left at Villa Wartholz. Nevertheless,

---

[31] "Blessed Charles of Austria and his relationship with the Sacred Heart of Jesus," The Catholic information page of the Community of St. Joseph, https://www.stjosef.at/artikel/sel_karl_v_oesterreich_herz jesu.htm.

he insisted on reciting the same prayer at the same time in the villa's private chapel. At around this time, he became an avid reader of *The Messenger of the Sacred Heart*.

His piety did not interfere with his growing knowledge of people—far from it. We have an interesting account of Charles's teenage years from Arthur Count von Polzer-Holditz, who would later play a part in Charles's life as emperor:

> I had known the future Emperor Karl from his earliest youth. I saw and spoke to him for the first time at a dance for young people given by Prince Alfred Windischgraetz on 6th February, 1902, at his house in the Renngasse in Vienna. The Archduke Karl was then still quite a child, a friendly fair-haired boy with candid blue eyes. His boyhood's friends were contemporaries of his own belonging to the most distinguished noble families, among them, Count Hans Wilczek, Prince Ferdinand Montenuovo, Count Draskovich, and Count Erdődy. I got to know him better when we met in the spring of 1904 at the hydropathic at Brixen. The Archduke had come there with his tutor, Count Georg Wallis, who had been my friend for many years, to recover his health after an illness. I spent several hours every day in the company of the Archduke, then a boy of sixteen. We took walks according to medical orders, made excursions on foot and wheel in the surrounding districts, played tennis, hunted for antiquities in the villages around Brixen, and generally whiled away the month's "cure" in all the ways we could think

> of. I hurt my eyes through an accident, and the young Archduke came to see me several times a day to help to fleet the hours I had to spend in a darkened room. In spite of the nearly twenty years' difference in our ages, he was very fond of being with me. I took great pleasure in his sunny nature, his gay and frank temper, and the kindness which found a friendly word or act for everybody. For all his youthful joie de vivre he liked serious conversation, I was often amazed at the clear and straightforward judgments he expressed on men and things. His judgments were always charitable, never malicious. He showed great appreciation for natural beauty and loved the mountains. But sentimentality was alien to his nature; he hated pose. He was absolutely genuine, sincere, and healthy-minded. It was the crown that first damped his spirit, as he bore the burden alone and faithfully.[32]

Fortunately, he had a few years left before that would happen. In 1904, Charles travelled around France and Germany and came to the conclusion that Alsace-Lorraine really would be better off as part of their old country.

It was typical of the young Charles—and, indeed, of the grown man—that he had no use for empty ceremony or show. When it was determined that he would join the Order of the Golden Fleece, he insisted on having the Order's old French statutes translated so as to see if he could swear to uphold them in the modern era. Satisfied that he could,

---

[32] Arthur Count von Polzer-Holditz, *The Emperor Karl* (New York and London: Putnam, 1930), pp. 37–38.

he swore. This would be true also for his entrance into the Order of Malta, his marriage, and his coronation as King of Hungary. Oaths were sacred things for him, in a way that it is perhaps hard for us to understand. It was not hard at all for Zita, whose great-uncle, as we have seen, refused the throne of France over a question of principle.

In 1903, the emperor appointed Archduke Charles as a lieutenant in the Uhlan Regiment "Archduke Otto" No. 1. Although it was on October 1, 1905, that his military training began in earnest with the 7th Dragoon Regiment, "Duke of Lorraine." The regiment had been formed in 1663 in light of the Ottoman threat to Austria and proved itself many times over the following two hundred and fifty years. The garrison was first stationed in Kutterschitz near Bilin in Bohemia and then, in 1906, was transferred to Brandeis-Altbunzlau. As with the Order of the Golden Fleece, Charles had no use for empty show and so threw himself into his military training, and he soon garnered many high ratings. On November 1, Charles was promoted to *oberleutnant* (first lieutenant), but it was a date that would prove tragic for him.

In the meantime, the health of Archduke Otto, Charles's father, had continued to decline. He had contracted syphilis around 1900, and at that time, he and Charles's mother ceased to live together. The disease began to cause him endless pain around 1904, and the heretofore popular archduke withdrew from public life entirely, moving to Egypt for a course of therapy. Upon improving, Otto returned to Austria, secluding himself at his castle at Schönau an der Triesting. Unfortunately, his reprieve was short-lived, and he fell ill again. The wreckage done to his nose had to be concealed by a prosthetic. As noted earlier, Otto lived the last few months of his life in a villa-turned-hospital at Anton Frank-Gasse 20 (today the Israeli Embassy) in the Viennese suburb of Währing. Desperately ill, Otto was nursed by his last mistress and, as we have seen, by his stepmother Maria Theresa of Portugal. Otto died on All Saints Day, 1906—the same day his son was promoted—attended by Bishop Godfried Marschall, the Auxiliary Bishop of Vienna. He died reconciled to the Church and with the sacraments, recalling on his deathbed that he had been enrolled as a Child of Mary.

One of Charles's strengths of character—and one that makes the now blessed a wonderful patron for children of broken or difficult homes—was his relationship with his parents. Different as they were—and even after they lived apart—Charles lived with both of them. Moreover, he was able to emulate the best qualities of each and leave the less pleasant ones aside. From his mother, he derived the deep piety and devotion that would characterize him from his early youth. Yet he did not emulate her dour and off-putting personality. From poor Archduke Otto, he received his easy and charming manner and quick wit. But he did not follow his promiscuous example.

The death of his father, however, gave him a new legal guardian, his uncle, Franz Ferdinand. As with Henry V and Robert of Parma (Zita's father), one cannot overestimate the influence of an uncle on his nephew. Indeed, it is impossible to understand Charles's efforts as emperor without grasping what Franz Ferdinand intended, had he lived to ascend the throne. On a personal level, of course, Charles learned what he knew of being a husband and father from watching Franz Ferdinand's relationship with his wife and children. He longed to have the same sort of home that his aunt and uncle had created. He shared his uncle's deep piety and, as we have seen, especially his devotion to the Sacred Heart. Charles also came to share his political views, both external and internal.

In terms of foreign affairs, Franz Ferdinand was a major proponent of a strong army and navy while still very much the leader of the "Peace Party" in Austrian governing circles. He was, in a sense, the counterpart of the onetime Russian Prime Minister, Pyotr Stolypin. Both men understood that their respective countries had more to lose than gain by conflict. Although a personal friend of Kaiser Wilhelm II, Franz Ferdinand had his doubts—well founded, as it turned out—as to whether his friend really had much control over Germany. Moreover, the archduke feared that too tight an alliance with Germany would end Austria's freedom of action. As the years went by, he conducted something of an independent foreign policy from his military cabinet's office in Vienna's Lower Belvedere Palace—the Upper Belvedere was his city residence. He had contacts in the Russian Foreign Ministry and, in 1913, would go on a hunting trip to England. At the party were the leaders of the then out-of-power Tory Party. It is not too much to suppose that he came to think that, when emperor, he might shift alliances when the Tories came back to power—perhaps a new Triple Alliance of Austria-Hungary, Russia, and Great Britain with the express mission of keeping Germany and France quiet and the continent at peace.

The same sort of peace Franz Ferdinand deeply desired for Europe, he wished to see at home. Having traveled through the United States and studied central European history, the archduke believed that the Dual Monarchy could not survive as it was in the long run. Among his "kitchen cabinet" at the Belvedere were specialists in various fields from among the different nationalities of the empire. He initially favored altering the Dual Monarchy to a Triune one (Austria, Hungary, and Greater Croatia, including Slavonia, Dalmatia, and after its 1908 annexation, which he had opposed, Bosnia). However, he eventually came to favor federalizing the monarchy, which would have meant allowing the Romanians, Slovaks, and Ruthenians of Hungary their own autonomous zones, something that the ruling party in Hungary, the liberals, could not be expected to accept. Indeed, there was no love lost between him and them, and from this arose the myth that Franz Ferdinand hated the Magyars. He certainly was not fond of the liberals nor of the Tiszas, the family that ran the party. Still, he had loved his time in the army in Gyor, Hungary, was close to the Catholic Party in the country and its leaders, the Zichys, and was very close to Jozef Lányi, a Hungarian priest who had taught him to speak Magyar. Indeed, Fr. Jozef baptized the archduke's children rather than the court bishop, who had opposed Franz Ferdinand's marriage to Sophie.

Count von Polzer-Holditz's comments on Franz Ferdinand's view of Hungary are particularly important here.

> There is no doubt that the Archduke had ideas about the internal constitutional structure of the Monarchy and the principles on which it should be reformed which were in sharp opposition to the principles of those in authority in Hungary. This very fact was a national crime in their eyes. None the less, although . . . influential Hungarian politicians feared the heir-apparent, because they were alarmed for their own power, it does not by any means follow that the Archduke hated Hungary. That was not the case. But I believe that I am not wrong in asserting that the then heir to the Throne rightly recognized that by maintaining Hungary intact he was safe-guarding the most precious jewel in his crown. For this reason he devoted special attention to Hungarian conditions. Nothing interested him more than what was happening in Hungary, nothing made him more uneasy than the short-sighted policy of the privileged leaders of Hungary, for, from the point of view of her future sovereign, he realized that this policy was bound to endanger the existence of Hungary in an extreme degree. The melancholy final phase shows how correct the Archduke's judgment was. It would, however, be a great mistake to think that the World War alone was responsible for Hungary's melancholy end. The World War merely hastened her ruin. It would have happened in any case.[33]

---

[33] Polzer-Holditz, *The Emperor Karl*, pp. 53–54. For the full quote, see Appendix II.

Given the enormous influence that Franz Ferdinand had on his nephew and the great love of Hungary that Charles would show until the end of his life, this would indeed seem to be the truth of the matter.

Franz Ferdinand's political opinions put him at considerable variance with the old emperor—and it is easy to see why. After the horrors of losing control over Germany and Italy to Prussia and Sardinia, being allied with them seemed a preferable alternative to Franz Joseph. Similarly, however cumbersome and difficult the compromise had been with Hungary, it had been the emperor's handiwork, and he could hardly be expected to look kindly on seeing all his efforts undone. As much as Charles may have agreed with his uncle, he understood Franz Joseph's position.

After his father's death, Charles began two years of intensive law studies at Prague University, staying at the city's Hradschin Castle. He also perfected his Czech. Franz Ferdinand was particularly happy that his young ward was studying Hungarian law as well as that of the other countries of the monarchy. In 1908, having come of age the year before, he moved to the Castle of Brandeis, both to be close to his regiment and because he liked the surroundings. Thus it was that he was in close proximity to Franzenbad, his aunt, and her companion, Princess Zita of Bourbon-Parma.

It will be recalled that there at the Archduchess Maria Theresa's hunting lodge at Sankt Jakob in Walde, Charles and Zita would go out shooting *capercailzie* and chatting. Much of the chat was, of course, romantic and would end, as we have seen, with their engagement. However, as Zita recalled,

> On one such outing the talk turned to politics and he said to me, "Dualism cannot be saved. Trialism is not just, and anyway does not go far enough. The only solution is a truly federal one to give all the peoples a chance."
>
> On another occasion I heard him say, speaking of an Emperor's duties: "A father makes no distinction between his children."
>
> This meant that he had no personal prejudices. . . . he was convinced that one group could not be favoured above the rest—as the Magyars and Germans were favoured under Dualism.
>
> We had up to seventeen nationalities, if one counted the tiny ones as well as the eleven main groups. He was prepared to give *all seventeen* their individual freedom if they wanted it. . . .
>
> And he went even further. He always stressed to me that it wouldn't even matter if one or the other nation wanted to declare itself a republic in this process. He used to point out to me that the three Hansa towns were, after all, republics within the German Reich. The essential thing for him was that, whatever constitutional form they chose, the nations should retain their link with the Monarchy and their identity with the State as a whole.[34]

These were not simply the conversations of a young man with his likely wife-to-be; they were those of a future

[34] Gordon Brook-Shepherd, *The Last Habsburg* (New York: Weybriaght and Talley, 1968), pp. 38–39.

emperor-king with a prospective empress-queen. For them to be a successful pair, they would have to share a common vision—and thanks to the history we looked at earlier, they did. Their view of the place of altar and throne was the same. But here we see subsidiarity in sharp relief, and this was already a part of Zita's political DNA.

Many of the counter-revolutionary authors of the restoration era, such as De Maistre and de Bonald, had inveighed against the abolition of the traditional French provinces during the Revolution. This continued to be a concern for French Legitimists throughout the nineteenth century:

> In the 19th century, decentralization became "the keystone of legitimist thought." . . . If, very early on, those nostalgic for the Old Regime denounced the centralization and standardization of the Revolution and the Empire as so many attacks on traditional franchises, they were nevertheless careful not to undo the administrative work accomplished between 1789 and 1815. . . . Henry V proposes in a letter of March 12, 1856 "a wisely decentralized municipal and departmental administration." . . . For the prince, "decentralization [can] no longer simply be the recognition of pre-constituted realities . . . it [must] also become a pedagogy implying respect for the family and the hierarchy. It is organic, communal, social, administrative, and not individualistic and political; it cannot become a subversive instrument."[35]

---

[35] Jean-Marc Guislin, "The participation of noble representatives in decentralizing debates in the National Assembly (1871–1875)," in Roger

Of course, Henry V was Zita's father's guardian and, as we saw, played for him the role that Franz Ferdinand did for Charles. But this sort of subsidiarity was not only the preserve of the French Bourbons. The motto of the Spanish Carlist Bourbons was *Dios, Patria, Rey, y Fueros* (God, Fatherland, King, and Provincial Liberties). The fourth of these were the charters peculiar to each Spanish province to which the older line of the Spanish Bourbons were committed. Needless to say, the Bourbons of Parma and the Two Sicilies were as committed to the freedoms of the small Italian States in the face of Sardinian-Italian expansion and centralization as were the Habsburgs of Modena and Tuscany. Provincial rights had also been part of Dom Miguel's struggle in Portugal. On both sides, to a greater or lesser degree, Zita's forebears had held out for the kind of monarchy that both Charles and his uncle wished to see in Austria-Hungary—not merely for the sake of ancient tradition but for contemporary advantage as well.

The close agreement of the happy couple was far deeper than political—it was religious. Both saw the salvation of the human soul as its highest good, and both were devoted to the Blessed Sacrament, the Sacred and Immaculate Hearts, the Rosary, and many other devotions. The *religion royale* of Zita's forebears dovetailed nicely with the *Pietas Austriaca* of Charles's forebears. For both, being a good spouse, a good parent, and a good ruler were interrelated religious duties.

Baury and Marie-Laure Legay, eds.,*L'invention de Decentralisation*, pp. 361–79.

This is one reason why trying to separate the religious and political viewpoints of either is to distort them.

So, they were deeply united in all the most important things—a key to making any marriage a success. As things stood on that lovely day on October 21, 1911, they would need their unanimity for the purpose of guiding their countries through the looming difficulties in good order and leaving to their own heir a better, stronger, and even holier monarchy than the one they would eventually inherit. Neither of them could have known how much more difficult would be the tests they would face or how much they would need each other. In the immediate, all they had to face were the rigors of the honeymoon and then adjustment to married life in a garrison town. Let us leave them for the moment in a setting so very happy that even Franz Joseph was positively cheery. It was a memory whose joy would soon be needed.

CHAPTER 5

NEWLYWEDS IN PEACE AND WAR

"Bless O Lord, this ring, which we are blessing in Thy name, so that she who wears it, keeping faith with her husband in unbroken loyalty, may ever remain at peace with Thee, obedient to Thy will, and may live with him always in mutual love. Through Christ our Lord."

—BLESSING OF THE WEDDING RING,
RITUALE ROMANUM, 1964

After their honeymoon, which took them from Trieste, down through Dalmatia, to Kotor (now Montenegro), and off to Bosnia, the happy couple made their way to Brandeis (now Brandys). There, they lived in a castle belonging to the Habsburgs while Charles performed his military duties, and Zita began learning Czech. But, on March 1, 1912, Charles's regiment was ordered to Kolomyia in Galicia (now Ukraine), near the Russian border. The regiment traveled slowly on horseback with its goods brought by wagon. Archduchess Zita took trains, stopping at each station where the regiment would halt for the night. In this slow manner, they at last arrived at the new garrison town. There, in Kolomyia, they lived in a small bungalow.

During their free time, they would motor around the area, exploring and enjoying whatever they could see. One day, their car broke down, and they hiked to the village of Nadvirna and ordered some food and drink at the local tavern. The landlady, having no idea who they were, mentioned that she had a boy serving in the army of Kolomyia. On determining they were going that way, she vanished, returning with five kronen she had saved for her son and a package of laundry. She asked, "Would you mind giving these things to him?" Without revealing their identities, they assured the mother that her son would get both. That evening, upon their return, the young trooper was amazed to be summoned to Charles's office, where he duly received his laundry and a sum of money that had grown considerably from what it had been.

Things changed when, in the summer, Charles was thrown from his horse and suffered a bad concussion; he was sent back to Villa Wartholz to recover. Zita came with him, and by their first anniversary, he was ready to return to duty. But Zita was also almost ready—to give birth. On November 1, 1912, Charles was promoted to the rank of major and reassigned to the 39th Infantry Regiment in Vienna. Moreover, Franz Joseph gave them the relatively undistinguished palace of Hetzendorf to reside in. But it would be at the Villa Wartholz, on November 20, that their eldest, Archduke Otto, named after his grandfather, would be born. Five days later, Franz, Ferdinand, and Sophie came to Reichenau. Franz would act as proxy godfather on behalf of the emperor at the baptism, which was held at the villa's private chapel.

The town gave itself up to celebration, and the entire monarchy was happy that there were now three generations of heirs behind the elderly Franz Joseph.

From this time on, Charles and Zita's life changed. Zita took over the role of imperial hostess, which Franz Ferdinand's wife was not allowed to take part in. Here, two things spoke well for both Zita and Charles, and his aunt and uncle came into play. It would have been quite easy, indeed, especially as the young couple had become so very popular, to set up a third center of intrigue to rival Franz Joseph's Schönbrunn and Franz Ferdinand's Belvedere. This they refused to do. Zita, however, began studying Magyar, and on January 3, 1914, their second child, Adelheid, was born.

It would have been very natural for Franz Ferdinand to have resented his nephew, who was taking his children's place, and Zita, who had supplanted his wife. Instead, their relationship became ever closer. The emperor did not keep Franz Ferdinand well informed of developments, which is one reason why he had developed his own staff at the Belvedere. But he often said, "When I am Emperor, I shall have Charles with me in the Hofburg, and let him work with me."[36] Despite often being left in the dark, Franz Ferdinand certainly knew what was going on in Europe. He was determined, once he became emperor—as we have seen—to have better relations with Russia and, perhaps, to even revive the "Three Emperors League" constructed by Bismarck, which had lapsed in his youth. In late 1913, he declared to an assistant,

[36] James Bogle and Joanna Bogle, *A Heart for Europe* (Leominster: Gracewing, 2004), p. 97.

> If we all go on arming like this, all of us in Europe will be ruined even before war breaks out. Europe must get a different constellation of alliances if it is to escape all the dangers of war. The only salvation for us is the Three Emperors' League, which I will continue to work for with all my strength. We also need the League for domestic reasons, in the cause of the conservative concept. What would be the point of fighting Russia? Not even Napoleon could succeed. And even if we beat Russia—which to my mind is totally [out] of the question—a victory like that would still be the greatest tragedy for the Austrian Monarchy.[37]

While Charles and Zita remained on very good terms with Franz Joseph, their relationship with Franz Ferdinand and Sophie deepened as they were a younger couple looking to the happily married elder duo for guidance and an example. Both couples shared a deep devotion to the Sacred Heart, and Franz Ferdinand had a pet project underway. Tyrol had been consecrated to the Sacred Heart since the province rose in rebellion in favor of Emperor Franz against the French and Bavarians in 1796. But there was no great shrine to the Sacred Heart in the province. In 1899, Franz Ferdinand attended the dedication of the Sacred Heart church in Botzen (Bolzano). Perhaps, as early as then, he began looking for a fit location for a shrine in honor of the land of the Sacred Heart. By 1912, the heir to the throne had found it.

[37] Jean Louis Thiériot, *François Ferdinand d'Autriche. De Mayerling a Sarajevo* (Paris: B. De Fallois, 2005), p. 244.

In Hall, Tyrol, there had existed, prior to 1782, the *Haller Damenstift* (Ladies Foundation of Hall), which had been an institution very much like the one in Prague presided over by Charles's cousin Maria Annunziata. It had been founded by Venerable Archduchess Magdalena of Austria (1532–1590). The sixth child and fourth daughter of Ferdinand I, Holy Roman Emperor (1503–1564) and Empress Anna of Bohemia and Hungary (1503–1547), she is the only Habsburg, other than Charles and Zita themselves, ever considered by the Church for beatification. Although both she and her two younger sisters wished to be nuns, they had to wait until their father, the emperor, died. After that bereavement, Magdalena founded the institution, dying there as abbess. It continued quite happily until Joseph II dissolved it as part of his war on the monasteries. Following that, it had gone through several uses, including as a barracks. In 1912, Franz Ferdinand bought the old building for fifty thousand crowns and donated it as a convent for the Daughters of the Heart of Jesus. He then began the refurbishing of the convent church with the intention of it becoming "the shrine" to the Sacred Heart in Tyrol—Austria's answer to France's Paray-le-Moniale or Montmartre. The date of dedication was fixed for July of 1914, and in preparation, Franz Ferdinand began making the Nine First Fridays devotion in March of 1913.

Although Franz Joseph had warmed somewhat to Sophie, creating her Duchess of Hohenberg in 1909 and sanctioning several trips abroad for the couple to take where they would be received as equals, she continued to receive innumerable snubs in Vienna—each of which Franz Ferdinand resented greatly. Even at the opera, Franz Ferdinand and his wife would be seated in separate boxes. It so happened that, one night, Charles and Zita ran into Sophie at the opera, and Zita kissed her beloved aunt-in-law's hand. Sophie pulled it away and asked her never to do so in public again: "It's just what people who want to make difficulties for me are looking for."[38]

It was partly for this reason that when Franz Ferdinand, as the Inspector General of the Imperial Army, was notified that he was to go on a tour of inspection in Bosnia in June of 1914, he was looking forward to it. The emperor had decreed that Sophie was to receive full honors as the wife of the heir to the throne at every place they would visit. One may perhaps detect not only the slowly increasing respect for Sophie on Franz Joseph's part but also the efforts of Charles and Zita with the old emperor, who loved the couple as much as his nephew did.

The two couples dined together frequently at Belvedere, but one dinner in early May of 1914, after this last tour had been assigned, took a rather chilling turn. After the dining was finished, Sophie took the three children up to bed. As soon as they had left, Franz Ferdinand said to Charles and Zita, "I must say this quickly, as I don't want your aunt to hear anything of this. I know that I shall soon be murdered. In this desk are papers which concern you. When it happens, take them; they are for you."[39] Asked if he was joking, Charles's uncle said that he was deadly serious, "after

[38] Gordon Brook-Shepherd, *The Last Empress* (London: HarperCollins, 1991), p. 25.

[39] Gordon Brook-Shepherd, *The Last Habsburg* (New York: Weybriaght and Talley, 1968), p. 27.

all, everything is ready. The crypt in Artstetten is now finished."[40] Sophie returned, and they all acted as if things were normal.

At this point, the question might well be asked: Who did Franz Ferdinand think might murder him? There was no shortage of candidates. Both German and Hungarian extremists saw him as an enemy; certainly, when he was murdered, folk of those persuasions were quite pleased. He disliked both the anticlerical French Republic and the Masonic Order intensely, and both were suspected of involvement. But his actual nemesis was Dragutin Dimitrijević, code name Apis, who was the head of Serbian Military Intelligence.

Apis had already established himself within Serbia as a force to be reckoned with. Since the 1830s, two families had vied with each other for control of Serbia—the Obrenovics, who were pro-Austrian, and the Karageorgevics, who were Russian allies. By 1900, Alexander I of the former house was on the throne in Belgrade. In May of 1903, Apis led a coup that resulted in the murder of the king and queen and several of their allies. He and his co-conspirators then summoned Peter Karageorgevic back from his Parisian exile, and he became King Peter I of Serbia. But he and the rest of the royal family were somewhat wary of their benefactor, to say the least.

That benefactor had an aim in mind. Apis wished for the union of all Serbs—in Serbia, Turkey, and Austria-Hungary—in one state under Russian patronage. Alexander's pro-Habsburg stance meant he had to go. When Austria

---

[40] Brook-Shepherd, *The Last Habsburg*, p. 27.

annexed Bosnia in 1908, it set Apis's plans back further, although the Balkan Wars helped by expelling Turkey from most of Europe and expanding Serbia by two-thirds. That left Austria-Hungary to deal with. The problem there was Franz Ferdinand.

However unpopular Franz Ferdinand might have been with the Magyar liberals, the Slavs within the empire—particularly the Croats and Serbs—loved him. For Apis, if Franz Ferdinand became emperor, all hope of the ethnic southern Slavs in the empire rebelling would be utterly lost. With the resources of Serbian Intelligence, of which he was now head, Apis created the Black Hand in Bosnia. This terrorist organization trained a number of young Serb zealots in the skills of assassination. One of these was a young man named Gavrilo Princip. He would be one of those tasked with attempting to murder the archduke and his wife when they made their official visit to Sarajevo on June 28, 1914.

Leaving their children behind at their Castle of Chulmetz (Chlum U Trebone) in Bohemia, Sophie and Franz Ferdinand began their journey to Sarajevo on June 23. The emperor left for his villa at Ischl, and Charles and Zita headed off to Villa Wartholz in Reichenau. Sophie was received ceremonially as the wife to the heir to the throne wherever the two went, and the military maneuvers went off like clockwork. On June 27, the happy pair checked into the Hotel Bosna in Ilidza, a spa resort town near Sarajevo, which they would tour the next day.

About three hundred miles away, Josef Lányi, who had been an auxiliary bishop in Nagyvarad/Grosswardein/Oradea went to bed in the episcopal palace. We saw earlier how he taught Magyar to Franz Ferdinand and baptized his and Sophie's children. But in 1906, he was made an auxiliary bishop for a Transylvanian diocese. He was archdeacon of the cathedral, and his noted diplomatic skills served him well as rector of a seminary riven by ethnic division. According to his own account,

> At a quarter past three on the morning of the 28th June, 1914, I awoke from a terrible dream. I dreamed that I had gone to my desk early in the morning to look through the post that had come in. On top of all the other letters there lay one with a black border, a black seal and the arms of the Archduke. I immediately recognized the latter's writing, and saw at the head of the notepaper in blue colouring a picture like those on picture postcards which showed me a street and a narrow side-street. Their Highnesses sat in a car, opposite them sat a general, and an officer next to the chauffeur. On both sides of the street there was a large crowd. Two young lads sprang forward and shot at their Highnesses. The text of the letter was as follows: "Dear Dr Lányi, Your Excellency, I wish to inform you that my wife and I were the victims of a political assassination. We recommend ourselves to your prayers. Cordial greetings from your Archduke Franz, Sarajevo, 28th June, 3.15 a.m." Trembling and in tears I sprang out of bed and I looked at the clock, which showed 3.15. I immediately hurried to my desk and wrote down what I had read and seen in my dream. In doing so I even retained the form of certain letters

> just as the Archduke had written them. My servant entered my study at a quarter to six that morning and saw me sitting there pale and saying my rosary. He asked whether I was ill. I said: "Call my mother and the guest at once. I will say Mass immediately for their Highnesses, for I have had a terrible dream." My mother and the guest came at a quarter to seven. I told my mother the dream in the presence of the guest and of my servant. Then I went into the house chapel. The day passed in fear and apprehension. At half-past three a telegram brought us the news of the murder.[41]

It very nearly did not happen. That warm June morning, on the way to the city hall, one of Apis's minions threw a bomb at the archduke's open car. With his usual *sang-froid*, Franz Ferdinand grabbed it and threw it under the car, where it exploded more or less harmlessly, although Governor Potiorek's adjutant was wounded and taken away to the hospital. The party then continued on their way to the city hall. There, the usual sorts of welcoming speeches were given, although they seemed a bit hollow in the light of what had just happened. The event concluded, and Franz Ferdinand informed the mayor and governor that he wanted to go to the hospital to see the wounded man. Orders were given to clear the streets, but these were not carried out, and Franz Ferdinand did not wish to wait, so he suggested that Sophie wait for him, but she refused. They set out again, but the driver, either not having been informed or forgetting the

[41] Alois Wiesinger, *Occult Phenomena in the Light of Theology* (Westminster, MD: Newman Press, 1957), p. 106.

change in plans, began to go on the previously publicized route. Once told that he was supposed to go to the hospital, he stopped and began to turn around. Apis's agent, Gavrilo Princip, having missed several opportunities earlier in the day, stepped forward and shot the archducal couple. Both died very soon—she of an internal stomach wound, and he by bleeding out from a severed artery. Unbeknownst to the crowd, their whole world had just died with the heir to the throne. In Reichenau, playing with their children, Charles and Zita were unaware that he was now crown prince. As with millions across the globe, those two gunshots altered things for them forever.

There was a wooden summerhouse in the gardens at Villa Wartholz, where Charles and Zita would eat lunch by themselves. This quiet time together was one of their greatest joys. Lunch had begun as usual, with the drinks and first dishes brought from the kitchen. On this day, however, there was a very long delay before the main course arrived. When it did at last, it was accompanied by a telegram signed by Baron Rumerskirch, Franz Ferdinand's adjutant. It revealed the tragic events at Sarajevo that morning. Zita watched Charles's face go white as he read the contents of the fateful missive. At the age of fifty, Franz Ferdinand could have been expected to rule into the 1930s; now, instead of decades, Charles and Zita would have only a few years, if that, to prepare to follow Franz Joseph. Moreover, there were the Hohenberg children to think of: as Charles had become Franz Ferdinand's ward when his own father died, so now his uncle's offspring became his responsibility. There was also the old emperor himself to think of. Although he and Franz

Ferdinand had been at loggerheads in both personal and political matters, there was always the possibility of ironing them out, especially as Franz Joseph's appreciation for his nephew's wife's virtues had been growing. Now there was no time left to heal rifts and no time to say whatever was unsaid. How would this affect him?

Charles called his great-uncle immediately at the Kaiser-villa in Ischl, where the old emperor had been enjoying his summer holidays. It was agreed that Charles and Zita would return to Vienna straightaway and meet Franz Joseph, who would come back as soon as he could. The couple returned to Schönbrunn. Zita waited at the palace while Charles went to Hietzing, the closest station, to pick up the emperor. Meeting him there, Franz Joseph and his new heir drove back to Schönbrunn in an open carriage through streets lined with silent, mournful people. There, they met Zita. When the trio were alone, Franz Joseph looked miserably at the young couple and, for one of the very few times Zita ever saw, gave way to his emotions. Referring to his brother, son, wife, and now nephew, he said "Is nothing to be left me?"[42] Franz Ferdinand and Sophie had to be properly buried, and so they would be.

That very night, violence broke out in Sarajevo as the Habsburg-loving Croats began taking revenge against the local Serbs, whom they considered sympathetic to the crime, even if not entirely responsible. The bodies of the murdered couple rested overnight in a makeshift chapel at the

[42] Erich Feigl, *Kaiserin Zita von Oesterreich nach Oesterreich* (Vienna: Amalthea, 1986), p. 169.

Konak—the residence of the Governor of Bosnia. They were then returned to Vienna by train, the car being saluted by troops at every garrison town the locomotive stopped in on the way. They arrived late on July 2 and were taken by torchlight to the Burgkapelle of the Hofburg, where the funeral was to be held. There had been some question, initially, of inviting all of Europe's sovereigns to take part. Who knows? Perhaps such a gathering, reminiscent of that for Edward VII in 1910, might have staved off conflict. However, the combination of needed security measures and timing led the Austrian government to recommend to the emperor that invitations only be sent to the ambassadors.

At 8 a.m. on July 3, the Schweizerhof of the Hofburg was opened up so that the public in their thousands might file by and view the coffins in the Burgkapelle. At the head of the archduke's casket lay his general's hat, sash, and sword. At the head of Sophie's casket lay a pair of white gloves and a black fan. Candles lit the scene, their lights reflecting off the jewels of the two coronets laid on a cushion by Franz Ferdinand's coffin, symbolizing the two crowns to which he had been heir. On Sophie's side, a similar cushion held her bejeweled badge of the Order of the Starry Cross—the unique female order of chivalry that would soon fall to Zita to head. At the end of the evening, ten each of the Life Guard and the Hungarian Guard appeared and drew their sabers. The emperor, Charles, and Zita entered the gallery to the right of the altar nearest the coffins, and other family members filled other places. Cardinal Piffl blessed the caskets with holy water and incense while the usual prayers were intoned. The next day, the coffins were transported to Artstetten, where they were entombed in the place Franz Ferdinand had so recently prepared for them. The obsequies done, Franz Joseph returned to the quiet of Ischl, and Charles and Zita to the Villa Wartholz. Yet while they enjoyed the last few weeks of summer peace, events were moving swiftly all around them.

One thing became clear: neither Franz Joseph, Tsar Nicholas, nor Kaiser Wilhelm were really interested in war, but most of their ministers and generals were. Wilhelm was on his yacht in the Baltic, and his chancellor advised he be kept there as long as possible for fear of his injecting some of his "pacificism" into the proceedings. As July wore on, the well-nigh universal wave of sympathy for Franz Joseph and Austria-Hungary turned into worries about the peace. Franz Joseph stayed on at Ischl, to which worried ministers would make daily pilgrimages from Vienna to keep him informed in a brief cursory manner as to how his ministers were proceeding. With its murdered head out of the way, the peace party vanished, but the same worthies who had tried to exclude Franz Ferdinand from any role in policy-making were set to do the same for Charles.

Indeed, life at Villa Wartholz continued with little change, as—unknown to Charles and Zita in the main—the war clouds gathered over Europe. Berchtold, the foreign minister, drafted an ultimatum to Serbia so reasonable that both he and Conrad von Hotzendorf feared that it would be accepted. But the Serbian Prime Minister was facing elections in November and could not afford to appear weak. Beyond that, there was Apis and his fellows. They had no scruples in murdering a Serbian king: What would they do to a Serbian politician, especially one who was about to turn them over to the Austrians?

So it was that the wave of sympathy in June had turned to saber-rattling by late July. Germany swore to stand by Austria-Hungary, so Austria-Hungary declared war on Serbia, Russia declared war on Austria-Hungary, Germany declared war on Russia, and France declared war on Germany. The system of alliances that was intended to keep the peace had instead ensured war in the most machine-like way possible. In keeping with a decade-old military plan to hit France first in the event of a two-front war, Germany violated Belgian neutrality and brought Great Britain and her empire into the war. In Sir Edward Grey's memorable phrase, "the lamps are going out all over Europe. They shall not be relit again in our time."[43] Nor have they been.

In retrospect, World War I has been called a European civil war. Certainly, this was true for Charles and Zita's immediate family. Ironically, both of Henry V's homes, Chambord and Frohsdorf, would be seized by warring governments as enemy alien property. France expropriated the former chateau from Zita's brother, and Austria-Hungary the latter from her Spanish Carlist cousin, Jaime. Despite his Spanish connections, the latter was considered French and was given the choice between house arrest in Austria in his sequestered castle or being allowed to leave for Switzerland. He angrily took the latter. But the cut came closer still. Although initially planning to join their brother-in-law

[43] Viscount Grey of Fallodon, *Twenty-Five Years: 1892–1916* (New York: Frederick Stokes, 1925), p. 20.

in the Austrian army to help punish Serbia for the murder, Zita's brothers, Sixtus and Xavier, changed their minds when France entered the conflict. They believed they must rush to their homeland's defense, and the old emperor understood and sympathized, as did Charles and Zita. They were allowed to leave by way of Switzerland. But in a typical show of republican pettiness, the French government refused to accept them. They enlisted in the Belgian army, under the command of their valiant cousin, Albert I, the *Roi-Chevalier* (King-Knight). Albert's personal gallantry would play an important role in the brothers' later activities, as we shall see. Their younger brothers, Felix and Rene, would enter the Austrian army, while the four youngest Bourbon-Parma children would stay with their mother, Maria Antonia, at Schwarzau. Sixtus's account of their parting on August 20, 1914, is at once painful and inspiring:

> Mother acts just like Zita and tries not to show her feelings but it must be absolutely terrible for her. She will stay behind all alone with the little ones. She says she will set up a hospital here. Suddenly, as we start to go, she breaks into tears. . . .
>
> And yet, sad as the evening was on the terrace at Schwarzau, we felt, as never before, how closely we belong together, bound to each other by indestructible ties. That was how we felt then, when Charles and Zita married. We swore then . . . to try and build a ring around them to protect them in these dreadful times,

> for we sensed what was coming. Now it is upon us. . . .
> No more. To-morrow we set out.[44]

Because of these connections—and even more when Italy entered the war against her peacetime ally—Zita would have much to suffer. Rumormongers and anti-Habsburg propagandists of many types would call her "the Frenchwoman" or "the Italian." They would constantly try to raise doubt as to her loyalty. This was in spite of the fact that, when she married Charles, she put him, his family, and his peoples above her own—it was laughable to think that she could have any affection for the French and Italian governments, who had murdered or exiled her forebears.

There was a great deal of discussion in government circles as to what role Charles should play in the war, not least because those whose incompetence, sloth, or other problems had caught Franz Ferdinand's attention were not keen on having his young disciple looking over their shoulders and reporting on them to the emperor. One thing was certain: Franz Joseph wanted Zita and the children to live at Schönbrunn, both for heightened security and as something of a comfort in the grueling days ahead. They would be housed in the east wing of the palace in the rooms once used by Franz Joseph's own parents.

Charles set out for the fortress of Premsyl to be with his regiment. However, it was decided after a few weeks that he would be recalled to Vienna and sent to various fronts as the "eyes and ears" of the emperor. After the Russians suffered a grueling defeat at Premsyl in late October, Charles was in

---

[44] Brook-Shepherd, *The Last Empress*, pp. 34–35.

Vienna to celebrate with Zita their third wedding anniversary. This would be the pattern of life for the next couple of years as "Charles the Sudden" would appear at a battlefield, survey the situation (often from a much closer vantage point than he was supposed to), and report back to his great-uncle in Vienna. Thus, Charles and Zita spent more time together than most married couples in their situation.

So it was that on February 8, 1915, their third child and second son, Robert, was born. Franz Joseph was extremely pleased with the new addition to the family, as he was with the child's father. But a new and bitter burden was added to the old man's plate on May 23. On that day, Italy, which had been Germany and Austria-Hungary's partner in the Triple Alliance but had opted to remain neutral,[45] came into the war on the side of Britain, France, and Russia. Where Italy's neutrality had been grudgingly accepted, her joining the ranks of the enemy was outright betrayal. Moreover, it opened up a new front in the south when Austria already had difficulties with just one.

On June 23, 1915, Charles was able to go to Hall to the Basilica of the Sacred Heart and fulfill his uncle's vow. The following day, in Vienna, news came that the Russians had been pushed back out of Lviv. A mob spontaneously poured into Schönbrunn Park and rushed up under the palace terrace to celebrate. Franz Joseph and Zita came out to cheers and applause, and the crowd went wild when Zita held little Otto up for all of them to see.

---

[45] This neutrality was permitted by the treaty because the alliance was only invoked if one of the members was attacked by an outside power, which clearly had *not* happened here.

When foreign dignitaries came to Schönbrunn to confer with Franz Joseph, it was Zita who acted as hostess. Additionally, what time she could spare from that and her children, she devoted to nursing wounded soldiers. Initially, she dealt primarily with those in Vienna hospitals, but increasingly, she went further afield. Charles, in the meantime, was sent to the Tyrolian front to face the Italians and commanded an army group there. As in Galicia, he demonstrated enormous courage under fire (to be fair, so too did Victor Emmanuel III of Italy, who, although not consulted about the war by "his" government, insisted on sharing the dangers of the men sent to fight in his name, thus gaining him the nickname of the "Soldier-King").

Franz Joseph would see another great-great-nephew born, Felix, on May 31, 1916. This was during an Austrian offensive on the Italian front, which was very successful, and in which Charles, commanding an army group, showed great prowess. But to relieve the Italians, the Russians unleashed a major offensive, which required half the Austrian troops to be recalled from Italy. They were successful in doing so, and the transfer did allow Charles a visit to Vienna to see his newest son. However, it put the Italian front back precisely where it had been.

In addition to her Red Cross and imperial hostessing efforts, Zita became the lonely old emperor's closest confidante. He spoke to her of old wars and battles, both political and military. It became apparent that the expulsions of Austria successively from Italy and Germany still pained him because he was, in his heart, really a native of that Holy Roman Empire that had apparently died almost a quarter century before he was born. He had no rancor toward Tsar Nicholas II and wore his Russian Order of St. George as he always had, despite it being an enemy decoration. Toward his German ally, Franz Joseph was never critical, but it was obvious to Zita that her elderly relative was not a deep lover of the new Germany nor really in sync with its ruler. Above all, he was not sanguine about victory. At one point at the beginning of the war, when Zita congratulated him on an early victory, he responded, "My wars have always begun with victories, only to finish in defeats. And this time it will be even worse and they will say of me 'He is old and cannot cope any longer. Then revolutions will break out and it will be the end.'"[46]

One can only wonder about the effect that these sorts of confidences had on the mind of the young archduchess. On the one hand, while raised in a happy home and family, her parents and other older relations had surely told her stories of royalty in defeat. Her ten times great-grandfather, Charles I of England, was murdered by Cromwell and the Puritans for refusing to consent to the abolition of bishops in the Church of England, for negotiating with Rome for reunion, and for defending his poorer subjects against the Enclosures. His son and grandsons, the Stuart claimants to the thrones of England, Scotland, and Ireland had, at various times, hazarded all for the sake of those thrones—and lost. Her great-great-uncle, Louis XVI, had gone to the guillotine praying, like Charles I, that his blood would not condemn his people. Her great-great-grandfather, Charles X, had been driven out of France by men who instantly began to misrule the

[46] Brook-Shepherd, *The Last Empress*, p. 39.

country, and her great-grandmother, the Duchesse de Berry, had risked her life to restore her son—but was undone by her own quest for personal happiness. Her great-uncle, Henry V, had refused the crown of France over a matter of principle, while her grandfather, Dom Miguel, and her Carlist cousins had fought civil wars in ultimately unsuccessful attempts to maintain their thrones in Portugal and Spain. Her father was driven from his throne as a boy, albeit into the happy and comfortable exile that was her childhood. Now, the current occupant of the throne to which her husband was heir was intimating that something similar awaited them.

What lessons might Zita have drawn from all of this? On the one hand, the more recent story of her forefathers was one of defeat, death, and exile. But it was much more than that because the tragedies of Zita's ancestors were not merely theirs and their families. In every case where their cause had gone down to defeat, the Church had suffered greatly, as had their people as a whole. For Zita, duty to God and her people was precisely what she had been called to as a princess at birth, as an archduchess by marriage, and as future empress-queen. Regardless of the odds they might face, whatever arose, it was that duty that required the young couple to fight as hard as they could—not merely for themselves and their children but for God and the subjects He would commit to their care. It is a safe bet that it was not a duty she or her husband were looking forward to. Yet looking forward or not, when the seemingly imperishable emperor did indeed die, it would fall to them.

In August of 1916, another neutral and former ally of Austria joined the enemy as Romania declared war. The Romanian politicians mistakenly thought that the Austrians, engaged as they were in Galicia and Tyrol, would be an easy foe to defeat. Instead, within three months, Austro-Hungarian troops were in sight of Bucharest. But Franz Joseph's health was visibly failing, and so Charles was called home. Nevertheless, the old emperor kept at his desk for a week, then ten days. It was on November 21, 1916, that the pneumonia was ready for its illustrious and most recent victim. At noon, Charles and Zita went to see the emperor. He was weak but coherent, saying how uplifted he was by a recent papal blessing and the Romanian victories. Later on, in the evening, they were called back, but Franz Joseph had sunk into a coma. They kept watch until a little after 9:00 p.m., when he breathed his last. As Empress Zita remembered,

> When it was all over, we filed out of the death chamber into the anteroom. No one knew what to say or do. . . . For a few moments there was utter silence. Then I remember the dear plump figure of Prince Lobkowitz going up to my husband and, with tears in his eyes, making the sign of the cross on Charles' forehead. As he did so, he said, 'May God bless Your Majesty.' It was the first time we heard the Imperial title used to us.[47]

It would not be the last time either. At the ages of twenty-nine and twenty-four, the young man and his consort were now faced with the seemingly impossible task of guiding their peoples through the current storm.

---

[47] Brook-Shepherd, *The Last Empress*, p. 41.

Chapter 6

THE YOUNG IMPERIALS

For God's sake, let us sit upon the ground
And tell sad stories of the death of kings;
How some have been deposed; some slain in war,
Some haunted by the ghosts they have deposed;
Some poison'd by their wives: some sleeping kill'd;
All murder'd: for within the hollow crown
That rounds the mortal temples of a king
Keeps Death his court and there the antic sits,
Scoffing his state and grinning at his pomp,
Allowing him a breath, a little scene,
To monarchize, be fear'd and kill with looks,
Infusing him with self and vain conceit,
As if this flesh which walls about our life,
Were brass impregnable, and humour'd thus
Comes at the last and with a little pin
Bores through his castle wall, and farewell king!

—William Shakespeare, *Richard II*,
Act 3, Scene 2

So it was, in the midst of an incredibly bloody war, increasing economic privation, and with less preparation than might have been hoped for, Charles and Zita undertook their royal responsibility. Yet, they had been prepared for it, in some sense, since birth. It was certainly true that Charles's accession had been possible, although unlikely when he was born. But Zita, as a royal princess of impeccable lineage, might well have married any number of monarchs—and that was also part of her upbringing. The training of both had emphasized loyalty to God, to the institution of monarchy itself, and to the peoples God would commit to them. We live in an age when—as seen by the ignorance of the institution displayed by the commentators in the media during coverage of the death of Elizabeth II and the accession of Charles III—few people in media, academia, or government—even in the remaining monarchies—really understand how Christian monarchy is supposed to work. Nevertheless, if one is to understand Zita and Charles on their own terms, it is essential to realize these things.

Any marriage, if it is to be successful and survive the strains of even ordinary life, requires the couple to have a similar vision regarding the basics of reality. Here, Charles and Zita were eminently suited for each other. As a sacrament, they saw their marriage as their road to Heaven—to mutual sanctification. There was no "you and me" but "us." It was for Charles to chart the course their family must take, and for Zita, with all her considerable talents and skills, to help him attain the goals he had decided upon. This meant giving him advice when she thought it necessary but supporting him in his choices, regardless of whether he heeded the advice. There could be no room on either side for resentment or recriminations; as it would turn out, this would be very much needed.

Similarly, they had the same view as regarded children. As she had learned from Robert and Maria Antonia, and he from Franz Ferdinand and Sophie, children must be welcomed with love, as souls given them by God to train and develop in accordance with His revelation and their future stations in life. This latter deprived Zita and Charles of one freedom most parents have in bringing up their families. While the majority of parents may help their children find their place in life in accordance with their own inclinations (so long as these are not sinful), this was not open to the imperial couple. Their family histories were littered with members—on and off thrones—who had pursued their own interests and pleasures to the neglect of their duties, and these had inevitably led to disasters, both personal and public. Some of these were close: Charles had the example of his own father to avoid, and for Zita, it was the Duchesse de Berry.

Underlying all of this was the practice of the Catholic Faith. Now, there are many individual ways of expressing Catholicism in everyday life. Fortunately, when they married, their devotional lives were already very similar. First and foremost was the Blessed Sacrament, the Holy Eucharist. Zita and Charles both loved the Liturgy of the Mass very much, attending daily and receiving Holy Communion as often as possible. They also loved Adoration of the Blessed Sacrament, which, as we shall see, would become a great consolation to them both. They were devoted to the Holy Cross—Zita, in particular, as a member of the Order of the

Starry Cross, about which we shall also see more—and to the Sacred Heart of Jesus. This is a unique devotion because of its many facets: personal, as we saw with Franz Ferdinand, who was making the Nine First Fridays and wearing a medal of the Sacred Heart when he was murdered; familial because families were urged to enthrone an image of the Sacred Heart in their homes to show the household's acceptance of Christ's rule over that family; and political. This last was expressed in the large number of royals who spread the devotion, the many militant groups struggling for the Church and monarch who had adopted it as their badge, and the various national consecrations to the Sacred Heart, culminating in Pope Leo's consecration of the whole world, which, as we saw, included the participation of the Habsburgs as a clan and Charles as an individual. The imperial couple was also very devoted to Our Lady—as seen at Mariazell and other shrines and as seen by their saying the Rosary daily, either as individuals or as a family.

For the new emperor and empress, their religious practices and beliefs could not be separated from their political action. From Westminster Abbey in London to Wawel Cathedral in Krakow, and from Palermo Cathedral to Bl. Charlemagne's church at Aix-la-Chapelle, their reigning ancestors had been anointed and crowned by the Church in emulation of King David. They had washed the feet of the poor on Maundy Thursday and marched with the Blessed Sacrament to show their participation in the kingship of Christ. All of these symbolized the sacred responsibility of the Crown, which had now come to them. But first, it was necessary for them to attend the last act of Franz Joseph's reign: his funeral.

According to ancient Habsburg ritual, the Requiem Mass was held at the Stephansdom in Vienna, after which the funeral cortege made its way to the Capuchin church on the Alt Markt, under which lies to this day the Kaisergruft—the imperial crypt. The imperial couple, dressed in black, marched in the midst of the funeral procession. But in all that darkly arrayed company, one figure stood out—the little Crown Prince Otto, his white clothing reflecting his blonde hair, looking for all the world like the light shining in all that darkness. When, at last, the mourning party arrived at the church, the chamberlain banged on the door with his staff. It opened, and a Capuchin friar replied, "Who goes there?" The chamberlain replied with all the sonorous titles of the deceased monarch:

> His Imperial and Royal Apostolic Majesty, Franz Joseph, by the Grace of God Emperor of Austria, King of Hungary and Bohemia, Dalmatia, Croatia, Slavonia, Galicia, Lodomeria, and Illyria; King of Jerusalem, etc.; Archduke of Austria; Grand Duke of Tuscany and Cracow; Duke of Lorraine, Salzburg, Styria, Carinthia, Carniola and Bukovina; Grand Prince of Transylvania, Margrave of Moravia; Duke of Upper and Lower Silesia, of Modena, Parma, Piacenza and Guastalla, of Auschwitz and Zator, of Teschen, Friaul, Ragusa and Zara; Princely Count of Habsburg and Tyrol, of Kyburg, Gorizia and Gradisca; Prince of Trento and Brixen; Margrave of Upper and Lower Lusatia and in Istria; Count of Hohenems, Feldkirch, Bregenz, Sonnenberg etc.; Lord of Trieste, of Cattaro

> and on the Windic March; Grand Voivode of the Voivodeship of Serbia![48]

"I don't know him," came the terse reply, and the door was shut in the chamberlain's face.

Undeterred, the chamberlain struck the door again with the staff. "Who goes there?" came the reply a second time.

"Franz Joseph, Emperor of Austria, Apostolic King of Hungary." Once more, this was answered with, "I don't know him," and the slammed door.

A third knock caused the door to open once more with the same question. This time, the chamberlain responded with, "Franz Joseph, a poor and sinful man." "Him I know," said the Capuchin, "Let him enter!" The casket was then brought inside, and Franz Joseph was laid among his ancestors until the last day.

Now, the new reign began in earnest. Emperor-King Charles was faced with a war he did not start or want and an exceedingly complicated domestic situation. It was known that he shared his uncle's views regarding the nationality situation, but this was extremely difficult in both the Austrian and Hungarian halves of his inheritance. Austria in those days included the country we know now (save Burgenland, which was part of Hungary then), Czechia, most of which is now Slovenia, South Tyrol, Trieste, Dalmatia with its Croatian population, Galicia with its mutually antagonistic Poles and Ruthenians/Ukrainians, and Bukovina, which, in addition to the two groups in Galicia, included Romanians,

[48] James Lyon, *Serbia and the Balkan Front, 1914: The Outbreak of the Great War* (London: Bloomsbury, 2015), chapter 1, note 1.

Germans, and Jews. Heterogenous as this crew was, they had universal suffrage. While very democratic in theory, this had made the Austrian Parliament very unwieldy in practice, since, as often as not, various national groups (especially the Czechs) would use their power to bring the work of Parliament to a halt. When this happened in the past, Franz Joseph would dissolve Parliament, rule by decree, and wait for tempers to cool before calling Parliament back into session. The Hungarian Parliament, by way of contrast, was much better run by the Liberal Party. This decorum, however, was due in no small part to the limited franchise for the Lower House: the Electoral Law of 1874 established "a complicated franchise based upon property, taxation, profession or official position, and ancestral privileges."[49] While this produced a much more gentlemanly parliamentary discourse, it also effectively disenfranchised Hungary's minority Slovak, Romanian, Serbian, and Croatian citizens, who together made up a majority of the inhabitants. Franz Ferdinand was keen on introducing universal suffrage to Hungary as well, and his nephew was very sympathetic to this idea.

On the evening of November 22, 1916, Charles issued the manifesto "To My Peoples." It began with praising his predecessor for his long service, devotion to duty, and so on. It then expressed the new emperor's confidence in his armies, his desire to maintain the constitutions of his realms, and to ensure equality for all his subjects before the law. This was alarming for some and not nearly enough for others, but it was, in a sense, boilerplate. Charles's own sentiments were

[49] *Encyclopædia Britannica*, 11th ed., s.v. "Hungary."

expressed in one place only: "I will do everything to banish, in the shortest possible time, the horrors and sacrifices of war and to win back for my peoples the sorely-missed blessings of peace."[50]

Despite Charles's hopes, internal peace—the reconciliation of the nationalities with each other—and external peace would turn out to be a sort of catch-22 problem for the new sovereign. Radical nationalists were already agitating for an Allied victory against the Central Powers; Pan-Germans wanted Austria much more closely tied to Germany; and the Hungarian leadership under Count Tisza was willing to sacrifice their new king if it meant that they would remain masters in their own house. Charles had much more loyalty to his people than their politicians had to him, but as always in an electoral system, the majority who loved their emperor-king had no way of expressing themselves politically save through those who nominally represented them or through spurts of violence that generally ended badly. This was particularly true in Hungary, where the official opposition to the ruling liberals had little effect on policy, and the non-voting majority had none.

By the Hungarian Constitution, Charles had six months at the latest before he would be required to be crowned and swear to maintain that document, which in some ways contradicted the Austrian Constitution. It had been Franz Ferdinand's intention, before he accepted the Holy Crown, to force some alterations to the charter in terms of electoral and

[50] Gordon Brook-Shepherd, *The Last Habsburg* (New York: Weybriaght and Talley, 1968), p. 49.

other reforms. But had he lived, he would have had the luxury of peacetime. Charles was in an unpleasant situation, to say the least. The Austrian half of the monarchy was dependent upon Hungary for grain and other resources; there had been bad harvests, and the Allied blockade was having a terrible effect on living conditions throughout Central Europe—and not least, Vienna. Tisza came to Vienna very quickly after the manifesto was issued and insisted that the coronation be carried out before the end of the year. Otherwise, he intimated, grain shipments and other necessities might not be forthcoming. Unhappy with this veiled ultimatum but sure that it could somehow be worked out by the politicians later, Charles consented.

Down through the centuries, a number of Habsburgs have been crowned multiple times—a precedent set by their predecessors as Holy Roman emperors. The record holder was probably Charles IV (1316–1378), who had five coronations: Bohemia, the Romans (Germany), Italy, Burgundy, and the Holy Roman Empire. Although not Holy Roman Emperor, Charles's great-great-uncle Ferdinand was crowned three times: Hungary, Bohemia, and Lombardo-Venetia. Franz Joseph lost the latter country and was never able to have the second coronation because of an inability to come to an accord with the Czech politicians as he did with the Hungarians, which allowed him at least one. However, it was in Budapest rather than Pressburg/Poszon/Bratislava, where they had been held since the Turkish conquest of the country. It was the ceremony for Francis Joseph at Budapest's Matthias Church that was the pattern for Charles.

The coronation, relayed by Anita Rádi in her article "Coronation of the Last Hungarian Kings," was as follows: Charles and Zita arrived in Budapest on December 27, 1916, with little Otto in tow. The three-day ceremony required extraordinary endurance and stamina from the royal couple, during which they had almost no time to rest. The grandiose ceremony of the coronation itself must have been very demanding, but Charles and Zita endured the long and detailed program without the slightest sign of fatigue.

According to tradition, Bl. Queen Gisela embroidered St. Stephen's coronation robe, and so, for hundreds of years, every Hungarian queen, including Franz Joseph's Elizabeth, was obliged to embroider a few stitches on the fabric during her coronation in order to prove her domesticity and skill. On December 28, Queen Zita made stitches on the coronation mantle in accordance with the millennial tradition. It was also on this day that the female members of the Hungarian aristocracy handed over the fancy Hungarian dress to the new queen. Thirty meters of satin were used for the fabric, thirty meters of taffeta, the same amount of flannel, and eighteen kilograms of gold were used for the lining. The intricately patterned lace veil was sewn from the dowry of the female members of the Esterházy family.

A small outfit was made for the heir to the throne, Otto. The celebrants were fond of the little heir to the throne with his golden curls and fairy-tale appearance. The outfit was made of golden silk with an ermine border and a white atilla with lace underneath. According to tradition, Charles wore the uniform of a Hungarian Hussar general at the coronation.

The ceremony was scheduled for December 30, at which time the entire area of Buda Castle was dressed in festive splendor. The buildings were decorated with flags and pine garlands, and decorative columns were erected on the streets. The storefronts of the businesses located there were already rented out well in advance at exorbitant prices, and many people sacrificed their entire fortunes to witness the famous event.

A huge crowd gathered at the foot of the coronation hill. There was the clatter of swords and the clatter of spurs, and the crowd awaited the arrival of the coronation procession in near ecstasy. The high clergy and state dignitaries appeared on horseback, and the wonderfully decorated horses pulled golden carriages with glass canopies. "Everyone trembled at the sight of the procession. This cavalcade of colors, splendor and brilliance contains a thousand years, all the wealth, light, faith and devotion of a nation,"[51] wrote the contemporary press.

Home Guard Hussars marched at the beginning of the procession, followed by the delegation from the capital, the lords of the court, the ensigns, and the ladies of the palace, displaying a centuries-old medieval tradition. The eighteenth-century carriage of the royal couple, pulled by eight white horses, followed the line of court carriages. The royal couple entered the church amid the roar of cannons and the ringing of all the capital's bells.

---

[51] *Budapest Newspaper* (Archive), https://adt.arcanum.com/hu/view/BudapestiHirlap_1916_11-12/?query=Szent+J%C3%A1nos&pg=615&layout=s.

Then the coronation ceremony began. The king knelt down and, kissing the Gospel, took the oath of justice and peace. He was then anointed with the consecrated oil on the golden tray, then St. Stephen's cloak was placed on him, and he was girded with his sword. The king turned to the congregation and drew his sword, making the usual crosscuts. At that, the cannon and volleys rang out outside. After that, Károly knelt before the altar, and then Prime Minister István Tisza, Deputy Palatine, and Prince-Primate János Cernoch crowned him with the Holy Crown. Then, they handed the king the scepter and the apple of the kingdom. "Long live the King!" shouted István Tisza, and the whole church was buzzing with excitement.[52]

Now, it was Zita's turn. Since the Coronation of Bl. Gisela, Veszprém has been considered the city of queens. Furthermore, according to tradition and records, the Bishop of Veszprém had the privilege of crowning the Hungarian queens. In the thirteenth century, however, the Archbishop of Esztergom tried to take this right away from the bishop of Veszprém. The legates of Pope Innocent III had to investigate, and the case ended with the confirmation of the rights of the Bishop of Veszprém. Zita's crown was originally made for Elizabeth in 1867 from the former crown of the wife of Ferdinand I, Maria Anna. For the new crown, many diamonds and precious stones were taken from Maria Theresa's former jewelry, but it was unfortunately lost after the dissolution of the Austro-Hungarian Monarchy. At any rate,

---

[52] As quoted in the article by Anita Rádi, "Coronation of the Last Hungarian Kings," December 31, 2019, https://ma7.sk/hagyomany/az-utolso-magyar-kiraly-koronazasa.

Zita was led by the hand of her chief courtier, Count Sándor Esterházy, and her train was taken by Prince Irma Esterházy and Count Sándor Apponyi.

After her coronation, Zita left the church with Otto, and the king performed the traditional ceremony of knighting the knights of the Golden Spur, who, at Charles's wish, were chosen from among the most decorated soldiers of the war. Not an order of chivalry as such, this group began in the Middle Ages as a type of knighthood given out by either the pope or the Holy Roman Emperor for services rendered. In time, the papal knights became an Order, which still exists legally but no longer has any living members. The imperial knighthood, on the other hand, became an honor only given when the later emperors were crowned at Aix-la-Chapelle and then Frankfurt. Since, after Emperor Franz, there were no further imperial coronations, Ferdinand, Franz Joseph, and lastly, Charles knighted them at their Hungarian coronations.

Then, the newly crowned king mounted his horse and rode up the coronation hill, built from the soil from each of Hungary's sixty-three counties on St. George Square. Charles then drew his sword and pointed in each of the four directions to show his willingness to defend the Apostolic Kingdom of St. Stephen and its peoples from any and all threats.

The coronation dinner took place in the royal palace, which was the last act of the series of ceremonies. This was a symbolic meal as the dishes were sent intact to the wounded soldiers and to the capital's hospitals. Due to wartime constraints, rather than the usual folk festival that had brightened the last coronation, free food was distributed to the poor.

The newspapers wrote of Queen Zita's charming smile and eyes with their deep, warm glow. They emphasized that the queen did not read her speech of thanks to her loyal Hungarians but spoke it freely in a clear, ringing voice. The Hungarians welcomed this with such cheers that the strong marble walls of the Buda Castle almost cracked. It was clear that the couple spoke from their hearts. Charles spoke perfect Hungarian. The queen's pronunciation was not yet perfect, but "so much desire radiated from her voice, so much warm, heartfelt joy from her eyes at the sight of her enthusiastic Hungarians,"[53] that it was felt she would surely master the Hungarian language in a short time.

Charles's coronation was the last great occasion for the parade of the special Hungarian costumes and the Hungarian aristocracy. The Hungarian ladies tried to dress from the family storerooms. Many of the dresses and gowns were old, coming from the eighteenth or nineteenth centuries. Few of the men had new clothes made, as they had ceremonial clothes, or perhaps they took out the clothes of their ancestors. Most of the women's costumes were made by József Girardi. This owner of the most prestigious Hungarian wardrobe shop later said in his reminiscences that 320 men and women worked in two shifts, day and night, on the 163 women's fancy Hungarian dresses ordered from him. Zita also received a pattern for her dress: a dress from the time of

---

[53] As quoted in the article by Anita Rádi, "Coronation of the Last Hungarian Kings," December 31, 2019.

Maria Theresa kept by the Pálffy-Esterházy family, of which she had to make a copy. The coronation was said to be the happiest day of the queen's life, and she had never worn a more beautiful dress.

The Coronation of Charles and Zita was, according to one witness, "the last time we saw St. Stephen's crown shining in its full light and the last time we saw the entire nation of Saint Stephen together in complete, compact unity."[54] While, for the Hungarians, it was an affirmation of their sacred nationhood, Zita later explained what it had meant for her and her husband:

> The thing that impressed both of us most about the whole ceremony was the moving liturgical side of it all—especially the oaths that the King took at the altar before his anointing to preserve justice for all and strive for peace. This sacred pledge given in the cathedral was exactly the political programme he wanted to carry out from the throne. We both felt this so strongly that hardly any words were necessary between us.[55]

In these sentiments, as in all else in his public life, Zita echoed her husband completely. For Charles and Zita, they meant to keep the oaths they took until death—from their wedding vows to Charles's oaths he took for the various orders of knighthood to which he belonged.

It was a tragedy for Tisza and other members of the Hungarian establishment that they did not take the oaths they

---

[54] As quoted in the article by Anita Rádi, "Coronation of the Last Hungarian Kings."

[55] Brook-Shepherd, *The Last Habsburg*, pp. 54–55.

made—to bear him and his heirs true faith and allegiance until death—as seriously. Not only would it have made Charles's quest for peace far easier, it would have provided a common ground upon which they could have met the Slovak, Croat, and Romanian leaderships in shared loyalty to their monarch. If they had reconciled, perhaps both what the Hungarians consider "the tragedy of Trianon" (the loss of a considerable amount of Hungarian territory at the peace treaty) and the horrible death of Tisza could have been avoided, as well as the hatreds and misunderstandings that separate these peoples to the present day. In any case, the Sabor (the Croatian Parliament)—Croatia being in a union with Hungary similar to Hungary's union with Austria—acclaimed Charles and Zita as their king and queen by virtue of the coronation in Budapest.

The coronation having finished, it was time for Charles to get started on what he considered his major goal—ending the war. Already, on December 16, a joint peace appeal by the Central Powers had been sent to the Allies, calling for peace on the basis of a return to prewar boundaries. Bethmann-Hollweg, German chancellor, was the primary author of the note, and he had several different political purposes in mind. There was, of course, the outside chance that the Allied leadership might accept it; in that case, the pressure on him by the naval leadership to begin unrestricted submarine warfare (a measure that both he and Charles thought would inevitably bring the Americans into the war) would end. If the Allied leadership did not accept it, then the presentation of the note would show not only the domestic populations of Germany, Austria-Hungary, Bulgaria, and Turkey that their governments were interested in peace but also those of Russia, France, and Italy, who were the hardest hit by the war. But Bethmann-Hollweg, despite being well-intentioned, was heavy-handed when it came to oratory. At the opening of the war, he had declared the conflict between the blocs to be "a fight to the finish between German civilisation and Slavdom."[56] Doubtless, this kind of talk excited the passions of German nationalists and Austrian Pan-Germans, but to then-Archduke Charles, who would one day rule Czechs, Slovaks, Slovenians, Poles, Croats, and Ukrainian/Ruthenians, this kind of talk seemed to veer between hateful and insane. Unfortunately, Bethmann-Hollweg's peace proposal followed a long rehearsal of the Central Powers' victories in the war, couching the start of peace talks as a sort of gracious gift.

Nevertheless, Woodrow Wilson, President of the United States, the most powerful neutral power, approved of the plan. The Allies, however, angrily rejected it as a cynical ploy. Charles, for his part, was emboldened in his decision to reach a peace accord, but, unfortunately for him and his peoples, he was hemmed in in several different ways. Although he had kept his great-uncle's ministers in power initially, it was obvious that there needed to be a shakeup in both the civilian and military sides of government. Unfortunately, there were very few men of real ability at his disposal. Ernest von Koerber, the chancellor whom Charles inherited, differed with his new ruler on two major points: he was against convoking the Austrian Parliament, which Charles wished to

---

[56] https://www.reichstagsprotokolle.de/Blatt_k13_bsb00003402_00012.html.

do, because he thought it premature, and he was against the immediate coronation in Budapest because he believed (rightly, as it turned out) that it would tie the emperor's hands in dealing with Tisza. He resigned the day before the ceremony in Budapest.

Charles looked to the remains of Franz Ferdinand's circle of advisors to find replacements. He appointed one of his uncle's closest friends, Heinrich Count Clam Martinic, as chancellor. The new chancellor had an agenda, but it was one that would prove impossible to attain. He wanted to see the Germans predominate in his native Bohemia; the Croats united in a single kingdom, equal with Hungary; Galicia separated from Austria and united with a resurrected Poland, conquered from the Russians as a new Habsburg kingdom; Hungary reined in from its powerful position; and the Austrian Parliament functioning normally again. He could accomplish none of these and would resign in August of 1917.

Another of Franz Ferdinand's old friends, Ottokar Count Czernin, was named foreign minister. Given the fatal role he would play in the lives of Charles, Zita, and their subjects, it is worth getting to know him a little better. Arthur Count Polzer-Holditz, Charles's old friend and now private secretary, shared his view of the man in his biography of the emperor:

> Czernin is not an easy man to describe . . . He was not lacking in gifts and talents, nor in understanding of the demands of modern times. Nevertheless, the bright sides of his nature were accompanied by

> the darkest shadows. He believed himself to be the statesman whom he brilliantly contrived, by an inimitable pose, to make himself appear. But he was not what he wanted to seem, and did seem, to be. He had never worked seriously, and had not at his command the degree of political experience and political knowledge he would have required for the difficult post he occupied. With his gifts he might perhaps have succeeded in remedying his deficiencies in a shorter time than others could; but he was hampered by his lack of self-discipline and industry, and, most of all, by his boundless over-estimation of himself. His faith in his outstanding talents and his political infallibility would never allow him to take anyone's advice.[57]

In time, these dispositions, along with Czernin's underlying instability, would ruin Charles's efforts. In the meantime, Charles assumed direct command of his armies himself, demoting his relation, Archduke Albrecht, Duke of Teschen, to his deputy. He moved the headquarters of the general staff to Baden bei Wien, a pleasant spa town outside of Vienna, and brought Zita, the children, and what remained of the court to the delightful castle of Laxenburg. The emperor immediately imposed a strict wartime food regulation on the court and upper classes so that more could be made available for the poor.

What wartime role did Zita play? It was twofold. In the words of Herbert Vivian:

---

[57] Arthur Count von Polzer-Holditz, *The Emperor Karl* (New York and London: Putnam, 1930), p. 128.

> The first act of the Empress on ascending the throne was to issue an appeal on behalf of children affected by the war. . . . She presided over the institution of *Kriegspathenschaft*, war-godmothership for children of men at the front, and was the means of assisting ten thousand mothers in Vienna alone, a work that eventually found imitators in most belligerent countries.
>
> There seemed no limit to her devoted efforts. She directed a fund to provide for war-widows and orphans, developed needlework guilds, créches, poor people's kitchens, homes for expatriated Galicians and other refugees, distributions of shoes and clothing for orphans throughout the Empire; met invalids from the front at railway stations, visited every ward and operation-room in Vienna, Budapest, Transylvania, and Tyrol, paying special attention to blinded soldiers and interesting herself in their future.
>
> Hutsuts were opened in her name for soldiers at the front, no less than three hundred during the first few weeks. Everywhere the cry went up: "Heaven be praised, we have an Empress once more.
>
> Cardinal Prince Bishop Piffl acclaimed her as "an Empress, who, from her childhood, revealed a loving, sympathetic heart for the needs of the people among whom she was brought up, and is now the guardian angel of all who are desolate or oppressed."[58]

[58] Herbert Vivian, *The Life of the Emperor Charles of Austria* (London: Grayson and Grayson, 1932), pp. 99–100.

Gordon Brook-Shepherd, who had the advantage of knowing the empress in her later years, fleshes out her wartime role a little more in his biography of her as regards her work with her husband on political and military matters:

> She would often "sit in," reading or sewing in a corner, on the prime minister's audiences and the military briefings presented to her husband every evening by a staff officer. She eventually received, on the emperor's orders, her own daily report not only from the diplomatic front but also from the battlefields. This led swiftly to the charge that it was the empress who was running the war as well as the empire. The reality was that, on the one occasion she did raise a military matter with her husband—and this in the humanitarian rather than the strategic field—it earned her the rarity of a rebuke. "You must leave such things to me, my dear. The truth is that I am a soldier, and you are not."[59]

The observations of Arthur Count von Poltzer-Hoditz, Charles's private secretary, on the role that Zita played during the war are important as an eyewitness account:

> When my report was made in the evening, the Empress was generally present. She sat apart as a rule, reading or writing letters. Her assistance was purely passive. Occasionally she would ask me to tell her about the position of this or that affair, never anything

[59] Gordon Brook-Shepherd, *The Last Empress* (London: HarperCollins, 1991), p. 50.

> of importance. It was only very seldom that she would make a remark if the Emperor was discussing political matters with me. Her remarks were always to the point, never irrelevant.
>
> Casual utterances of the Empress showed me that she felt a great interest in Hungary. She regarded it as politically the more stable part of the Monarchy. It was quite natural for her to feel like this; she saw the national heedlessness, the dissensions in the Austrian Parliament, and, in contrast to this, the unified national idea in the Hungarian Parliament. . . . The choice of the Imperial entourage had been arranged in a manner very favourable to Hungary. And the Empress was a crowned queen in Hungary, her husband a crowned king. She knew the almost mystical reverence of Hungary for the sacred crown of St. Stephen. Did she discover that this mystical reverence was for the crown rather than for its wearer?[60]

It is also worth noting that these Hungarians she prized so greatly were from the same group as those to whom Franz Ferdinand had been close, and many would reappear again when the imperial couple most needed them.

On domestic political matters, Zita was certainly Charles's principal confidante and, when the going got tough, his main source of strength. She was thus a consort as well as a wife. While she played no part in the empire's exertions on the battlefields, she did, as we shall see, have a leading role in what it tried to achieve on the peace front. Yet here,

60 Polzer-Hoditz, *The Emperor Karl*, pp. 208–09.

Charles stood, if anything, a pace in front of her, and he would have gone forward with or without her help. Fortunately for Charles, that was a dilemma he never had to face.

At Baden and Laxenburg, a slimmed-down version of the imperial court was maintained, and no luxuries, such as chocolate or white bread, were served unless foreign dignitaries were present. The emperor sketched out the outline of a new Social Welfare Ministry—the first in the world. With Charles's permission, Zita had the imperial carriages used to bring food to the poor in Vienna, and despite the jibes of press and rumor, the popularity of the new sovereigns continued to rise among the common people. January 1, 1917, could be greeted with some hope that the New Year would provide a way to external peace.

However, this hope would be rudely disturbed in the first week of the New Year, when Czernin paid his first official visit to Berlin on January 5. The earlier mentioned pressure to commence unrestricted submarine warfare had grown considerably in the face of the Allies' contemptuous rejection of the peace offer. Czernin found that both Generals Hindenburg and Ludendorff, now *de facto* rulers of Germany as well as managers of the war, had agreed to it and had persuaded Kaiser Wilhelm. The naval chiefs assured the German leadership that if allowed the right to fire at will on neutral shipping with the U-boat fleet, they would strangle the British Isles within three months. Bethmann-Hollweg (and Charles, when he found out about the scheme) was certain it would bring the United States into the war. Both Charles and Zita also opposed the move on moral grounds. However, the admirals were certain that Britain would surrender by the spring of 1917, so there would be no war for them to enter.

A German naval delegation headed to Vienna to put the case to Charles directly and met with the emperor, his two prime ministers, and his chiefs of staff on the one hand and with Czernin and the Foreign Office on the other. Both the emperor and the prime minister repeated their worries about the campaign bringing in the Americans—an action, in Charles's opinion, that would definitely lose the war for the Central Powers. At the official lunch given in honor of their German visitors, Admiral von Holtzendorff made the rather rude comment to Zita, "I know you are against the Uboat war, just as you are against the war in general."

Her Majesty replied in an annoyingly (to the admiral) calm voice, "I am against war, as is any woman who would rather see people happy than suffering."

The admiral replied haughtily, "Suffering—what does it matter? I work best of all when I have an empty stomach; then it's a case of tightening the belt and holding out."

"I do not like hearing talk of 'holding out' when one is sitting at a fully laden table," was Zita's frosty reply, which effectively ended the conversation.[61] But when the visit was over, the admiral informed Charles in no uncertain terms that his opinion did not matter anyway, and that the order to deploy the U-boats had been sent out.

This incident fixed several things in the couple's mind: The first was that their German allies regarded Austria-Hungary as a third-rate ally whose wishes and needs were not to

---

[61] Brook-Shepherd, *The Last Empress*, p. 64.

be taken seriously. The second was their loss of faith in the abilities of the German government and military to bring the war to a successful conclusion. If Austria-Hungary was to survive the conflict, it would need to do so through an independent policy. Charles and Zita must seek peace, regardless of whether their allies could be persuaded to accept it. It would have to be done secretly; there could be go-betweens such as Zita's brothers, Sixtus and Xavier, now fighting with the Belgians. It would also be preferable if Germany could be brought into the peace process, but Austria-Hungary's survival was dependent on a quick end to the war, as the alliance of various nationalist groups with the Allies showed. The longer that the war continued, the more likely the monarchy would break apart, and that, although they did not realize it, would do far more damage to the peoples of the monarchy than it would to the monarch.

Charles regularly visited all three fronts on which his troops were engaged throughout the year 1917. As he was now emperor, there was no one who could tell him to stay away from the front, and he risked his life on several occasions. These must have been nerve-wracking times for Zita, but she could not or would not attempt to talk him out of it, especially when so many other wives' husbands were risking their lives for their emperor.

Just before the Bourbon-Parma brothers departed for France in 1914, Charles and Sixtus had met at Schwarzau. They had agreed that a German victory would ultimately be a defeat for both France and Austria. Around that time, Charles, in a conversation with Zita, had likened the alliance with Germany to tying an iron pot and a clay pot together—the clay pot would be broken to pieces. Even before his coronation, the new emperor believed that his brother-in-law would be the best confidential mediator between himself and the Allies. He asked Zita's mother to arrange a meeting with her son in Switzerland. The Duchess of Parma, in turn, wrote to her son and the Queen of Belgium asking for permission for Sixtus and Xavier to visit her in Switzerland.

On January 29, the duchess was reunited with her two oldest sons in Neuchâtel, Switzerland. They were staying at the house of Maurice Boy de la Tour (7 Rue du Pommier), a convinced Francophile who gladly lent his house to the representatives of France and Austria for the talks. The duchess bore a letter from Zita asking her brother to help the emperor in seeking peace. Sixtus replied that he felt that there were four requirements on the Allied side: surrender of Alsace-Lorraine to France without any colonial compensations, the reestablishment of Belgian independence, the restoration of Serbia with Albania so that she could have an outlet to the sea, and Constantinople and the Straights to go to Russia. Sixtus then returned to Paris and informed the president, Raymond Poincaré, of Charles's desire for peace. Poincaré told him to continue the talks. The brothers returned to Neuchâtel.

Charles entrusted the next part of the negotiations to his close personal friend, Count Tamás Erdődy. Having been serving in the army, the count was asked to report to Charles directly on February 8. When he did so, the emperor asked him if he would be the confidential courier between him and his brothers-in-law. Erdődy agreed and prepared to depart.

He now faced the problem of obtaining civilian clothing and a corresponding passport in the midst of a war. After these things were accomplished, he had to visit Czernin, who handed him a sealed courier bag. He then reported back to the imperial couple and received a city map of Neuchâtel from Zita on which she had handwritten the route between the train station and Rue de Pommier 7 where Sixtus and Xavier of Bourbon-Parma were waiting for him. He would then hand them two letters from the emperor. Charles pointed out to him that, apart from Erdődy, Zita, and himself, only Czernin knew anything about the existence of the letters.

On February 8, Erdődy took the evening train from Westbahnhof by way of Innsbruck and Feldkirch to Switzerland, where he initially stayed in Zurich. On February 10, in Bern, he met the Austrian envoy, Colonel von Einem, to whom he handed the sealed messenger bag given to him by Czernin. The colonel, who did not know the reason for Erdődy's trip, warned the courier that Switzerland was a playground for enemy agents who would not shy away from murder for the purpose of gathering information. He used February 12 for a trip to Interlaken, and on February 13, he continued by train to Neuchâtel as "Mr. Waldmayer, merchant from Bregenz." With a letter in reply from the two of them, he set out again on the way back, which took him through Zurich, Bern, Innsbruck, and Salzburg on the night of February 15. The following day, he returned to Vienna, where he met Charles the next morning to hand him the letter from his two brothers-in-law.

The emperor's letters accepted all of the points in Sixtus's proposal, save for the restoration of Serbia. Rather, he called for a federation of Serbia, Montenegro, Bosnia, and Albania that would have a Habsburg archduke as its king. The unsigned note from Czernin, however, indicated that Austria was bound to remain attached to Germany, Bulgaria, and Turkey and that a separate peace was out of the question (it was typical of Czernin to withhold his signature from correspondence that might cause him difficulties later). Despite that caveat, Charles declared that the plan be pursued "with all speed."[62]

The problem that would follow Charles continually throughout the negotiations was that both his ministers and the two generals running Germany had absolutely no doubt of the Central Powers' final victory, something that the more realistic Charles doubted ever more with each passing day and came to disbelieve in entirety when the United States entered the war. What neither he nor his brother-in-law knew was that the British and French had already—in the secret treaty by which they induced Italy to enter the war—promised the Italians Trentino, Istria, Trieste, and Dalmatia. So, by this stage, neither the emperor's allies nor his enemies were really in a position to negotiate in good faith. Blissfully unaware of this, he and his relations soldiered on for peace.

Sixtus had brought the Austrian acceptance of the four proposals to Poincaré. The French president was aware that neither Britain nor France wanted anything from Austria; moreover, Russia only wanted the Turkish Straits. His hands

---

62 Brook-Shepherd, *The Last Habsburg*, p. 67.

were tied regarding Italy, whose demands, which the Allies had agreed to honor, were secret. It was his hope that if an accord was brought about between the three original Allies and Austria, either the Austrians or the Italians could be persuaded to accept or renounce them. Meanwhile, in late February, when Kaiser Wilhelm visited Vienna, Charles told him that an opportunity had arisen to make contact with the Allies to find an end to the war. When Wilhelm asked who the go-between might be, Charles replied, "That is something I cannot divulge, but I can guarantee his discretion."[63]

On March 3, Charles made a decision entirely unrelated to the search for peace but nevertheless fated to have very serious—if beneficial—repercussions, albeit long after his death. He appointed the Romanian Catholic military chaplain, Iuliu Hossu—now, like Charles, a blessed—to be Bishop of Gherla. Fr. Hossu's cousin, Captain Iustin Hossu, fought in the Imperial and Royal Army on the Serbian Front and later died a hero's death on the Russian Front. After hearing the news of his cousin's death, Fr. Hossu voluntarily enlisted as a chaplain, at the rank of second lieutenant, in the VII Army Corps at Timișoara. At the beginning of December 1914, Fr. Hossu left Timișoara for Vienna, together with Infantry Regiment 64 to guard the imperial capital. This regiment had four Orthodox and four Greek Catholic chaplains. In Vienna, he provided spiritual assistance both to the soldiers guarding the Schönbrunn Palace and to the inmates of the infirmaries for the wounded brought from the fronts. It was

[63] Brook-Shepherd, *The Last Habsburg*, p. 74.

this service that undoubtedly brought the future victim of Communist imprisonment to the emperor's attention.

The next step was to bring Sixtus and Xavier directly to Laxenburg to carry on face-to-face negotiations. This had to be done with the same cloak-and-dagger methods as were used for Erdődy's visit to Neuchâtel. On March 13, Erdődy received a telegram of which he immediately informed the emperor:

> "Bertrand [Sixtus] is expecting you on the 20th Greetings." On the evening of March 16, Erdődy set out again for Switzerland. After a stopover in Bern, the Count travelled on to Geneva on March 19, where he handed a letter from Zita to Sixtus and Xavier that evening. It read, "Do not let yourself be deterred by considerations which would be justified in private life. Think of all those unhappy people who are living in the inferno of the trenches, who are dying there by hundreds every day. Think of them and come."[64]

The next day, Colonel von Einem also arrived in Geneva, where he visited the Austrian Consulate General together with Erdődy for two passports made out to "Josef Pfister, Kaufmann from Brünn" (for Xavier) and "Engineer Stefan Blattner from Prague" (for Sixtus). On March 20, Erdődy and von Einem returned to Bern, while the two princes drove separately to Fribourg and spent the night there. On March 21, Erdődy and the two Bourbon princes traveled on the same train, but in different compartments, towards the

[64] Polzer-Holditz, *The Emperor Karl*, p. 230.

border. They crossed the border separately; Erdődy crossed the border near Feldkirch, while Sixtus and Xavier von Bourbon-Parma were greeted by the governor of the Principality of Liechtenstein, Leopold Freiherr von Imhoff, and smuggled by way of the principality into Austria-Hungary. There, they were received again by Tamás Erdődy and traveled on together to Vienna. On the evening of March 22, the adventurous journey came to an end, and the two princes spent the night in Erdődy's apartment at Landskrongasse 5, Vienna.

Zita's brother, Rene, was also involved and brought Erdődy and his two brothers to Laxenburg Castle in his car the following day, arriving at 8 p.m. Erdődy had previously agreed with the castle captain that they should enter the castle through a back entrance. They proceeded to the second floor—by way of a small circular staircase, which was then called the Blue Staircase but is now called the Sixtus Staircase because of this event—where the imperial couple was already waiting for them. Charles, Zita, Sixtus, and Xavier were finally reunited after almost four years—and what horrible years they had been! The four young people embraced and must have been ecstatic to see one another again. There then followed a conversation about the French demands. There was mention, at last, of Italian demands (which had been revealed to Sixtus prior to his departure), but these were dismissed as unimportant.

Count Czernin arrived at 9:30, and Zita withdrew from the room. The four points that the French had demanded and to which Charles had agreed in principle—that Belgium would be restored; Serbia also would be resurrected with an outlet to the sea; Alsace-Lorraine would be returned to France; and Russia given the Straights—were discussed. Given that the tsar's hold on power in Russia was now unsteady, this question would be tabled until things became clearer. Czernin had no difficulty with Belgium and Serbia, but Alsace-Lorraine was another question. Here, Czernin was rather cold and, despite Charles's titular role as Duke of Lorraine, was unhappy at the thought of agreeing to give away German territory without their knowledge or consent. At length, he left, and Erdődy, Sixtus, and Xavier drove back to the Landskrongasse, where the princes spent the night again. Sixtus and Xavier realized that Alsace-Lorraine was precisely the question they would need to probe with Czernin—there was no way the French would accept anything less than that province's return.

The following day, Czernin came to the Erdődy apartment. While the foreign minister kept lecturing them about the need for prudence and Germany's power, he assured them that he stood completely behind the emperor in this venture. That afternoon, Sixtus and Xavier went back to Laxenburg Castle with their brother Rene to speak with Charles and Zita, during which time Erdődy again personally kept watch. Charles had been drafting and redrafting a written commitment to send back to the French government. The brothers joined in with Zita, and, from time to time, they called Czernin to consult him on particular points, although he would not see the final version.

The letter was couched as a personal note from Charles to Sixtus and spoke of the horrors of the war over the past few years and of Charles's high regard for the French and the bravery of the French troops. Then came the crux of the matter:

> I ask you to pass to the President of the French Republic, M. Poincaré, the secret and unofficial message that I will use all means and all my personal influence to support France's justified demand for the return of Alsace-Lorraine. Belgium must be restored as an independent state, keeping all its African territories, quite apart from the compensation for the losses she has suffered. The sovereignty of Serbia will be restored and, in order to demonstrate our goodwill, we are willing to guarantee her an appropriate natural access to the Adriatic Sea as well as economic concessions.[65]

There was, of course, no mention of the Italian issue. Although unofficial, the note was in Charles's own handwriting and signed by him. When the letter was handed over, the emperor told Sixtus to explain to President Poincaré, when delivering the message, that if anything should come out through France's fault, he would categorically deny the whole letter and, to prove his allegiance to Germany, would be compelled to send divisions to the Western Front. He also asked his brother-in-law not to leave the original of the letter with any of the Allied rulers but to keep it himself.

Pleasant as this interlude had been, it was necessary for Sixtus and Xavier to return to Paris with the letter as soon as possible. On March 25, Erdődy took the train back towards the Swiss border with Sixtus and Xavier. The following day,

---

[65] Brook-Shepherd, *The Last Habsburg*, p. 72.

he said goodbye to the two, who were taken back by Leopold Freiherr von Imhoff and smuggled into Switzerland. From there, they returned to France as swiftly as possible. Sixtus delivered the letter to Poincaré on March 31. Unfortunately, the premier, Aristide Briand, who was pro-Austrian and especially favorable to Charles, had resigned and was replaced with Alexandre Ribot, who was not. Nevertheless, Ribot immediately went to Folkestone to show it to Lloyd George. The British Prime Minister joyfully declared upon reading it, "This is peace!"[66] But Ribot insisted on consulting the Italians, which was a breach of faith that would have dire consequences.

The day that Sixtus and Xavier left, Czernin headed north to Berlin on a pre-arranged visit. He spoke to Bethmann-Hollweg about the talks without naming the French envoys and saying that they had occurred in Switzerland. Alsace-Lorraine had been discussed, he declared, as had the Italian demands, which Czernin dismissed out of hand. If the French were open to a second session, would Germany consider ceding a part of the disputed provinces? The German chancellor responded firmly in the negative, and the foreign minister returned to Vienna rather unhappily. Fortunately for his peace of mind, he did not know the contents of the letter Sixtus had brought back with him.

In any case, Czernin had now to prepare himself for a state visit by Charles and Zita to Germany on April 3. On March 29, eager to share with his ally what he believed to be the progress made with the Allies, Charles sent a cipher

---

[66] Brook-Shepherd, *The Last Habsburg*, p. 80.

message to Wilhelm. He said he wished to bring Zita to meet the Empress Auguste Viktoria (the two kaisers' wives having never met) at Homburg, where the German imperials were staying. However, he would also bring Czernin as he had "high political matters" to discuss. Wilhelm, of course, knew what that meant but asked his advisers if they had any idea of what it could be. They all replied in the negative.

Alongside Zita and Czernin, Charles brought his new chief of staff, General Arthur Arz von Straussenburg, to meet Wilhelm, Ludendorff, and Hindenburg. Zita would also be able to meet those who had become Germany's real rulers, the two generals. Charles had counseled Arz to emphasize to the duo Austria-Hungary's military difficulties; instead, they converted him to their belief in eventual victory. While Czernin spoke of compensating Germany with parts of Galicia in return for ceding part of Alsace-Lorraine to the French, Charles, in separate conversations, spoke of uniting Russian Poland with Galicia in a resurrected Polish kingdom. The German side, at the very least, sensed an exploitable confusion and division in their Austrian allies.

Ludendorff had the bright idea of exploiting the confusion in Russia even further by sending the revolutionary Vladimir Lenin from Switzerland through Austria-Hungary and Germany. Charles flatly refused to have anything to do with the scheme and declared that it was not only bad for the Russians but for the Germans and Austrians since Lenin's kind of revolution was unlikely to respect borders. He refused to allow Lenin to come through his territories and advised the Germans to drop the idea. They did not, with the result that all the world has had to bear. He did manage, however, to spare Italy a similar fate since the Germans were ready to send a similar figure to Italy, but for the same reason, Charles forbade it.

There was a minor score for humanity. Since her brothers were in the Belgian Army and had his confidence, Zita knew very well that King Albert—even though most of his country was occupied in sometimes brutal fashion by the Germans—was as anxious for peace as she and Charles were; hence, his permission for the Bourbon-Parma brothers to attempt their secret diplomacy. The king, too, had tried various means of convincing both his British and French allies and, through his contacts in Switzerland, the German enemy of the need for peace. While the Belgian government was safely ensconced in Le Havre, Albert and his Queen, Elizabeth, were risking their lives just behind the lines at a castle in De Panne, Belgium. It was not just that the king commanded from the front but the Germans bombed the castle in which they were staying on Albert and Elizabeth's name days, November 15 and 19, in the years 1914, 1915, and 1916. Despite this, the king continued to call for a peace based on "no victors, no vanquished."[67]

Zita revealed the terrible fact that the king and queen were being directly menaced to Auguste Viktoria and invited her to consider what it would be like if the Allied air forces targeted Homburg. Outraged, Auguste Viktoria agreed to go with Zita and demand that Hindenburg halt the bombing. Confronted by two angry empresses, the usually unflappable

---

[67] Jean Stengers, "Le Roi Albert en 1916," https://www.persee.fr/doc/barb_0001-4133_2002_num_13_1_23485.

combat veteran denied that any such thing was happening but promised to look into it and put a stop to any such activities if they were going on. In any event, he did look into it, and the bombing stopped.

Returning to Vienna, the news that Charles had dreaded awaited them. Citing Germany's policy of unconditional submarine warfare, President Woodrow Wilson had asked for and obtained a declaration of war. The opposition was quite small—its leader was Senator Robert LaFollette of Wisconsin, who pointed out that Great Britain had done the same thing by mining "war zones" in international waters and that if the Americans tolerated the violation of the freedom of the seas and the rights of neutrals on the part of the British, they must extend the same treatment to the Germans. His arguments did not avail much; about the only saving grace was that Austria-Hungary was not mentioned.

Charles had Czernin draft a memorandum addressed to Charles himself, with the idea of Charles then sending it to Wilhelm to "keep him informed." After exploring the dire state of the Austrian military and declaring that they could not take more than one more winter, the memo insisted that peace must come by the following spring or autumn at the latest. Revolution had broken out in Russia, and it could very well spread to the Slavic subjects of the empire—and even to the Germans. Czernin's note then declared that the politicians in Germany were unwilling to face facts, thanks to the military's predominance and the latter's misplaced confidence in the U-boat. Czernin concluded in a sadly prophetic manner: "If the monarchs of the Central Powers are not capable of making peace within the next few months, their peoples will make it for them over their heads, and then the waves of revolution will sweep everything away for which our sons and brothers have fought and died."[68]

Wilhelm's response to Charles's cover letter was to assure him that the situation was well in hand, the U-boat strategy was working, and victory was in their grasp. From this point on, Charles and Zita became convinced that the only way the empire could be saved was a separate peace. It was a hard choice, to be sure, and fraught with peril. On the one hand, the imperial couple was convinced that the Germans would simply refuse to see reality until it came crashing down around them. On the other hand, they were convinced that many in Germany—and a number of Austrian Pan-Germans—would welcome any attempt by Austria-Hungary to leave the alliance as an excuse to snuff out the monarchy's independence. The trick would be to secure peace with the Allies swiftly and present Berlin with a *fait accompli* that could not be undone. This would require good faith on the side of the French, British, and Italians. It would soon be demonstrated that this was as likely as clear thinking on the part of the German general staff.

Two weeks after his return from Laxenburg, Sixtus spoke to Ribot and discovered that Italian Foreign Minister Sidney Sonnino would be included in the upcoming negotiations planned at Saint-Jean-de-Maurienne. Sixtus feared that the Italians would reveal the secret negotiations, the Germans would react badly, and the Austrian population would be similarly agitated—his sister and brother-in-law might be in

[68] Brook-Shepherd, *The Last Empress*, p. 75.

personal danger if this happened. Sixtus met Lloyd George on the morning of April 18, 1917, at the Hotel Crillon in Paris. As with Poincaré and Ribot, Lloyd George gave his word of honor to keep the Austrian peace move secret. The following day, at Saint-Jean-de-Maurienne (on the southern slope of the Massif de la Vanoise), the premiers' railway carriages were moved to a side track, and talks took place in the carriages. Lloyd George, Ribot, Boselli, the Italian premier, and Sonnino took part. Ironically, Sonnino had brought Italy into the World War with the secret Treaty of London; he would later admit that he would have brought Italy in on the side of the Germans and Austrians if they had promised Italy more than the Allies did. Ribot and Lloyd George could only present the Austrian case in the most general terms because of the secrecy oaths they had taken.

Sonnino refused to negotiate with Austria, declaring their proposal to be some sort of trick to divide the Allies. In response, Lloyd George emphasized that the British Admiralty was very much in favor of peace with Austria. Sonnino replied that he feared there would be a revolution if Italian participation in the war did not bring the promised territories. On his return to London on April 20, Lloyd George stopped once more in Paris and informed Sixtus of the result and declared that the Allies could only enter into negotiations once Austria declared its readiness to cede Trieste, Istria, Trentino, and Dalmatia to Italy.

However, while Sonnino was being imperious at Saint-Jean-de-Maurienne, King Victor Emmanuel III, who was serving at the front, Chief of Staff General Luigi Cadorna, former and future foreign minister Tommaso Tittoni, and former Prime Minister Giovanni Giolitti were all too aware that the Italian Army was at least as debilitated as the Austrian soldiers in the "white Hell" of the Italian front. Although preparing for another offensive—the soon-to-be Tenth Battle of the Isonzo—neither the king nor his chief of staff was anxious for a continuation of the war, given that they were fighting it while Sonnino and the other ministers were safely in Rome and not confronted with the conflict's misery. Bypassing "their" government entirely, the king and general sent an emissary to Charles with an offer of a separate peace based solely on the cession of Aquileia and Italian Trento to Italy. At the same time, separate peace offers came from Prince Gyorgy Lvov, head of the Provisional Government of Russia, which had ruled the country since Nicholas II's abdication in February. Not wanting to endanger Sixtus's peace mission, Charles decided not to respond to either, trusting in the assurances of the French and British prime ministers. It was a fateful decision.

Looking at the correspondence between Wilhelm II and Nicholas II on the eve of the war; Franz Joseph's warning his ministers of the consequences of war at the time and his declaration just before his fatal illness that "I'll look on for another three months, and then I'll put an end to it;"[69] King Albert's ongoing efforts at peace; Victor Emmanuel III's overtures; and, of course, Charles's endeavors for a solution, a certain uneasy conclusion begins to form that if Europe's sovereigns had been left to settle things on their own, without

---

[69] Polzer-Holditz, *The Emperor Karl*, p. 220.

interference from "their" governments, the war would have been much shorter if it would have happened at all.

Regardless, the emperor asked his brother-in-law to come to Vienna a second time. On April 24 and May 4, 1917, Erdödy met Sixtus again in Switzerland. A letter from Zita made it clear that Vienna had two different demands from Italy before making a decision and wanted to be clear as to which was to be followed up. Sixtus came on May 7, and the situation seemed positive. He returned with a second letter from Charles to Ribot, but there would be no answer. The Allies had decided that rather than a separate peace with Austria-Hungary, the monarchy's destruction would be the best way to bring Germany to heel. It was a short-sighted policy, and many would die as a result. Anatole France, who could hardly be considered a conservative, observed the following, as a result of what came to be called the "Sixtus Affair":

> No one will ever persuade me that the war could not have been ended long ago. The Emperor Charles offered peace. There is the only honest man who occupied an important position during the war, but he was not listened to. In my opinion his offer ought to have been accepted. The Emperor Charles has a sincere desire for peace, so everybody hates him. Ribot is an old scoundrel to have neglected such an occasion. A King of France, yes, a King would have taken pity on our poor people, bled white, extenuated, at the end of their strength. But democracy is without heart,

> without bowels. A slave of the powers of money, it is pitiless and inhuman.[70]

The same, as we have observed, might be said of the governments of every one of the combatant nations, each claiming to reflect the "will of the people."

Nevertheless, May 7, 1917, was a pleasant day at Laxenburg. Sixtus departed in a good mood. But as Russia staggered toward collapse, the Germans became ever surer that victory was just around the corner. At the same time, the Allies gave up on the negotiations; and on June 20, Lloyd George broke his oath by showing Sonnino the entire correspondence. On June 25, Sixtus returned to the Belgian Army, thoroughly tired of the whole business.

Meanwhile, as absorbing as all of this had been, Charles was also trying to salvage the empire's internal situation. There had been, in the early years of the war, a very foolish tendency by certain of the German and Magyar elements of the monarchy's civil and military leadership to cast severe doubt on the loyalty of the Slav populations of the empire. To be sure, there were temptations that way. For example, the Czechoslovak National Committee in Paris under Tamas Masaryk was certainly working with that goal as were the Yugoslav enthusiasts. However, many of the cited leaders were playing directly into the hands of their opponents. There were military tribunals looking for, finding, and trying any example of disloyalty they could and then administering draconian, and sometimes capital, punishments.

---

[70] Vivian, *The Life of the Emperor Charles*, p. 132.

In this atmosphere of distrust, heightened by the economic woes of the populace, rumor and misinformation were rife. One of the lies seized upon by Pan-Germans and Czech Nationalists alike was that of the "desertion" by the Prague 28th Infantry Regiment to the Russians in the 1915 Carpathian fighting. Supposedly, the regiment deserted *en masse* to the invader. They were lionized as heroes by Masaryk and his crew and denounced as traitors by elements of the Imperial and Royal High Command. Their name and number were struck off the regimental list of the army. The truth was that they had been exhausted and poorly supplied when ordered to take up new positions. After days of digging in the snow, they were suddenly attacked by a Russian division and, almost to a man, died fighting loyally for their emperor-king—as Russian records plainly show. Ironically, one battalion of the regiment had been sent to the Italian front and highly distinguished themselves there until the end of the war—the name and number being revived for them. Apart from Masaryk and company, the real traitors were the commanders who refused to supply them properly and blackened their posthumous reputation to conceal their own incompetence. This was not the only case.

The truth was that from Tyrol to Transylvania, there was loyalty to the dynasty in every ethnic group of the monarchy, but it was beginning to fray in an atmosphere of economic want and suspicion. Charles and Zita were very much aware of the real situation, thanks to their inveterate traveling around the empire. But complicating things even further was that the Austrian Parliament was still out of session. Recalling it not only meant that the constitution would be operating again, but that the quarrelsomeness and ineffectiveness of the politicians would be resumed. Nevertheless, on January 31, 1917, Czernin received a letter from the presidium of Český svaz (the Czech Union, a major Czech party in parliament) declaring,

> Your Excellency! With regard to the response of the Entente States to the President of the United States of America Wilson, in which the states at war with our monarchy cited, among other things, the liberation of Czechs from foreign rule as one of the goals which they want to achieve by force of arms, the President of the Český svaz rejects this insinuation, which is based on completely incorrect assumptions, and declares that the Czech people, as always in the past, so also in the present and in the coming time, sees its future and the conditions of its development only under the scepter of Habsburg. Signed: Frantisek Staněk, Dr. Bohumír Šmeral, and Jindrich Maštalka.[71]

What makes this document even more remarkable is that the second named was a Marxist Socialist, and both he and the last signatory withdrew from political life after 1918 in loyalty to the Habsburgs.

So it was that the new emperor did have a fund of loyalty to seek to build upon. But his opposition, to a large degree, was to be found on all sides: specifically, any public figure who was more interested in the good of his own nationality

[71] Chamber of Deputies Parliament of the Czech Republic, https://www.psp.cz/sqw/hp.sqw?k=1228.

than that of the whole. Unfortunately, there were very many of these plentifully scattered about in all the higher echelons in both halves of the monarchy. In the end, they would get what they wanted, and they and their peoples would pay a heavy price for it. Those who advised the emperor against reopening Parliament were fearful that this selfishness and agitation would dominate the legislative body.

However, there was the issue of the Hungarian Parliament to deal with first. Due to Hungary's electoral laws, 407 of the 413 seats in the lower house were held by Magyars, even though they were little more than 50 percent of the population of the kingdom. While this had bothered both Franz Ferdinand and Charles during peacetime, as emperor, Charles had witnessed (and decorated for valor) heroic feats of bravery on behalf of the monarchy by Croats, Serbs, Slovaks, and Romanians. It was not merely a question of maintaining but rewarding their loyalty to the Apostolic Kingdom. However, bound as he was by his oath to the current Hungarian Constitution, all Charles could do was attempt to convince Count Tisza of the necessity of altering the franchise. For Tisza the politician, this would mean ending the mastery of the Magyars (and his party) over their own country; for Charles the monarch and soldier, this would mean justice for an element of his subjects who had proven their worth in wartime. The two points of view were irreconcilable and led to a heated interview between the two on May 22, which resulted in Tisza resigning and joining the opposition. His most obvious replacement, Count Gyula Andrássy, who believed in electoral reform, was dedicated to maintaining the alliance with Germany. Given Charles's desire to break free of that particular embrace, he settled upon

Count Móric Esterházy. Although Esterházy shared Charles's views, he was something of a novice in politics. He was, however, able to cobble together a minority government. Unable to overcome the opposition to electoral reform, he resigned after two months. His replacement, Alexander Wekerle, took over his cabinet and kept his ministers but would not attempt anything further.

Meanwhile, on May 30, the Austrian Parliament was reconvened. Although the opening session was far more decorous than the last in 1914, Charles was immediately faced with demands. Fr. Anton Korosec, the priest-leader of the Slovenian Catholic Party, rose to demand the union of the Slovenes of Carniola and Carinthia with the Croatians and Serbs in Croatia, Dalmatia, and Hungary in a new Third Partner State with Austria and Hungary. The Polish delegates called for the same for their nationality, whereupon the Ukrainian-Ruthenian Yevhen Petrushevych declared that no part of his people's lands should go to any Polish entity. Frantisek Staněk wanted a third kingdom of the Czechs and Slovaks, which, like Korosec's demand, would intrude upon Hungarian territory.

The basic problem that faced Charles and Zita was this: the nationalities that were so combative with each other at home were fighting doggedly as comrades in the war. Peace was needed if the internal situation was to be sorted, but the intense division within and between the nationalities regarding a separate peace and the intransigence of both the Germans and the Allies was making that peace an ever more distant prospect. To untie or slash this Gordian knot would have required either a strong base of support or powerful allies; the emperor had neither.

The following day, Charles delivered his speech from the throne. He affirmed constitutionalism and the design of the constitutional and administrative foundations of all public life. Together with the deputies, he wanted the free national and cultural development of peoples with equal rights. He stressed his readiness for peace and his right to make peace. Charles also dealt in detail with war victims and the financial possibilities for making amends for war damage with the care of the bereaved from war casualties and with the war disabled. He promised the establishment of the Ministry of Social Affairs, measures for public hygiene, youth welfare, aid for large families, social security, and worker protection legislation—such as the regulation of women and child labor. These were all measures that he and Zita had discussed in detail, pooling their shared experiences on the home front and his on the battlefields.

However, since it was national autonomy that was the big issue in most of the delegates' minds, the nuts-and-bolts measures that affected their peoples as they really lived were of secondary importance to them. Since, as we have noted, Charles was not in a position to promise anything concrete in this area until and unless there should be peace, none of them were very happy with the speech; though it received great acclaim from the popular press. It was certainly true that with Clam-Martinic's and Polzer-Hoditz's assistance and building upon materials left behind by his murdered uncle, Charles had, in fact, drafted a program for the federalization of the empire. But as things stood, it simply could not be released. As a result, Clam-Martinic could not put together a coalition, his budget was defeated, and he resigned on June 21, 1917.

On June 23, 1917, Charles asked his old tutor, Dr. Ernst Seidler to form a provisional government, which would be replaced by a parliamentary government in the autumn. The new prime minister's tasks were limited to tax reform and ongoing administrative business, feeding the people, and supplying coal to industry. After his inaugural speech three days later, he was able to get through the budget for four months. Parliament again heatedly discussed the constitutional questions and declared the right of self-determination of the nations as the basis for a lasting peace. Thereupon, Seidler read out Czernin's answer with the reference to the emperor's sole right to conclude peace (Art. V of the Basic Law of 1867). The reactions were explosive. The emperor's sole right to make peace was disputed, arguing that Charles had not sworn to the constitution.

If he could find ministers to do what he wanted, they could not get his measures through either parliament. It was a thankless task—and yet Charles was well aware of this. As he told one confidante during this crisis,

> What does the Gospel say? The children of this world are wiser than the children of light. The children of this world are those who think only of an immediate advantage. They are wise and hold me bound. And the children of light, who see further, cannot set me free. Ministers shelter themselves behind their constitutional responsibility and I cannot question that, though I know very well that eventually I shall be the

> one to shoulder the blame. The late Emperor Franz Joseph often impressed upon me that the whole business of ministerial responsibility is nothing but a farce. In reality, it is we, only we, who are held responsible. His late Majesty often told me never to forget that.[72]

Stymied on both fronts, there was one measure Charles could take that he did not need either the Hungarian or the Austrian Parliaments or governments for. This was his imperial and royal prerogative of mercy. Since the war broke out, there had been many charges of treason. The most notable had been Dr. Karel Kramar, a member of Parliament who—as we now know but was not proved at his trial—was in touch with Russians from the outbreak of the war. Arrested in 1915, he was handed over to a military court and convicted not on his actual activities, which apparently were unknown to or undiscovered by the prosecution, but merely on various statements he had made. For this, he was sentenced to death, which Franz Joseph commuted to hard labor. This was, of course, only the most famous of the 115 Czechs and 94 Germans who had been convicted, in Charles's mind, unjustly. In his own notes, the emperor wrote, "The military courts had issued so many hasty, unjust convictions, so many that were not sufficiently well-founded political processes, that with the abundance of cases an individual pardon was impossible."[73] He discussed it with Zita,

---

[72] Polzer-Holditz, *The Emperor Karl*, p. 278.

[73] As quoted in Elisabeth Kovács, *Untergang oder Rettung der Donaumonarchie?*, book 1, chapter 9, https://www.elisabethkovacs.com/neue-forschungen-zu-kaiser-karl/band-i/kapitel-ix-innere-probleme-oesterreich-ungarns-der-ersten-haelfte-des-jahres-1917/.

who believed that granting a blanket amnesty in the current situation was a very bad idea. Nevertheless, he went ahead, and on July 2, the amnesty released all those convicted of high treason, *lèse majesté* ("insulting the Monarch") disturbance of public order, insurrection, riot, and acts of violence against any assembly appointed by the government or against any court or public authority. The civil rights of those affected were restored. However, excluded from the amnesty were those who had evaded criminal proceedings by fleeing abroad or by deserting.

As Zita had feared, neither those pardoned nor their confederates were grateful. Worse still, in Austria, the military authorities felt discredited by their commander-in-chief. The opponents of the amnesty included the German ambassador Count Wedel, the Austro-Hungarian Foreign Minister Czernin, and Wilhelm II—to say nothing of those who were now that hapless emperor's real masters, Hindenburg and Ludendorff.

The latter two wished to reduce Austria-Hungary to precisely the state of vassalage that Western propaganda claimed it already was, and the enemies of the monarchy in the Allied capitals (including nationalists like Masaryk) asserted that its destruction was a necessary part of defeating the Germans. This latter claim was one reason why the desire to secure a separate peace with Austria slowly ebbed away on the part of Western politicians. Seeing in Zita an opponent, they surreptitiously joined a wide array of individuals inside and outside the empire, and on both sides of the war, in a smear campaign against her. Moreover, the overthrow of the Russian Provisional Government by Lenin's revolutionaries in November seemed to confirm Hindenburg's and Ludendorff's initiative in sending the arch-Communist back to Russia— discrediting Charles's judgment in their eyes even further. The new regime sued for peace; the bitter fruit that Germany, in particular, was to reap from this harvest lay far in the future. The German and Austro-Hungarian governments agreed to a ceasefire, and talks were to begin at the town of Brest-Litovsk.

Ironically, it was a military success that would set the stage for Austria's ruin: the German and Austrian victory at Caporetto (October 24 to November 19, 1917). The Italian Army collapsed, and the forces of the Central Powers drove the Italians all the way back to the Piave River. But with the Allied blockade having reduced the amount of food that could be spared the victorious soldiers, and with the Italians digging in behind the wide and deep river, they could go no further.

This victory had two unfortunate results: it contributed to the fall of the Ribot government in France and the appointment of Georges Clemenceau as premier in his stead. A horrible man in his own right, he had a particular hatred of Catholicism and monarchy alike—and particularly of the Habsburgs. Worse yet, he was now the custodian of the explosive Sixtus letters.

The worst was yet to come, as the second unfortunate result ensued. The defeat of the Italians worried Woodrow Wilson greatly, and he believed it might be necessary to rush American troops to Italy to shore up his ally. But, of course, this could not be done if the United States were not at war with Austria-Hungary. So, on December 5, 1917, as part of his State of the Union message, he asked the combined Congress for a Declaration of War against the Dual Monarchy, stating that this was necessary to "clear away with a thorough hand all impediments to success." The president further claimed that Austria-Hungary was "the vassal of the German government" and was the "instrument of another nation." [74] Of course, this was not true at the time, nor was the claim that the Austrians had boarded and sunk an American schooner. The witnesses claimed that the captain of the submarine had been speaking "Austrian." Later, it was determined to have been a German U-boat. In any case, there was only one vote against the measure—the Socialist Congressman Meyer London from New York. Senator LaFollette of Wisconsin was out of the chamber when the vote was taken but declared that he, too, would have voted against it.

As Charles and Zita enjoyed Christmas with little Otto, Adelheid, Robert, and Felix at Laxenburg, they must have been glad to see the difficult year of 1917 pass away. They would spend New Year's at the hunting lodge at Eckartsau, little realizing how much time they would spend there later nor how much worse for them and all of Europe 1918 would be.

---

[74] Woodrow Wilson, "State of the Union Address," December 4, 1917, https://www.infoplease.com/primary-sources/government/presidential-speeches/state-union-address-woodrow-wilson-december-4-1917.

Chapter 7

ANNUS HORRIBILIS

This afternoon was the colour of water falling through sunlight;
The trees glittered with the tumbling of leaves;
The sidewalks shone like alleys of dropped maple leaves,
And the houses ran along them laugh-
ing out of square, open windows.
Under a tree in the park,
Two little boys, lying flat on their faces,
Were carefully gathering red berries
To put in a pasteboard box.
Some day there will be no war,
Then I shall take out this afternoon
And turn it in my fingers,
And remark the sweet taste of it upon my palate,
And note the crisp variety of its flights of leaves.
To-day I can only gather it
And put it into my lunch-box,
For I have time for nothing
But the endeavour to balance myself
Upon a broken world.

—Amy Lowell, "September, 1918"

However grateful Charles and Zita might have been to see 1917 depart, the New Year would offer challenges to the young couple that might have unhinged any individual, let alone shattered innumerable marriages. The fall of the Russian government and the beginning of peace talks with their Communist successors ironically ended German interest in peace talks with the West. Images of total victory danced in the heads of Germany's two warlords; the more far-seeing Charles envisioned yet another element of disaster, not just for the multi-national empire but for Germany as well.

Ironically, the New Year did seem to bring new opportunities—and those from a most unexpected source: President Woodrow Wilson. On January 8, he laid out his famous Fourteen Points for a future peace in a speech before a joint session of Congress. Point number ten was especially relevant: "The peoples of Austria-Hungary, whose place among the nations we wish to see safeguarded and assured, should be accorded the freest opportunity of autonomous development."[75] This struck Charles and Zita as being precisely what they wished themselves—the rest of the points also accorded with Charles's views—although he knew that such matters as the restoration of Belgium and the return of Alsace-Lorraine to France would be difficult for his German ally to accept.

At Charles's urging, on January 24, Czernin delivered a speech in Budapest in which he declared the Austrian government's acceptance of the Fourteen Points that applied directly to Austria-Hungary, and he maintained silence on those that did not. By this time, Zita and Charles believed

---

[75] Gordon Brook-Shepherd, *The Last Habsburg* (New York: Weybright and Talley, 1968), pp. 135–36.

Czernin to be allied sufficiently with Hindenburg and Ludendorff so as to assist with a German takeover of the monarchy if the Austrians began to make serious steps toward a separate peace.

There were several meetings in February in Switzerland with different Catholic and non-Catholic international bodies. These would form an excellent opportunity to open up clandestine negotiations with the Americans. Charles, without consulting Czernin, prevailed upon Heinrich Lammasch, a member of the International Peace Movement and a former functionary of the International Court of Justice in the Hague, to bring his proposals for both a separate peace and a federalization of the monarchy to George D. Herron. Herron was an American peace activist and former Protestant minister who was employed by the British and American governments and had acted as a go-between during several previous attempts at peace negotiations on the part of various players. Lammasch and Herron met in a castle near Bern that was owned by another committed peace activist. The Austrian transmitted his emperor's views. He then asked Herron to tell the Americans that if they found these sufficient, then Woodrow Wilson should signal his willingness to negotiate in a speech that would make this clear. Herron agreed to do so and dutifully passed on the information.

On February 11, Wilson duly delivered an address that welcomed Czernin's speech while contrasting it unfavorably with the reply made by his German counterpart. This was the signal agreed upon of which Czernin, of course, was ignorant. The president went on to boil his peace terms down to four: Peoples should not be moved arbitrarily;

their national claims would have to be met; they themselves would have to be liberated from autocratic rule; and in the interests of enlightened humanity, the United States wanted to create a new world order dedicated to freedom. Around the same time as Wilson made his speech, Lammasch, in Switzerland, was informed that the United States intended to provide Austria-Hungary with financial support as soon as it began peace negotiations and ended the war. Given the situation—the starvation in Vienna and the Austrian half of the monarchy, and the ominous rumbling of strikes—this seemed to spell a way out for Charles and his countrymen.

But German intelligence was on the job. They informed the German foreign secretary, Richard von Kühlmann. He informed Czernin, with whom he was conducting negotiations with the Russians and Ukrainians at Brest-Litovsk. Czernin assured his German colleague that there would be no separate peace and that he was offended that Charles had done business behind his back.

The always unstable Czernin had more woes, however. In return for agreeing to cede Austrian-occupied Chelm, which was part of Russian Poland, to the newly independent Ukraine and to establish a new autonomous province in the Ruthenian parts of eastern Galicia, Ukraine was to open its granaries to the starving Austrian markets. When this agreement became public on February 1—although Czernin returned to a cheering crowd in starving Vienna—the Poles in the monarchy were outraged. Declaring themselves betrayed, Poles rioted in Krakow, Lemberg, and Czernowitz. However, because, in the end, Ukraine could not deliver the grain, the deal was quashed. All that remained was Polish disaffection with the empire. Yet the anti-Charles propaganda campaign had worked so well that, during the debate over this latest development in the Austrian House of Lords, speech after speech not only defended Czernin but obliquely castigated the emperor for not being sufficiently pro-German and victory oriented. As with everyone else in this sad drama, they would receive their reward.

In the meantime, the Communists had delayed their side of the negotiations. At length, the six-month ceasefire ended, and the German and Austrian troops surged forward, rapidly occupying large areas of Russia. This brought the Reds back to the peace table. On March 3, 1918, the representatives of Kühlmann and Czernin signed the contract. The Russians signed under protest, and they stuck to the dictated peace, they agreed to the withdrawal of their troops from Livonia and Estonia, demobilization, the release of civilian prisoners and prisoners of war, and peace with Ukraine. They pledged to evacuate Finland, the Aland Islands, and Ukraine, cede eastern Anatolia to Turkey, recognize the independence of Persia and Afghanistan, and revive the 1904 German-Russian trade treaty. Both sides waived reimbursement for war costs and agreed to resume consular and diplomatic relations.

We have not touched on a number of attempts at peacemaking that had been going on in the previous years, the most famous of which was that of Pope Benedict XV. There had been several clandestine attempts as well between lesser members and functionaries of the Allies and Central Powers of which the Sixtus affair had concerned us most closely. But, in the immediate aftermath of the Russian defeat, Hindenburg, Ludendorff, and those who thought as they did, such as Czernin, were filled with renewed confidence and certainty that military triumph in the West was in sight. Certainly, the end of the war in the East meant that many troops deployed there could be flung at the Western Front—and such an offensive was certain to succeed, was it not? Thus, Czernin was in an arrogant and overconfident mood, while Charles and Zita, having just been explicitly warned that a separate peace meant direct occupation by Germany, were not.

As a result, the imperial couple were both caught off guard and horrified by a speech Czernin gave on April 2, 1918. He had given a typescript version of the speech to Charles and Zita to read two days earlier, but they were not prepared for what would follow. Entertaining the municipal council of Vienna at the Foreign Ministry on the Ballhausplatz, Czernin unfolded his version of the current political situation. The foreign minister first dealt with the peace treaties in the East, emphasizing their economic advantages for Austria and defending the treaty with Russia. Then he spoke of the war in the West and the American overtures toward a separate peace. He emphasized Charles's supposed loyalty to Germany and then absolutely endorsed German policies and the start of the western offensive, which—made possible by the German soldiers transferred from the Eastern Front—had begun on March 21.

Czernin blamed the French for the renewed fighting and claimed that Clemenceau had initiated the peace contacts and had asked whether or not negotiations were possible. The Count then declared that there was no problem in beginning peace talks—save only for the French demand for

Alsace-Lorraine. This was of course not true, since it was Austria-Hungary that had opened the door for talks.

Clemenceau's reaction was volcanic, and he denied being the one who had shut down the negotiations. Czernin, in turn, called him a liar. It is important to recall at this point that during the negotiations with Sixtus, it had been agreed by both sides that the matter was to remain secret. Despite these solemn oaths sworn by Clemenceau's predecessor, he began hinting that he had proof of earlier negotiations in which the Austrian side had agreed to the cession of Alsace-Lorraine. To Czernin's continued denials, on April 9, Clemenceau declared that he had possession of a letter in which Charles himself had agreed to it with the approval of Czernin.

Now, it had been agreed as part of the cloak-and-dagger arrangements the previous year that if it looked as though the French were going to reveal Sixtus's negotiations, Charles would send a telegram to Wilhelm denying it, and the French would take this as a signal to desist. In response to Clemenceau's statements, on April 10, Charles sent his brother kaiser the agreed-upon telegram.

The French had violated their agreement to destroy the correspondence. Worse yet, two days after Charles's ill-fated telegram to Berlin, Clemenceau published the whole of the correspondence. This was certainly a perfidious act of betrayal; moreover, it would destroy any chance of a separate peace. This was something even the Americans saw, and Secretary of State Lansing commented,

> There was always the possibility of outcomes arising from the Austrian Emperor's evident desire for peace

> at any cost. Clemenceau's folly destroyed this possibility. Through this crazy act, Charles was forced to share the lot of the Kaiser [Wilhelm II]. Everything we've done is in vain. We can forget all the unofficial conferences we had. Given the French leader's blatant stupidity, we have to get used to the new situation he has created.[76]

Yet, if Clemenceau was treacherous and stupid, Czernin became unhinged. Part of the difficulty lay in the fact that there were a number of versions around—the French, the Austrian Foreign Office, and Charles himself had different ones, and no one could be entirely sure which had been considered binding. On April 13, Czernin came to the Kaiserhaus at Baden where the imperial family was staying. He insisted on Charles signing a "Declaration of Honour," which he himself had composed. According to its text, Charles was to swear "on his honor" that he had only ever written a private letter to Prince Sixtus, not to be shown to the French government, that there was no mention of either Belgium of Alsace-Lorraine in it, and that Clemenceau's text was falsified. This would in effect exonerate Czernin of all knowledge regarding the second letter. That is to say, he would confirm Czernin's statements on his honor and declare Czernin to have been ignorant of anything that would have gotten him in trouble with Berlin.

When the emperor angrily refused to sign the letter, Czernin threatened him with the prospect of a German invasion,

---

[76] Papers of Robert Lansing, Manuscript Division, Washington, Library of Congress, fol. 143–44.

intended to end all Austro-Hungarian ability to conduct independent policy. He also promised to keep the signed document purely for his family records and not to reveal it to the Germans. This was all irrational enough; but when Charles continued to refuse, Czernin threated to commit suicide. The emperor commented on the affair in his diary:

> I gave him this word of honour because I saw that Czernin was not quite normal at the time . . . and because the announcement of the content to Germany that he threatened would have led to a serious conflict with this state, if not to a war, and finally also the negotiations with the German Emperor about Alsace -Lorraine-Galicia I could not betray to the local public.[77]

When the meetings of that day—April 12, 1918, were at last over, the emperor retuned to Czernin, demanding that he take responsibility for the negotiations as foreign minister—which he had previously agreed to do, after all, and as the constitution demanded. He refused, again citing the danger of a German takeover. Charles, in response to all of this, had a minor heart attack.

Czernin's irrationality was mixed with a certain cunning. Between urging that all three of them make a suicide pact, he also suggested that Charles make him regent due to his ill health—in which time, he would make all amends with

---

[77] As quoted in Elisabeth Kovács, *Untergang oder Rettung der Donaumonarchie?*, book 1, chapter 18, https://www.elisabethkovacs.com/neue-forschungen-zu-kaiser-karl/band-i/kapitel-xviii-graf-ottokar-czernin-und-die-clemenceau-oder-sixtusaffaire/.

Germany; that is, subject the monarchy entirely to its ally. He finally left, but Charles called the police to see if he could be detained. They replied that he could only be arrested if he committed a crime. So it was that the emperor had to accept a huge blackening of his reputation with nothing to show for it.

Czernin, of course, resigned and was replaced with the colorless but efficient civil servant, Count Burian. Burian, too, was pro-German, but he sincerely believed in the victory of the Central Powers. Nevertheless, the amount of subjugation that Austria-Hungary was now forced to accept was not to his liking.

So far as Hindenburg and Ludendorff were concerned, Charles and Zita's duplicity and unreliability were proved before the world. The German leaders were intent on taking over the management of their ally and increased pressure to that effect, with help from the Pan-Germans within the empire. In May 1918, antidynastic rumors were rampant. They were spread by Poles and Czechs and penetrated from the army to the early Austrian layers of the high nobility. The archdukes were also against the empress because she had criticized their unfair war profits. Those of them married to princesses from Germany or Spain (Archduke Friedrich, Archduke Joseph, and Archduke Leopold Salvator) agitated alongside Czernin against the so-called "Parma course" of Emperor Charles. Workers threw stones at Empress Zita's car, and court officials plotted against them.

On May 11, after enjoying Zita's birthday two days before, Charles went to Spa to confer with Wilhelm and his two military masters. There was no question as to what would emerge from this meeting. The memorandum signed the next day created a long-term political alliance serving the defense and security of the two empires and plans to develop an alliance of arms and, step-by-step, a customs and economic union. Seven points, attached to the agreement and signed by Hindenburg and Arz, formulated the foundations for the Armed Forces Association. Every man capable of bearing arms would be required to undergo military training. The principles of organization and the training and use of the troops and their armament would have to be unified, the exchange of officers would be mutual, and preparations for war would have to be made jointly. The uniform expansion of the railway network was designed. The armament plans for the wars of the future were on the table. In a word, Austria-Hungary's independence was indeed over in large part.

From this point on, the Allies began not only to look at Austria-Hungary as merely an appendage of Germany but to actively look for her abolition. Tamas Masaryk, who had been so fearful at Charles's granting of amnesty for its effect on his cause, was quite happy, and he had reason to be. Secretary of State Lansing, knowing full well what would come of Clemenceau's stupidity, so hated the now-dominant Germans that it altered his view of Austria-Hungary completely:

> If Germany is permitted to continue this mastery after peace is declared, which seems to be the plan, the Prussians will have to all intents won the war, for, if Austria is permitted to remain in possession of the territory now within her borders, the German Emperor will control millions of people utterly hostile to the

> Germans, who will be in a state of servitude. Submission of these various nationalities to Austria-Hungary by the terms of this alleged agreement would mean submission to Germany. The Poles, the Czechs, the Jugo-Slavs and the Roumanians would become serfs of the German. Such a state of affairs must never be. . . . When, therefore, the Emperor Karl showed that a separate peace was vain and when he became a vassal of Germany, a revision of policy became necessary. From that moment Austria-Hungary lost its right to exist as an Empire including these oppressed races. Karl at German Grand Headquarters signing away his birthright lost any sympathy which had been felt for him before that event. . . . In view of the new state of affairs it seems to me that Austria-Hungary must be practically blotted out as an empire. It should be partitioned among the nationalities of which it is composed. As a great power it should no longer exist. Stripped of these nationalities and of the territory occupied by them, Hungary would undoubtedly desire to become an independent kingdom and Austria would be merely an arch-duchy weak and insignificant as she should be. Over this helpless state Karl would be ruler. Such a result would be a destiny which Austria and the Hapsburgs richly deserve. To announce this policy and to give it publicity in the Austro-Hungarian Empire are the next steps in carrying out this policy.[78]

---

[78] Papers of Robert Lansing, Manuscript Division, Washington, Library of Congress, fol. 148–50.

Such was the fruit of Czernin's foolish tirade in Vienna. Nevertheless, despite it all, Charles and Zita still had a country to attempt to save and obligations to fulfill. They did not, however, know of the American sword of Damocles that hung over them.

That grim spring had been lightened somewhat by the birth of another son, Karl Ludwig, on March 10. One cannot help but think of the fortitude of the imperial couple as well as their continuing love for their offspring and each other. In these months in the little Kaiserhaus in Baden, world affairs, the disasters, and seeming triumphs in the war were intermingled with the cares and pleasures of their domestic lives. One can see how the family circle provided both Charles and Zita respite from care and spurred them on to struggle ever harder for a decent future for their children, both those who called them "Mother" and "Father" and those who addressed them as "Your Majesty."

Another happy interlude came from a visit to Pressburg/Pozsony/Bratislava, the former Hungarian coronation city and present-day capital of Slovakia. The imperial couple, along with young Otto and little Adelheid, came from Vienna by way of the Danube steamer *Franz Joseph*. At their arrival, thrones had been set up by the riverside statue of Maria Theresa, who had been crowned Queen of Hungary in the city. Charles, Zita, and the children were seated and received greetings from various local dignitaries and the cheers of the crowd. After speeches thanking them for their welcome, the imperial family got into a carriage and were driven up to the Coronation Hill, past thousands of cheering locals. After more speeches, they were driven through many more cheering crowds to the palace of Archduke Friedrich (now the Slovakian presidential palace). There, they were met by the local Catholic, Protestant, and Jewish religious leaders and the commander of the military garrison. After a tour of the cathedral and several other sites, they returned to the ship. The demonstrations of loyalty were heartening, but as Zita recalled decades later,

> The reception was such that we asked ourselves: 'Is it all a dream?' In a sense of course, it was. In the midst of all this joy there was for us sadness, because we both knew that the cheering, though genuine, was deceptive. It had no substance, and the emperor warned me against forming any illusions. He knew that, however much the ordinary people waved and cheered, the empire could not go on much longer without peace abroad and reform at home.[79]

What neither could know was that 2,331 miles away in Yekaterinburg, Russia, Nicholas II and the Russian imperial family would be murdered by the Communists the next day. Both the Austrian offensive on the Piave and the German offensive in the West were stalled by mid-June. While the Austrian defeat was imminent due to a tactical miscalculation by Conrad von Hotzendorf, the disruption in weapon and food supplies caused by strikes and shortages turned what would have been a setback into a catastrophe. The Allied push on the Western Front was slow but steady,

---

[79] Gordon Brook-Shepherd, *The Last Empress* (London: HarperCollins, 1991), p. 109.

and given the starvation rampant throughout the Central Powers, there could no longer be any question of a war of attrition. July 1 saw a huge defeat for both Charles and the Hungarians, albeit on the diplomatic front rather than the battlefield. This was the recognition by France of Masaryk's Czechoslovak Council as having "special status." This was the beginning of the Allies' commitment to dismembering the Austro-Hungarian monarchy. The British government issued an official statement on August 9, recognizing the Czechoslovak National Council "as the trustee of the future Czecho-Slovak Government."[80]

On August 15, Charles and Wilhelm, their foreign ministers, and their top generals met to discuss peace. Only Hindenburg and Ludendorff remained unconvinced of the need to end hostilities. On the American side, General Pershing convinced Lansing, and so Wilson, that the Central Powers were near collapse and that they would be offering peace terms within a few weeks. Rather than seizing upon this opportunity to end the bloodshed, their consensus was to continue hostilities until the Central Powers were willing to surrender unconditionally, which Pershing estimated would happen before Christmas. They were quite correct, as we see now, but it is telling that the prospect of ending even a few months of bloodshed and suffering on both sides was not an appealing prospect.

Robert Lansing summed up the situation to Wilson on August 25, 1918:

---

[80] "Text of British Recognition," *The Bohemian Review*, Official Organ of the Bohemian (Czech) National Alliance of America , 2:9, (September 1918), 142.

> The continued success of our arms, which has continued unabated for the last six weeks, convinces me that the Central Powers will very soon make peace proposals. It is in their interest to do so while still holding extensive areas which they might consider bartering objects. The pinnacle of their military triumph has been reached and from now on General Foch will withstand the offensive and drive the Germans back. Under these circumstances, we must prepare a negotiation proposal. I am disposed to believe that the Central Powers will attempt this through the mediation of the Pope, Spain, Switzerland, Holland or Sweden, and doubt that any of them are prepared to act. If they don't negotiate we can expect the rapprochement of Austria-Hungary, because Germany is not defeated enough to do it herself. As soon as the proposal comes from Vienna, it should be rejected briefly. We can then wait for Germany to seek peace directly, and I believe that Germany's government, under the advice of its military, will undertake it.[81]

So certain were the Americans of the end of Austria-Hungary that on September 9, they recognized the Czecho-slovak National Council as a *de facto* government. Lansing had predicted precisely what happened—Germany proposed mediation by the Queen of the Netherlands. On September 14, 1918, on Emperor Charles's own initiative, the Austro-Hungarian government issued a peace note to all

[81] Papers of Robert Lansing, Manuscript Division, Washington, Library of Congress, fol. 148-150.

the belligerent nations. It made reference to Pope Benedict's peace plan and called for the warring states to attend at a conference in a neutral nation. This would set the stage for a final treaty. It was the last major address of the imperial and royal government to the world.[82]

That very day, the French-led coalition army on the Salonika Front launched an offensive against Bulgaria. Four days later, Charles, in concert with King Ferdinand of Bulgaria, issued another peace appeal to the Allies, offering to separate from Germany and to cede Transylvania and all Romanian-speaking lands in the monarchy to Romania, if Romania as a whole joined them in a Danubian Federation. This, too, was rejected out of hand. Starting from Salonika, the Allied forces attacked the Bulgarians east of the Vardar. Within ten days, the Bulgarians were defeated. On September 26, 1918, the Vienna government knew that the game was lost. The following day, Bulgaria had to request an armistice, conclude a separate peace, and break the alliance with the Central Powers. On October 3, King Ferdinand abdicated in favor of his son Boris. From then on, Bulgaria and Wallachia were transit areas for the Entente.

Things had deteriorated so badly on the Western Front that Hindenburg and Ludendorff now insisted on peace talks being undertaken. The German Chancellor, Count Hertling, resigned on October 1. His successor, Prince Max von Baden, appealed to President Wilson for an immediate ceasefire on October 3. The Austro-Hungarians joined

---

[82] Elisabeth Kovács, *Untergang oder Rettung der Donaumonarchie?*, book 1, chapter 20, https://www.elisabethkovacs.com/neue-forschungen-zu-kaiser-karl/band-i/kapitel-xx-der-weg-zur-aufloesung/

the appeal. An agreement was reached between Vienna and Constantinople, and secret contacts with Washington were sounded out through their own ambassador in Bern.

It became rapidly apparent that the Allies, while willing to deal with the Germans, had no desire to do so with Austria-Hungary: dismemberment alone would suffice. It was still Charles and Zita's hope—and that of many other ordinary people throughout the monarchy—that something could be saved, although without a doubt, the Polish, Ukrainian, and Romanian areas would be lost as well as some or all of the territories desired by the Italians. The politicians of Vienna had lost the will to fight Charles any longer, but this had come far too late to do any good. As a sign of things to come, on October 6, the southern Slav deputies of the Austrian and the Hungarian parliaments came together in Zagreb as the National Council of the Slovenes, Croats, and Serbs, declaring themselves the representatives of the southern Slavs within the Habsburg monarchy. Ten days later, Charles issued a proclamation, "To My Faithful Austrian Peoples":

> Since I ascended the throne, I have constantly endeavoured to achieve for all my peoples the peace they long for and to show to the peoples of Austria the paths along which they may, unhindered by obstacles and conflict, bring their powerful national identities to richly beneficial fruition. The terrible struggle of the world war has hitherto impeded the work of peace. . . . In accordance with the will of its peoples, Austria is to become a federal state in which each nationality shall

> form its own polity on the territory on which it lives. . . . This reshaping, which shall in no way affect the integrity of the lands of the holy Hungarian crown, is intended to give each individual national state its independence.[83]

Under the pretense of forming such national councils, the vultures were soon to circle what they believed to be a dying corpse. On October 21, the German-speaking members of the Austrian Parliament held a constituent assembly at the Provincial Government of Lower Austria building in Vienna, in accordance, as they claimed, with Charles's manifesto.

Those present at the assembly comprised representatives of the German-speaking Austrian and Bohemian lands, having been elected at the last parliamentary election in 1911. Since that body had been suspended from 1914 to 1917, there had been no further elections, but Charles had extended its mandate until the end of 1918. While the majority were Pan-Germans or Christian Socials, the Socialists, under their cunning leader, Karl Renner, would soon become dominant. This was the first appearance of this shady character on our stage, but sadly, it would not be the last.

That same day, despite expressly excepting Hungary from his decree, Charles was at last able to prevail upon the Hungarian Prime Minister, Wekerle, to approve the union of Croatia, Slavonia, and Dalmatia into an independent (albeit under the Habsburg Crown) Kingdom of Croatia. This the

83 Emperor Charles I, "To My Faithful Austrian Peoples!," quoted from Wolfdieter Bihl, *The First World War 1914–1918. Chronicle–data–facts* (Vienna: Böhlau Verlag, 2010), p. 230.

Hungarian government officially ratified the next day. On October 23, Charles, Zita, and the children traveled to Hungary, ostensibly to dedicate the new University of Debrecen but also to shore up the loyalty of the Hungarian government. They stayed at Gödöllö, since Budapest was already too dangerous. After they arrived, Charles officially ended the military alliance with Germany by a telegram to Wilhelm. Various candidates presented themselves to Charles to be made Hungarian Prime Minister, the most odious of these was Count Karolyi. The next day, the Hungarian government revoked the Compromise of 1867 and reduced the link with Austria to a personal union under a common monarch. Two days later, the imperial couple made a hasty return to Vienna (to Schönbrunn rather than Baden) because of the serious situation there. But they left their children behind to show their confidence in their Magyar subjects, thinking they would return to them on November 13.

In Bohemia, Allied backing of Masaryk's group led to the émigrés taking over the political leadership. On October 28, their representatives in Prague declared independence. That same day, a National Council was formed in Hungary headed by Count Michael Karolyi. Its declared goals were a quick end to the war, secession from the Habsburg monarchy, the introduction of universal suffrage, and land reform. Karolyi's government demanded that Hungary should retain its historical borders—the non-Magyars, such as the Slovaks, southern Slavs, and Romanians, had already declared their own independence. As in 1848, however exciting independence might be for the Hungarian leadership, it would inevitably be followed by the same demands being made by the subject minorities. But this time, there would be no dynasty to smooth things over. Violence broke out throughout Hungary.

The following day, in Vienna, Charles appointed a new government with Heinrich Lammasch (whom we saw negotiating for Charles in Switzerland) as chancellor. On the same day, the Hungarian government recalled the Hungarian regiments from the Italian front. This led to chaos in the Austrian ranks there, and since the order included the Hungarian Lifeguards on duty at Schönbrunn, it left the imperial family unguarded. When word of this reached the young cadets at the officers' academy in Wiener Neustadt and the artillery school at Traiskirchen, they marched to the capital to take up guard duty. That same day, the southern Slavs finally renounced their allegiance to the dynasty. They declared Article I of 1868, the Croatian-Hungarian Compromise, to be abolished and proclaimed themselves the sovereign national state of the Slovenes, Croats, and Serbs.

On October 30, the so-called "Provisional National Assembly" proclaimed the state of "Deutschösterreich" or German-Austria. The new state, like independent Hungary, Czechoslovakia, Croatia, Poland, and Romania, had no fixed borders, being created supposedly as an expression of the self-determination of peoples. Completing the confusion that day, Slovak representatives ratified the foundation of Czechoslovakia and the incorporation into it of what had been Upper Hungary in the Svätý Martin Declaration, named after the town where the delegates had met.

The members of the German-Austrian regime faced two possible options: the first was to attempt the creation of a kind of Danubian Federation with their former partners in the monarchy, while the second was to be annexed to Germany. Karl Renner favored the second. The rioting and mayhem continued in Hungary, and as a result, Count Tisza was shot by the Communists on October 31. Though he had often been a hindrance to the plans and hopes of both Franz Ferdinand and Charles to avoid the very situation that at last overwhelmed his country, he was certainly an able man and a true lover of Hungary. However short-sighted he had been, his murder was an unconscionable crime—how many more would suffer at the hands of that same evil, unleashed with Lenin in that sealed railway train? His fate, however—although unknown at the time to the guardians of the royal children at Gödöllő—shows how dangerous things had become. Count Joseph Hunyady called their caretaker, Captain Walla, from Vienna puzzled. "Are you still in Gödöllő? Don't you know that the revolution has broken out in Budapest? You and the children must take off immediately for Vienna, and I will travel from here to meet you."[84] Little Otto, tired of waiting and dressed in a little Hungarian officer's uniform, grew impatient to leave and stepped out on the steps of the royal castle. A group of rather unfriendly soldiers had gathered and laughed when they saw the six-year-old in his uniform. Not realizing that they could have harmful intent, Otto smiled at them and saluted. They saluted back and began cheering the little tyke—and continued to do so as the royal party departed. Avoiding Budapest, the group

[84] "This is Just the Present, and the Future Is Promising," Otto Von Habsburg Foundation, https://habsburgottoalapitvany.hu/en/this-is-just-the-present-and-the-future-is-promising/.

was able to return to the imperial capital without incident, much to Charles and Zita's relief.

Two governments were now active in Vienna: the imperial government under the leadership of Lammasch and that of Renner's German-Austria, a self-proclaimed government with neither a constitution nor defined borders. Nevertheless, even if the other fronts had dissolved, the Italian Front remained, and what was left of the Austrian Army remained under Charles and Lammasch, to whom responsibility fell to end the fighting. An armistice was negotiated, which was due to take effect on November 3. On that day, the Austrians laid down their arms. The Italians then claimed that the armistice was actually set for the next day. Swarming over the front, the Italians took 360,000 prisoners during these last hours of hostilities.

One Austrian commander who was not caught napping, however, was the redoubtable Croatian Field Marshal Svetozar Boroevic, who had managed to pull his troops out of the wreckage of the Italian Front and bring them to Velden in Carinthia. He sent several telegrams to Charles, offering to bring his army to Vienna to maintain order. Obviously, had he done so, the situation in the capital would have altered remarkably—and no doubt a man of such flexible principles as Karl Renner would have immediately sworn undying loyalty to the emperor and maintained it so long as those troops were around. Unfortunately, the telegram was sent via the commander of the Vienna garrison, Johann von Kirchbach auf Lauterbach, who had gone over to Renner on November 1. Not only were the telegrams not passed on to Charles, but Boroevic's offer of aid was twice refused in

Charles's name; though Zita declared, years after the war, that he would certainly have accepted it had he known. Von Kirchbach auf Lauterbach's action can only be considered treason to the emperor to whom he had sworn allegiance. Of course, he was far from alone in this.

The armistice-related orders and conferences lasted until 4 a.m. on November 4. A telegram from Charles to Wilhelm brought them to a close. The imperial couple went to Mass in the castle chapel at 4:30 a.m., this being Charles's name day. At 10 a.m., the customary emperor's name day Mass took place at St. Stephen's Cathedral. Except for a few stalwarts, the representatives of the old regime appeared in civilian clothes, Renner's minions stayed away, and depression hung over everyone. Tears ran down the cheeks of many in the congregation as they sang the *Te Deum* and *Gott Erhalte* ("God Save Francis the Emperor") for what many, if not most, must have felt would be the last time.

That day, a Communist revolution broke out in Kiel, Germany. Spreading rapidly through the country, it forced the abdication of Germany's princes, and at last, Wilhelm himself on November 11—the day the Armistice was signed and the fighting ended on the Western Front. Events in Vienna would take a somewhat different turn.

The Czechs, however, were not done with the memory of their former rulers. On the anniversary of the Battle of White Mountain (November 8, 1620), more than three hundred thousand Czechs burned the symbols of the Habsburg dynasty there:

> Six speakers declaimed against the Habsburgs, against the Catholic religion and against the Vatican in the open air. The crowd returning to the city [Prague] demolished the precious column in the Old Square, dedicated to Ferdinand III. Built in 1650 in honor of the Mother of God and the liberation of the city, this column was adorned with a statue of the Mother of God, which the crowd destroyed under the mistaken belief that it was erected in contempt of the Czech people.[85]

So it was described by Apostolic Nuncio Valfrè di Bonzo from Vienna, underlining the aggression of the Czechs toward everything German and toward Catholicism. The nationalist-minded Italian worried about the proposed separation of church and state and the pace at which the reformers were promoting the Hussite church. He foresaw the *Kulturkampf* ("culture conflict"). Parallel to Masaryk's return to Prague, Czech priests in America informed the local Apostolic Delegate Giovanni Bonzano of Masaryk's great influence on Wilson and of his intention to implement the American model of separation of church and state in Czechoslovakia.

The same day that the Czechs were taking out their fury on the Virgin Mary's column in Prague, a visitor arrived at Schönbrunn—Admiral Nicholas Horthy. As with Karl Renner, the Hungarian naval officer would play a major role in the forthcoming drama of both the Habsburgs and Europe.

---

85 "Prague: Will the Marian Column on Old town Square be Resurrected?" https://www.kirche-in-not.de/allgemein/aktuelles/20200407-prag-mariensaeule-neuaufbau-rudolf-grulich/.

He was already well known to the imperial couple, having been Charles's adjutant at their wedding—an occasion which must have seemed to have been ages before, while only a scant seven years had passed—but the world had changed.

In any case, as the last Commander-in-Chief of the Imperial and Royal Navy, the hard task of surrendering the fleet to the new South Slav government had fallen to the admiral. Shaken by the task, he had come to see his king and offer him support. Horthy was loyal to the very end, and he would do all in his power—even if it meant dying—to see Charles restored to his thrones. Charles was very much impressed with the naval officer's sincerity. He then took his leave, but time would show, in the end, just how much this naval hero's oath was worth.

At midnight, after the departure of Horthy, Charles summoned his two adjutants, Baron Werkmann and Count Hunyadi. He told them that he would not abdicate but was all too aware that the defenders of the monarchy were very few. He might be overthrown, but he would never abdicate. A few days earlier, the Christian Socials had declared themselves loyal. Were they still?

Werkmann went into town to investigate, calling on each of the major politicians very late at night. He returned by 2 a.m., but as Charles was already in bed, Werkmann and Hunyadi made their report to him when he rose at 6 a.m. The consensus was that the Social Democrats were ready to strike to bring down the monarchy, the Pan-Germans were effectively neutral, but the Christian Socials were still loyal. It was recommended that Msgr. Johann Hauser, the head of the party, be consulted. Charles then wrote a letter to

Cardinal Piffl, asking him to solicit Msgr. Hauser's support. Werkmann went off to the archbishop's palace to deliver the note. Piffl read it, spoke to Hauser, and then called to assure Charles of his and Hauser's support. The cardinal added that Hauser assured him he could certainly hold the party loyal to the emperor. The wily monsignor, however, immediately went back on his word and spent November 10 and 11 advocating a republic to his party members in preparation for a vote on the matter in the assembly on the twelfth.

On the tenth, Lammasch's cabinet, still legally in power, met to consider their options. That morning, Renner sent a demand that the emperor abdicate immediately, or else he and his henchmen would declare Charles deposed. While the cabinet refused, they asked the emperor the following day to sign a decree, withdrawing from the affairs of government. Meeting with him in the Blue Chinese Salon, they showed him the manifesto they wished him to sign. He called Zita in to read it, and her response was electric. She glanced at it quickly rather than reading it.

"Never! You cannot abdicate."

Charles replied calmly, "This is not an abdication."

Zita continued, "A Sovereign can never abdicate. He can be deposed. He can be declared to have lost his rights. Very well. That is force. It does not compel him to admit that he has lost his rights. He can submit to force according to time and circumstances, but abdicate! Never, never, never! Rather will I be struck down here with you. Then Otto will succeed us. And if we all fall—why, there remain other Habsburgs!"[86]

[86] Brook-Shepherd, *The Last Habsburg*, p. 213.

Of course, she was simply repeating what both she and Charles believed. Their anointing and oaths were as binding as those taken at their baptisms and wedding and could be no more renounced than those sacred obligations. But she reread the document, and Baron Werkmann explained that abdication was in no way meant by that document; rather, it was a temporary move and would give them time to regroup. Zita agreed, and part of the manifesto, as signed, reads as follows:

> Since my accession to the throne, I have striven incessantly to relieve my peoples from the horrors of a war, for the declaration of which I was in no way responsible.
>
> I have not hesitated to restore constitutional life and have opened the way to the independent national development of my peoples.
>
> Ever filled with unchangeable love for all my peoples, I will not place myself as an obstacle to their progress.
>
> Henceforward, I recognize the decision which concerns the future government of German Austria.[87]

Since Schönbrunn was about to be taken over by the republic-to-be as government property (and to save the young cadets from possible harm), Charles and Zita resolved to leave the capital for one of their private homes. Their choice settled upon Eckartsau, a hunting castle near the Hungarian and Czechoslovakian borders. The woods were filled with game, and its location meant that they could stay in touch with

---

[87] Brook-Shepherd, *The Last Habsburg*, p. 214.

events in the neighboring countries as well. Zita described the leave-taking from Schönbrunn that evening:

> The emperor and I went down with our children to the palace chapel, where we said a short prayer that we might one day return here. After that, we went up to the so-called Hall of Ceremonies, where those who had still remained behind were gathered. We said goodbye to them, and thanked them one by one.
>
> Then down the stairway to the small inner courtyard below where the cars were waiting. Along the sides of the arcades, drawn up in two ranks, were our cadets from the military academies, with tears in their eyes, but still perfectly turned out and guarding us to the end. They had really lived up to the motto Empress Maria Theresa had given them: "Loyal for Ever."[88]

For Charles, of course, this was an unprecedented thing for a Habsburg—save for the precipitate flight of his thrice great-grandfather from Vienna after his defeats by Napoleon at Austerlitz and Wagram in 1805 and 1809. But Zita's father had had to flee Parma, her grandfather Lisbon, and her great-grandmother Paris. She knew all too well this bitter road. Worse yet, she would taste it a number of times more before she died. One senses that she defied it—all the exile in the world and all the depositions imaginable would not deflect her from what she believed to be her duty. Behind all developments in the world of politics, she saw the hand of God prodding her to be ever stronger, as though her

---

[88] Brook-Shepherd, *The Last Empress*, p. 132.

salvation depended upon it. In this, she was one with her husband, who would begin and end each day with prayer, as she did. They both attended Mass daily, whenever possible. If anything, their religiosity deepened as adversities multiplied.

Two days later, a Hungarian delegation arrived at Eckartsau, headed by Cardinal Csernoch—the same prelate who had crowned Charles less than two years before. This was perhaps the worst choice of chairmen. To be pressured to abdicate by the very man to whom Charles had sworn his unbreakable oath must have seemed either very funny, very sad, or merely grotesque to the anointed Hungarian king. In the event, what they brought back to Karolyi was a note saying, "I do not wish to stand in the way of the Hungarian nation, for whom I still feel the same unchanged love. Consequently I resign my part in the business of state and accept this decision as regards the new form of government in Hungary."[89] With that bland statement, they and their master in Budapest would have to be satisfied. It was even less than what Lammasch had gotten out of Charles. Both "withdrawals from government" in Austria and Hungary envisaged free referenda on the form of government. Neither ever took place. Three days later, Hungary was declared a republic.

At this point, however, as we have seen the political establishments in all quarters of the monarchy swiftly changing coats, centuries of loyalty vanished overnight. Indeed, it is very doubtful that a majority would have been in favor

[89] Brook-Shepherd, *The Last Empress*, p. 134.

of ending the only system they had ever known. Indeed, while referenda have often been fixed, the new authorities in the various successor states would not risk it. As in most democracies, the majority must simply accept whatever their representatives deign to give them. But from Tyrol, where Giovanni Menato, Mayor of Castello Tesino, had hung out the double eagle, to Transylvania, where poet Ioan Slavici was imprisoned for a year due to his continuing loyalty to the Habsburgs, there were individuals who refused to change their coats. Croatian Field Marshal Boroevic, remaining staunch in his loyalty, stayed in Vienna, so too did Stjepan Sarkotic, the last Governor of Bosnia. The Slovenian politician Ivan Sustersic was of like mind. Certainly, there were many monarchists in both Austria and Hungary—we shall shortly meet some of the latter. Yet so it was even in Masaryk's Czechoslovakia—his son Jan remained in the imperial army until the war ended and did not conceal his Habsburg loyalties until his death. Nor were such lacking in the other nationalities. But a Polish noncommissioned officer would have a particular importance as regarded Charles's ultimate legacy. Sergeant Major Wojtyla would name his son Karol—the future Pope St. John Paul II—after his beloved emperor. This role could and should be endlessly expanded.

At the moment, however, this reservoir of loyalty could do little good for the immediate position of the imperial family. Before her marriage, Zita had the support of her wealthy family, and after her wedding, she and her husband had the resources of Austria-Hungary behind them. Now, the two of them in Eckartsau had only themselves to rely upon for their future and that of their children and of the fifty or so loyal courtiers who stayed with them. For food, there was game in the woods, but as the security situation worsened in Vienna and poachers increased, the future looked uncertain. The Spanish flu came in December, nearly killing Karl Ludwig and leaving Charles very sick. The empress would later recall,

> Christmas 1918 was a rather sombre festival—especially as the emperor, who was anyway suffering from repeated heart attacks and overstrain, had gone down with a severe attack of Spanish influenza ten days before and was now really ill. All the children caught it as well; some only mildly, it is true, but some severely—Karl Ludwig, for example, who was then barely eighteen months old, very nearly died.
>
> However, we did our best to make it a cheerful occasion.
>
> The emperor got up for Christmas Eve but was so weak that he had to remain seated in an armchair while the presents were being exchanged. He was quite exhausted afterwards and his temperature went up again. That same night, we heard, there were toasts drunk to the emperor that night all over the capital.[90]

They would do so again when New Year's Eve came, ending at last this truly horrific year. Zita, Charles, and their children did not know what would face them, but husband and wife were resolved never to abdicate and to do what they could for their peoples so long as they were able.

---

[90] Brook-Shepherd, *The Last Empress*, p. 136.

Chapter 8

AFTER THE FALL

"It is as the seers of Byzantium foretold, the prophets that spoke incessantly of the fate that was coming, of the final days of the City. The weary Byzantine knew that the doom so often threatened must some day surely envelop him. And what did it matter? It was needless to complain. This world was a foolish travesty, haunted with pain, and with sorrowful memories and foreboding. Peace and true happiness lay beyond. What was the Emperor, the Peer of the Apostles, what even was Constantinople itself, the great City, dear to God and to His Mother, compared to Christ Pantocrator and the Courts of Heaven?"

—Stephen Runciman[91]

At first, the new year of 1919 did not seem too different from the horrible year that had just passed. But, for Karl Renner, the imperial family remained a threat of some sort—even bereft of money and soldiers—as long as they were ensconced at Eckartsau. A coward, after all, can never be sure of his safety. He was, however, sufficiently sure of himself to go to Eckartsau and demand that the emperor abdicate the throne and leave the country. Without

[91] Stephen Runciman, *Byzantine Civilisation* (London: Methuen, 1966), pp. 299–300.

bothering to notify Charles that he would be descending on him, he set off for the castle in the first week of January. When he arrived, Charles was informed, but since Renner had made no appointment, Charles did not see him. One of the emperor's aide-de-camps, Captain Emmerich von Schonta, sat the hapless chancellor down and gave him a snack. Renner told the captain with great solicitude that he was afraid the damp river air might be bad for the emperor's lungs and that there were all sorts of dangerous people in the neighborhood, intimating it would be best for Charles to leave. But Schonta assured Renner that Charles was pleased with the air and that, with thirty rifles on hand and the men to use them, they did not anticipate any difficulties at all—the more so since, after all, the government was responsible for the safety of the imperial residence and their effectiveness could not be questioned. Finally, Renner demanded that Charles stop being addressed as "Majesty." To this demand, Schonta brightly responded that Renner should stop being called "doctor." With that, the peppery little demagogue flounced off. Frustrated for the moment, the little man was only checked, not stopped.

A campaign of harassment ensued against the imperial family. January was not yet over when betrayal came from an unexpected quarter: Cardinal Piffl, the Archbishop of Vienna. Elections to the constituent national assembly were scheduled for February 16, 1919. In preparation for this, the cardinal—who had been quick to drop the title of "Prince Archbishop," which he and his predecessors had enjoyed for centuries—penned a pastoral letter for the faithful of

"German-Austria" regarding the current political situation to which the archbishops and bishops of the country assented.

In this screed, Piffl declared that the Church was not integrally connected to monarchy; Catholics could be republicans. The unpublished letter was brought to the emperor, who asked Piffl to employ the clergy in persuading Catholics to vote for a restoration. He pointed out that without the monarchy, Austria would be secularized, as shown by the fact that the new regime had already legalized divorce and Freemasonry, and that in any case he himself had not abdicated. Piffl was unconcerned, and had the letter read.

As Elisabeth Kovács explains, the letter called on Catholics to work together to build a happier future for society and the fatherland, citing St. Paul's Epistle to the Romans and Leo XIII's 1885 encyclical *Immortale Dei*. The participation of the people in the government could "not only contribute to the benefit of the citizens, but also be their duty. The assertion that the Church begrudges the states their new order is unfounded and empty slander."[92] Piffl "then went on to claim that the emperor himself would have given the Austrians the right to self-determination and had entrusted the current representatives of the people with the reorganization of state affairs."[93] That Charles had agreed to abide by a referendum on the monarchy was true, but it would never be held; the assertion that he had approved the current

[92] As quoted in Elisabeth Kovács, U*ntergang oder Rettung der Donaumonarchie?*, book 1, chapter 23, https://www.elisabethkovacs.com/neue-forschungen-zu-kaiser-karl/band-i/kapitel-xxiii-eckartsau/.

[93] As quoted in Elisabeth Kovács, *Untergang oder Rettung der Donaumonarchie?*, book 1, chapter 23.

representatives of the people was simply a lie. But lie or not, who could possibly doubt the word of a cardinal of the Holy Roman Church?

In the meantime, Renner's regime stepped up its pressure on the court at Eckartsau. Poachers in the woods multiplied, and various unsavory messages were posted on the estate's fences from time to time. Carts from Vienna taking provisions to Eckartsau began to be raided by police and troops in Vienna. There were also further agitations from more remote players. The Communists unsuccessfully attempted to assassinate the Czechoslovakian prime minister, and their Magyar brethren were demonstrating ever more in Hungary. There began to be a real danger that the Habsburgs might suffer the same fate as the Romanovs.

In early February, however, things changed. Sixtus was in Paris and very concerned about the difficulty the family was facing. He appealed to President Poincaré to do something, but the French president declared himself unable to help. Sixtus and Xavier then went to London, where Sixtus was able to see the king and queen. George V felt a tremendous amount of guilt over the deaths of his cousin, the tsar, and the Russian imperial family. He assured Sixtus that he would do something immediately.

The king was as good as his word. On February 15, a telegram was sent to Colonel Sir Thomas Cunningham, the British military representative in Vienna; it reached him in Prague. He was ordered to send a trustworthy officer to Eckartsau, "who should endeavour by every means in his power to ameliorate the conditions of life of the emperor and the empress and give them the moral support of the British government."[94] There was attached to it a report indicating plots to assassinate the imperial couple. Cunningham lost no time in returning to Vienna and chose Colonel John Summerhayes of the Royal Medical Corps to act as the emperor's honorary escort.

On February 20, Cunningham and Summerhayes drove out to Eckartsau. The larger situation was looking very bleak indeed. Karolyi's regime in Hungary was becoming increasingly like that of Kerensky in Moscow, which through its weakness paved the way for the Bolshevik takeover in 1917's October Revolution. So it was that Karolyi was losing ground daily to the Communists. The Czech Legion had occupied Bratislava, and the tension between the two countries was rising. The Renner regime maintained two battalions of the Volkswehr (People's Guard), infiltrated by Communists, that were stationed in Hainburg and Grossenzersdorf. Chief of Police Schober, whose ten detectives were guarding Eckartsau, was aware of a conspiracy. In this atmosphere, the arrival of Summerhayes was happily greeted by Charles and Zita. The emperor wrote George V a letter in French, thanking him for his assistance and pronouncing himself very grateful for this timely assistance. Addressing the king as an equal, Charles wrote further that "the situation in the whole world is very difficult, above all for us sovereigns." He signed off, "From Your Majesty's good brother and cousin, Charles."[95]

---

[94] Gordon Brook-Shepherd, *The Last Empress* (London: HarperCollins, 1991), p. 137.

[95] Brook-Shepherd, *The Last Empress*, p. 138.

On February 16, the election took place. The results in the assembly were 72 Social Democrats, 69 Christian Socials, 26 Pan-Germans, 1 Czech, 1 bourgeois democrat, and 1 Zionist. Charles appealed once more to Piffl, "Let us pray a great deal, patriotism and loyalty must be preached to the faithful, it must now be said clearly and distinctly: We want a monarchy, because throne and altar are inseparably linked."[96] The cardinal had decided differently long ago—mere gratitude was not in his nature. The Christian Socials had split into monarchist and republican wings. Charles sharply criticized their behavior, writing further, "The Christian Social Party should take courage and at least vote against deposition, expulsion, etc., because if the dismissal is decided unanimously, restoration is very difficult. I wrote this only so that I would not have missed something by omitting a warning that would have weighed heavily on my conscience for the rest of my life."[97]

The Renner regime had informed Colonel Cunningham as early as February 19 that they wanted the imperial couple to leave the country. Julius Deutsch, spokesman for the Social Democrats, demanded the abdication of the emperor. It must have occurred to someone in the London Foreign Office that Summerhayes—as a subordinate of the occupying power as represented by Colonel Cunningham, which was charged with dealing with the Renner regime—might be in an invidious position if he was also charged with

---

[96] As quoted in Elisabeth Kovács, *Untergang oder Rettung der Donaumonarchie?*, book 1, chapter 23.

[97] As quoted in Elisabeth Kovács, *Untergang oder Rettung der Donaumonarchie?*, book 1, chapter 23.

protecting the emperor from that regime. Whitehall notified Cunningham that they were sending another officer and, in their message, warned him, "It is an instruction that you have nothing further to do with this matter and that above all you refrain from giving advice to the new officer, or to the Emperor, or to anyone else."[98] As it happened, it would turn out that the officer selected was quite literally perfect for the job.

On February 21, Lieutenant-Colonel Edward Lisle Strutt was enjoying the hospitality of the Hotel Danieli in Venice. Strutt was the scion of two aristocratic clans: his father, the Honorable Arthur Strutt, was the son of the 1st Baron Belper. His mother, Alice Mary Elizabeth Phillipps de Lisle, was the daughter of the noted Catholic convert, Ambrose Phillipps de Lisle, Lord of Grace Dieu Manor in Leicestershire. Strutt had learned German at the University of Innsbruck before the war and had many friends amongst the aristocracy, including Franz Ferdinand, with whom he shared a love of mountaineering. A born adventurer, he had served in the Boer War, earning the Queen's South Africa Medal and four clasps and the King's South Africa Medal and two clasps. Strutt's gallant service on both the Western and Salonika Fronts during the war had gained him Chevalier, Order of Leopold (Belgium); Chevalier, Order of Romania; Croix de Guerre (Belgium); Croix de Guerre (France) with four palms; and Officer, Légion d'honneur; and last, he was made Companion of the Distinguished Service Order (DSO) in 1918. In a word, he was not an easily

[98] Brook-Shepherd, *The Last Empress*, p. 138.

frightened individual. Many years later, after being asked if he hated the English given what they had done to his family, Otto replied, "One could—but then there was Strutt!"[99] The last part of his statement was made with a tremendous smile.

The man who would make such an impression on the young archduke left Venice by train the day following his reception of the order. The train journey took him through Rijeka, Zagreb, and Ljubljana to Vienna. Arriving at the Hotel Bristol, where he had habitually stayed before the war, he ran into Czernin, whom he had also known. Unaware of the part that his old friend had played in Charles's ruin, they had an amicable chat. On the twenty-seventh, he set out for Eckarstau in a six-seat automobile from the imperial garage. Lunch was soon to be served when he arrived, and he found to his great joy that one of Charles's adjutants, Count Hunyady, was another old prewar friend. When taken to his room, he saw a particularly poignant reminder of past times—a framed photograph of himself with Franz Ferdinand and the archduke's aide, Karl Baron Rumerskirch, at St. Moritz before the war.

In his diaries, Strutt recorded his first impressions of his two new charges. Of Charles, he wrote,

> The emperor is of medium height, very slightly built, with quite a good-looking, well-bred but weak face. . . . He was wearing full field-marshal's uniform, with a handsome sword and a mass of medals, decorations, and "plaques." Amongst them I recognised the

---

[99] Gordon Brook-Shepherd, *Uncrowned Emperor: The Life and Times of Otto von Habsburg* (London, Hambledon and London, 2003), p. 47.

> Order of the Golden Fleece, the Iron Cross, and our own GCVO! . . . I may say here that I almost always spoke French to the emperor and he replied in German. His English, he told me, was very indifferent, but his French was excellent as regards pronunciation, if rather deficient in vocabulary. The emperor's appearance describes his character; an eminently lovable, if weak, man, by no means a fool, and ready to face his end as bravely as his ancestress, Marie Antoinette.[100]

Strutt would certainly come to love the emperor, and he would come to radically revise his opinion concerning Charles's weakness. But if he found himself coming to love his charge, Zita conquered him:

> She was very simply dressed in black wearing her wonderful pearls (I came to know those pearls very well later) and looked pale and ill. About medium height and with a slim figure, she looked younger than her age, twenty-six. The first impression I had was of extraordinary strength of character, softened by her own remarkable charm. Determination was written in the lines of her square little chin, intelligence in the vivacious brown eyes, intellect in the broad forehead half hidden by masses of dark hair. Without extraordinary claims to beauty, the empress would always attract attention in a crowd. . . . Nor did I ever hear one word of complaint from her, who certainly felt

[100] Herbert Vivian, *The Life of the Emperor Charles of Austria* (London: Grayson and Grayson, 1932), p. 178.

> her position more deeply than her husband. No more affectionate and devoted couple than these two could possibly be found. So much for the foul lies of the gutter press.[101]

Indeed, she must have been deeply aware of her position. Unlike Charles, who was after all, heir to a throne that, despite rocks and shocks over the past two centuries, had, until this moment, maintained itself successfully. His family tradition had trained him for every foreseeable circumstance, save utter defeat. Zita, however, had been raised with stories of her forebears' successive ejections from the thrones of France, Spain, Portugal, the Two Sicilies, and Parma; she herself was born in exile. Such a background could not help but give her a ready-made set of responses to such a situation. For a gallant soul like Strutt, the urge to serve and assist this couple would soon outweigh and eventually outlast his government's official assignment to them.

Strutt and Charles would hunt for deer and woodcock in the woods for dinner. But things were getting worse on the outside. The Communists were becoming ever more powerful in Hungary, and the Karolyi regime was ever feebler in the face of the menace. Charles appealed directly to George V and the Foreign Office, asking for troops ("Americans if not British, but no French or Italians"[102]) to block the Bolsheviks and set up a Danube Confederation strong enough to put down the Bolsheviks at home—and to keep Russia at

[101] Vivian, *The Life of the Emperor Charles*, p. 179.
[102] Gordon Brook-Shepherd, *The Last Habsburg* (New York: Weybright and Talley, 1968), p. 234.

bay if, as was beginning to look likely, the Reds triumphed in the civil war now raging in that country. As during the war, Charles's sense of what was likely to happen was far keener than that of the political leadership of his and the other European nations. And as during the war, that would avail him and his peoples little.

In the meantime, Renner's regime was now officially inaugurated on March 15. That very day, Strutt had received an order from the Foreign Office: "Most desirable to get the Emperor out of Austria without delay. All possible steps to be taken to expedite departure."[103] Now, if the Allies had ignored the emperor's warnings, they had not forgotten him. On March 12, the issue of his exile was discussed before the inter-Allied war council at Versailles; Lloyd George spoke up for Charles, emphasizing that the young emperor was not responsible for the war; rather, he had inherited it and done his best to get out of it as Lloyd George knew quite well. The British Prime Minister declared that Charles had been treated with great brutality and was in mortal danger. Switzerland would be a preferable place of exile to any Allied country. The discussions made it clear that the Allies had no intention of punishing Charles as they did not believe him to be guilty of anything save defeat. Foreign Secretary Arthur Balfour was asked to confidentially request the Swiss Ambassador in London to offer the imperial family hospitality and to assure that Switzerland would have no trouble receiving the Emperor of Austria. When the Swiss government declared that they were prepared to give the Emperor

[103] Vivian, *The Life of the Emperor Charles*, p. 182.

of Austria a residence permit as a "refugee and private person," the Foreign Office ordered Strutt to get the "ex-Kaiser" out of Austria immediately and to speed up his departure for Switzerland.[104]

Charles had steadily refused to consider leaving, but he finally agreed on the condition that he would not have to abdicate. This gave Strutt two seemingly irreconcilable problems: Charles and Zita would leave only if they were not forced to abdicate, but would Renner and his gang allow them to leave under those circumstances? Strutt went down to Vienna on March 17 to see what the regime had to offer. They informed him that Charles and Zita had three choices: they could abdicate, in which case they could remain as private citizens of Renner's republic; if they refused to abdicate, they must leave; but if they refused to do either, they would be imprisoned. Obviously, the threat the young couple posed to Renner and his henchmen must have been extreme.

Strutt then ordered the imperial train to be made ready to take the imperial family out of the country whenever he gave the order. He then returned to Eckartsau on March 18 and offered the plan he had in mind to Charles, that he should accompany the emperor disguised as a British officer for Switzerland, whereupon Strutt would return for Zita and the children. Zita refused, point blank.

The following day, an incident occurred that steeled Strutt to do what he must. A cart with provisions for Eckartsau was waylaid by regular soldiers, and the driver was sent back on foot to Eckartsau with a nasty note. Strutt confronted

[104] Vivian, p. 183.

Zita and explained his fears for the family and the fact that their country was hostile at the moment. Yet he promised to get them all out without any need for abdication. Zita said nothing, and finally, Strutt blurted out, "A dead Habsburg is no good to anyone, whereas a live one, with a family, may yet be." She then smiled, took his hand, and said, "We will leave under your orders."[105] So it was that she accepted with her husband the must-trodden, long road to exile that so many of her family, down to her own father, had had to take.

Charles had one last card to play, and that was to move to Tyrol in a sort of internal exile. Strutt went down to Vienna on March 20 to run the idea past Renner. Strutt had come to know the little man for the bully he was, and in his diary, Strutt described him as "a hairy, cunning-looking rascal with intelligent eyes."[106] Having accurately taken his measure, Strutt entered the newly minted chancellor's office, wherein Renner sat at his desk, eyeing him. Strutt shouted at him, "Please stand up when I enter your room!"[107] This shocked the Socialist placeholder, and Strutt sat at his desk to address him, Renner standing all the while. But if the British officer had exposed the coward in the chancellor, he could not get him to accept Charles's proposal. Indeed, from the standpoint of Renner and his gang, that would have been the worst possible outcome. Charles, as with all the Habsburgs down to the present, had a special relationship with the Tyroleans; even today, it remains a center of monarchist sentiment. The imperial family resident there would

---

[105] Vivian, p. 187.
[106] Vivian, p. 186.
[107] Vivian, p. 186.

be an infallible recipe for an attempt at restoration; Renner was not a fool. Strutt returned to Eckartsau and relayed the bad news, explaining that there was no alternative but exile in Switzerland. Charles responded, "Only promise me that I shall leave as emperor and not as a thief in the night."[108] Strutt promised, but it would require some effort to keep.

On March 22, Strutt returned to Vienna to make some final arrangements regarding the imperial train. He was given a note asking him to come to Renner's office. Knowing what sort of a creature Renner was, Strutt supposed there would be some sort of last-minute trick. As a defense, he wrote and signed a message to the War Office in London on an official British Mission telegram form, put it in his pocket, and went to see what sort of a surprise Renner had for him.

The chancellor stood up to see him but declared that Charles and Zita would not be allowed to leave Austrian soil without abdicating, thus, true to form, reneging on the agreement Strutt had made with Renner and his regime. Strutt pulled out the telegram draft that he had written and placed it in front of Renner. To his horror, the wily little man read,

> En Clair, To Director Military Intelligence London
>
> Austrian Government refuses permission for departure of emperor unless he abdicates. Consequently give orders to re-establish blockade and stop all food trains entering Austria.
>
> (signed) Strutt[109]

---

[108] Vivan, p. 187.
[109] Vivian, p. 189.

Once again, Strutt had the measure of his man. Against this bluff—for utter bluff it was—all the hot air flew out of the chancellor. Renner threw up his hands and said, "Grosser Gott!"[110] He then said, "All right, he can go."

"Without conditions?"

"Yes," he snapped.[111] Strutt left, taking care to take his bluff with him.

On Sunday, March 25, the imperial train—reassembled with a full set of saloon cars, a dining car, and the rest—set off on its final journey, sporting both the double eagles on the train cars and the Union Jack at the head; aboard was an escort of six British MPs and a sergeant. The train pulled into Kopfstetten station, two miles from Eckartsau, at 3:45 p.m. The family was attending Mass offered in the castle chapel; seven-year-old Otto was serving. When the Mass was over, all present sang the imperial anthem—many openly sobbing.

All afternoon, the family's things were loaded aboard the train; Strutt took charge of various extremely important items, papers, jewelry, and the like. At 6:35 p.m., the imperial couple (Charles in his field marshal uniform) came down the stairs to say farewell to the servants, gamekeepers, local officials, and peasants. They all fell to their knees as Charles and Zita walked to the two motor cars that would take them to the station. Twenty minutes later, they had arrived; their headlights illuminated some two thousand people who had come to see them off. Four or five wounded veterans

---

110 "Holy God."

111 Vivian, p. 189.

were waiting by the entrance to the saloon car doors. As they climbed into the car, Charles said to Strutt, "After 700 years."[112] He then sighed and said, "Sacred Heart of Jesus, I trust in you!"[113] Later, in the dining car, Zita turned to Strutt and asked, "My family have been exiled from France, Italy, and Portugal. Then I became an Austrian subject, and now I am an exile from Austria. Colonel Strutt, tell me, to what country do I now belong?"[114] For once, the quick-witted colonel had no reply. It was a question that would also afflict her son Otto; many years later, he would come up with a novel answer.

The imperial train passed westward without incident at any of the stations, save at Innsbruck where a group of the Italian occupying soldiers had to be warned away. While on the train, Charles composed the Feldkirch Manifesto, so called from the name of the last large town before the Swiss frontier where the emperor signed it. In this document, he declared that all of his renunciations were invalid because they were made under pressure.

When the imperial couple arrived in Switzerland, they were greeted by representatives from the Swiss government and two of Zita's brothers. Wartegg would be their new home while in exile. The train left for Austria just as quickly as it had arrived. All but one of those train cars would be

---

[112] Vivian, p. 190.

[113] Ildefons Maria Fux, "Blessed Charles of Austria and His Relationship with the Sacred Heart of Jesus," The Catholic Information Page of the Community of St. Joseph, January 22, 2005, https://www.stjosef.at/artikel/sel_karl_v_oesterreich_herzjesu.htm.

[114] Brook-Shepherd, *The Last Empress*, p. 145.

destroyed in World War II; the lone survivor may be seen in Prague's National Technical Museum. It has been used the past few years, however, to bring several of Charles and Zita's descendants to the annual "Audience" at Brandeis—an observance wherein Czechs from all parts of the country come to honor the imperial couple's memory. No doubt this development would have been a great comfort to them, if they could have known it would one day happen!

The imperial couple and their children lived at the castle Schloss Wartegg for about three months. The Bourbon-Parma family who owned the castle would have to give it up in 1924, but for a short while, it was a pleasant place of exile in which Charles and Zita could relax and plan for the future. Three weeks after their arrival, Colonel Strutt departed for his next assignment in Constantinople. But he would see the imperial family again. While still at Wartegg, Charles, Zita, and the children received a very pleasant visit from a monk of Disentis Abbey, Fr. Maurus Carnot. The family had first become aware of the monk when Otto celebrated his First Communion in 1918. Fr. Carnot wrote a short poem celebrating the event and sent a copy to the imperial family in Vienna, and he received a very nice note from Zita in return. When they found themselves in exile, he hurried to visit them to see "whether those who had been cast out might not be in need of consolation, a small ray of joy."[115] Apparently, he was successful to some degree, for they remained strong friends ever after.

[115] "Habsburger," http://www.pater-maurus-carnot.ch/html/habsburger.html.

Charles and Zita then had to move their family to Lake Geneva, due to an abundance of caution. Today the clubhouse of a golf club called the Domaine Impérial, the Villa Prangins was constructed in 1860 on the orders of Prince Jerome Napoleon (1822–1891)—son of Jerome Bonaparte, brother of Emperor Napoleon and a former King of Westphalia. In 1859, the prince bought some of the land that his uncle had previously owned in Prangins, namely three hundred hectares to the east of Promenthoux. He commissioned Emile Trélat (founder of the Paris School of Architecture) to design a relatively modest Villa Prangins. But after the fall of his cousin Emperor of the French Napoleon III in 1870, Prince Jérôme divided the estate and sold the villa to his English friend, Charles Lucas. For a while, several proprietors succeeded one another, during which time, Villa Prangins was partially destroyed by fire in 1899 and reconstructed the following year. Jules Couchoud, a master printer from Lausanne, acquired the property in 1910 and set about restoring it with the elaborate touches and adornments of the period—but then sold it almost immediately to Ashton Clarke, a wealthy Parisian. He, in turn, rented it to Charles and Zita in 1919. This pleasant spot would function as a palace in exile for the next two years. Just one day after their arrival in Prangins, their majesties invited the former Polish Regency Councilor, Prince Zdislaus Lubomirski, to a dinner with Count Revertera, who had acted as an emissary for Charles several times during the war. The prince then wrote to England about the emperor's financial problems caused by the Austrian Habsburg laws and about the emperor himself. He was amazed to find the emperor extremely calm. Judging by Charles's optimism and his deep faith in the future, he was concentrating on the resurrection of the old monarchy in a Danube Federation and putting his and his family's problems behind the problems of his people, whose fate completely occupied him.

In the villa's chapel, the imperial couple placed a statue of the Sacred Heart in front of a lamp that constantly burned. First Friday was celebrated with solemnity: In the morning, a *Missa Cantata* was offered by Court Bishop Ernst Seydl, who had accompanied the family into exile. The two older archdukes, Otto and Robert, served as altar boys. After the Mass ended, little Karl Ludwig would say his prayer aloud, "Sacred Heart of Jesus, I trust in you. Have mercy on the fatherland, enclose all loved ones in your heart, and soon bring us all back home happily!"[116] To be sure, the homeland for which they prayed was the entirety of the old monarchy and all its peoples. In the evening, the family prayed the litany of and consecration to the Sacred Heart. Then they would sing the song *Auf, zum Schwure, Volk und Land!*:

> *Up to the oath, people and country, raise your heart and hand to heaven!*
> *What you vow to the Savior is tested in eternal loyalty ("Yes, we swear again today, Jesus' heart to you eternal loyalty").*

[116] Ildefons Maria Fux, "Blessed Charles of Austria and His Relationship with the Sacred Heart of Jesus," The Catholic Information Page of the Community of St. Joseph, January 22, 2005, https://www.stjosef.at/artikel/sel_karl_v_oesterreich_herzjesu.htm.

Always miraculously powerful, you were always the people's treasure,
in times of need and danger of war you shielded the people and altar
("Therefore we pledge anew, Jesus' heart to you eternal loyalty").
We stand firm and strong to our God in spite of scorn and ridicule;
We hold fast to the faith, our people's most beautiful adornment
("Therefore we pledge anew, Jesus' heart to you eternal loyalty").
On the wide earth, there is no more beautiful covenant.
Our enemies blaspheme too, loyalty is the custom of Christians
("Therefore we vow anew, Jesus' heart to you eternal loyalty").

In addition, there was a Sacred Heart prayer service in the house chapel every Friday. In the children's room, there was a small house altar with a picture of the Sacred Heart, in front of which the children said their prayers. But not only the children found help through the visible sign of Christ's humanity. The emperor himself had a picture of the Sacred Heart on his desk as well as near his bed. He also had pictures of the Sacred Heart painted and framed in silver for his mother-in-law and sisters-in-law to be given as Christmas gifts.

In truth, this was the closest that the imperial family would ever have to a time of normal life together. But this domesticity was only a part of what was happening.

Charles's political thoughts were not merely the yearnings of an exile. Less than an hour away from the villa was the city of Lausanne, home of Hungarian author Felix Valyi, director of the *Revue politique internationale*. Together with Count Gyula Andrássy, who had been driven from Hungary, and several other Hungarian Legitimists in the area, they set up the *Agence Centrale*. Its aims "were to inform Western politicians of the true situation in the region of the destroyed monarchy, to keep in touch with the supporters of the emperor in the different Successor States, and to realise Emperor Karl's plans by influencing the international press regarding the necessity of a Danubian Confederation."[117] Within two months, the agency had branch offices in Prague, Belgrade, Budapest, London, and Paris. In addition, the emperor and his supporters were trying very hard to influence the Allies by preventing a project dear to Renner's heart, the union of Austria with Germany. At this time also, the Communist menace from Hungary was surging in neighboring countries. Hungarian and Croatian committees were formed by refugees in Vienna—the latter headed by the ever-loyal Field Marshal Boroevic—to restore Charles in their respective countries, while a Hungarian anti-Communist government in exile had formed in Arad, headed by Count Karolyi, who was assisted by Admiral Horthy.

[117] Zoltan Becsi, *Forbidden Federalism* (Reno: Helena History, 2020), p. 31.

But, amid this intrigue, family life was not neglected. In the mornings, Zita spent time with the children, and Charles spent time with them every afternoon. Often, the family would take day trips—not least to Schloss Habsburg, two and a half hours away in Aargau, where the family had first come into prominence. This pleasant period was punctuated on September 5 when another boy was born, Archduke Rudolf. No doubt these revisits of the House's original home at least partly inspired the child's being named after the first very prominent member of the line.

In the meantime, the victorious Allies had been conducting peace negotiations at Versailles with Germany, at the nearby Trianon Palace with Hungary, and at St. Germain with the representatives of Austria. Without doubt, the proceedings were dominated by the Allied leaders—Woodrow Wilson for the United States, Lloyd George for Great Britain and her empire, Clemenceau for France, and Orlando for Italy; George V and Victor Emmanuel III were as excluded from "their" ministers' diplomacy as Nicholas II and Wilhelm II had been before the war. The elected representatives of the people were able to conclude peace treaties as ultimately disastrous for Europe as had been the tsar and kaiser's peace treaty being vetoed by "their" governments before the war. But Charles's warnings did have some effect. The treaty of St. Germain, ratified by the Austrians on October 17, forbade the name "German-Austria" and the union of the country with Germany. Renner would have to wait nineteen years before delivering his homeland to its northern neighbor.

But things were heating up in Hungary. The reign of terror that Bela Kun and his associates had unleashed was directly responsible for the establishment of both the Hungarian committee in Vienna and the government-in-exile in Romania. The Hungarian Communists had invaded Slovakia and set up a short-lived Soviet Republic there—and the attempted takeover in Vienna would have made a land bridge to the equally abortive Bavarian Communist regime. Horthy had turned up in Szeged on June 6, where anti-Communist forces were gathering under the protection of French occupation forces. He made contact with Charles, who approved him as minister of war in the government-in-exile. Horthy then assumed command of all the Conservative troops who were gathering, especially those of Major Ostenburg and Colonel Lehár, both well-known for their loyalty to Charles.

On August 1, 1919, the Romanians—tired of the whole farce—invaded Hungary, and the counterrevolutionaries joined them. Bela Kun fled to Vienna, and Admiral Horthy rode into Budapest on a white horse. There was a month of experimenting with different cabinets, but the Romanians remained firmly in charge for the rest of the year. Meanwhile, correspondence continued to be received from loyal Austrians, Hungarians, Slovaks, Croats, Slovenians, and even Czechs, assuring them of their continuing loyalty.

In the meantime, life continued as per usual at Prangins, with daily Mass, the devotions to the Sacred Heart earlier referred to, and excursions with the children. Thanks to their relationship with Fr. Carnot, the older children were able to have a winter holiday at Disentis Abbey; Charles and Zita joined them on December 30 for a Mass commemorating the third anniversary of their coronation at Budapest. How much had happened since that day! But it reminded them—as if they had needed such a reminder—of their duties and obligations as crowned and anointed King and Queen of Hungary. Surely, 1920 would be better than 1919.

Back in Budapest, Horthy was maneuvering to make his temporary military dominance of the country permanent and political. On March 1, he had himself elected regent of the reconstituted Kingdom of Hungary. He dispatched Captain Bela von Revhegyi to Prangins to assure Charles and Zita of his undying loyalty and the temporary nature of his office. Charles and Zita had discussed the possibility of Charles simply coming onto the scene amid the unrest in Hungary. But the problem with this—and Horthy alluded to it in his letter—was that the Allies had made clear their distaste for a Habsburg on the throne. They even barred Archduke Joseph from being regent. Since, at that time, Hungary was literally negotiating for its life at the Trianon, the time for the great return would have to be after the treaty was signed and after whatever possible damage was done.

When the text of the treaty was received in Budapest on May 5, one could have been forgiven—from the Hungarian point of view—for thinking that nothing could have been worse. Two-thirds of the kingdom and over half the population were given to the successor states: Czechoslovakia, Yugoslavia, and Romania. Alongside the Magyars and Germans, who would now dwell in these new countries, many of the Slovaks in the first-named country and the Slovenians and Croats in the second were already feeling buyer's remorse. Quite far from settling the national problems that had agitated the monarchy, they were exacerbated under the new regimes. If anything, this development reinforced

Charles's conviction that only a federation under his headship could restore some element of civility and cooperation to the region. But for that to happen, he had to begin the process by being restored somewhere—and Hungary was the obvious candidate for such a nucleus.

In May of 1920, as soon as he read the contents of the treaty, Charles sent the newly minted regent (who had assumed the title of duke, that being the customary rank of a regent in the past) a letter, reading,

> In the interests of maintaining and consolidating Hungary's territories, I intend, during the course of this year, to take over the reins of government again. I therefore request Your Serene Highness [in deference to his self-assumed Dukedom] to inform me, from your clear understanding of the situation, the most suitable moment for my return to the throne.[118]

But Horthy had moved—after seeking Charles's permission—from the Hotel Gellert to the Royal Palace in Buda. He did not yet occupy the royal apartments, but he began acting as sovereign in various ceremonial ways. When Charles sent him manifestos for publication, he did not publish them, and his letters became ever more vague. Then, at last, he ordered the armed forces to swear allegiance to him personally without ever mentioning the king or dynasty.

In the summer of 1920, however, outside events began to push some of the Allied leaders to think in the direction of restoration. Like Hungary, Poland was threatened by Russian

---

[118] Brook-Shepherd, *The Last Empress*, p. 157.

Bolshevism. While negotiations were taking place at Versailles over Poland's western borders, Marshal Pilsudski attempted to seize as much territory as he could on the eastern frontier—ignoring allied warnings of Soviet strength. Initially successful, he was driven all the way back into Poland. Had it not been for the "Miracle of the Vistula," an unexpected victory on August 18, 1920, Poland would have fallen to the Soviets.

> At this point, the utility of a Habsburg restoration came to be seen by many in the French government—especially Aristide Briand; he did not trust the Czechoslovaks to remain loyal to the Entente should the Soviets win in Poland. Through intermediaries, Charles was informed of this change of heart. At the beginning of September, Charles approached Pope Benedict XV to assist him in regaining his throne for the sake of his peoples, each of whom were threatened religiously and politically in their new states. While he was the natural defender of the Church in his realms, his adherents required outside support and could not be expected to act without it. He concluded his appeal: Far from rushing things in a moment of impatience, I trust in Providence the attentive observer of all events. My intention is to contribute as much as possible to the salvation of my peoples, to bring their destiny in line with my rights that have not been statute-barred.[119]

---

[119] As quoted in Elisabeth Kovács, *Untergang oder Rettung der Donaumonarchie?*, book 1, chapter 24, https://www.elisabethkovacs.com/neue-forschungen-zu-kaiser-karl/band-i/kapitel-xxiv-restaurationsversuche/.

The pope indicated in his reply that he favored such a restoration as the best way to safeguard Catholicism in the lands of the former Monarchy. But there was little he could offer in terms of practical help. All the various sources consulted—the Hungarian and Austrian bishops, Admiral Horthy himself, and various magnates—declared that the time was not yet ripe. But the Soviets were getting fiercer, and various adherents in the different countries—albeit few of the more powerful—assured him of their support. Moreover, despite all of the various Entente diplomats decrying any possibility of a Habsburg restoration, and making various threats should one succeed, hidden behind it all were the French tacit assurances of support.

It was obvious, as 1920 drew to a close, that if anything was to be done by way of a restoration, Charles would have to do it himself. He took the children to Disentis for New Year's. But he contracted a severe cold, and as a result, rather than attending Mass at the abbey as he had planned, Fr. Carnot offered it for him in his hotel room. In light of what 1921 would bring Charles, Zita, their family, and their peoples, it seems oddly prophetic.

Chapter 9

RETURN OF THE KING?

"Then let us seek help from over sea. Is there no Christian prince in Neustria or Ireland or Benwick who would come in and cleanse Britain if he were called?"

"There is no Christian prince left. These other countries are even as Britain, or else sunk deeper still in the disease."

"Then we must go higher. We must go to him whose office it is to put down tyrants and give life to dying kingdoms. We must call on the Emperor."

"There is no Emperor."

"No Emperor . . ." began Merlin, and then his voice died away. He sat still for some minutes wrestling with a world which he had never envisaged.

—C.S. Lewis, *That Hideous Strength*

A number of things were agitating the British and the French. The most obvious of these was what the Soviets—frustrated in Poland—might do next to export their revolution. This concerned Briand, now the French Foreign Minister, tremendously. Although unable to do anything about them, he was aware of Charles's various notes to members of the peace treaty negotiating terms regarding the need for a Danubian Federation under the Habsburgs. This would not only serve as a buffer against the Soviets in his view, but a Habsburg Central Europe allied to France would be a counter to a resurgent Germany, first and foremost. Each of France's allies in central Europe—the so-called Little Entente: Poland, Czechoslovakia, Romania, and Yugoslavia—were unstable, thanks to the nationality problems they had so happily taken on from the Habsburgs. But none of the dominant nationalities in each of those countries could command the loyalty of their minorities in the way the Habsburgs had been able to do. Briand feared that, somehow, a militant Germany might collapse—a fear that would be decisively proven two decades later. Moreover, while Hungary was strategically essential to any defense of central Europe from either Germany or the Soviet Union, nothing could overcome the mutual antipathies between the Magyars and their neighbors save, perhaps, the House of Habsburg.

But Briand also did not trust his southern ally, Italy, whom he feared was trying to patch together a sphere of influence from the defeated countries: Austria, Hungary, and Bulgaria. Here again, a Habsburg Federation allied with France would eliminate any danger from that direction. As Briand well knew, Charles's wartime experiences with varying kinds of German and Italian betrayal had made him immune to blandishments from either of those quarters.

These considerations may be why Briand, in the presence of the devout Catholic and staunch royalist Marshal Lyautey, informed Sixtus that the Italian government was planning to marry the Hungarian Habsburg Archduke Joseph's son to Victor Emmanuel III's eldest daughter, Princess Yolanda of Italy. They wanted to establish an Italian-Hungarian Habsburg dynasty "to annoy the Serbs"[120] (ironically, she would be the only one of the king's four daughters to marry a nonroyal). Briand declared that if Charles returned to Hungary now, Great Britain and France would have a loyal friend in him and a French princess as Hungarian queen. Austria would follow very soon. In Briand's opinion, "It was time for the Emperor to show energy."[121] Of course, the French would protect the renewed Hungarian kingdom against their clients of the Little Entente—if Charles succeeded. If he failed, Briand would deny everything. This conversation took place on February 14. Sixtus telephoned Prangins immediately and informed Charles of Briand's views.

Obviously, the time had come to do something! But who to rely upon? Who indeed but the redoubtable Colonel Strutt? As it happened, Strutt was staying in St. Moritz with his wife at the time. Charles summoned him to the villa, and on February 22, he and Strutt spent two hours in the park of Villa Prangins discussing Briand's invitation to make a royal *faît accompli* in Budapest. The British and French would not make the slightest opposition—the latter, in the person of Briand, being anxious for him to make the attempt.[122]

---

[120] As quoted in Elisabeth Kovács, *Untergang oder Rettung der Donaumonarchie?*, book 1, chapter 24.

[121] As quoted in Elisabeth Kovács, *Untergang oder Rettung der Donaumonarchie?*, book 1, chapter 24.

[122] See Elisabeth Kovács, *Untergang oder Rettung der Donaumonarchie?*, book 1, chapter 24.

Charles was to be in Hungary between March 15 and 30. Charles refuted all of Strutt's objections, urging him to go to Paris to check for himself. On February 23, Strutt met with Sixtus in Paris. Zita's brother-in-law was filled with enthusiasm and explained that Xavier would accompany Charles to Hungary. Strutt's assignment was to attempt to cross the border unchecked and unnoticed at Martinsbrück in the Engadine. Strutt agreed and went to St. Moritz. Although he was able to manage the border crossing unnoticed, once he returned to Charles's company, he consulted various friends in high military and diplomatic circles, all of whom gave him the most negative response to the idea. He passed this on to Charles, who simply thanked him and said he looked forward to seeing him. In the meantime, the imperial family had grown by one more member: Charlotte was born at Prangins on the night of March 1 and 2, being baptized the following day by Bishop Nandor Rott of Veszprém, whom we last saw crowning Zita as Queen at the coronation in Budapest. When Strutt returned to Prangins on March 4, Charles was ready to start the attempt at restoration

What followed was truly worthy of a romance novel.[123] At noon on Maundy Thursday, March 24, Charles set out from Prangins. His aides knew nothing—he had been at Mass that morning. Zita then said that he was not well and was to be left alone. He may have climbed unaccompanied from Prangins by way of Nyon into the French Jura and crossed the border on foot. A car was waiting at Gex, which took

[123] Elisabeth Kovács provides details of this epic narrative in chapter 24 of her first volume, similar to the above.

him to the train station in Strasbourg, where he boarded—in best interwar mystery story fashion—the Orient Express to Vienna. Sleeper room number twelve had been reserved from Paris. Awaiting him on the train were Xavier and his Spanish friend, Count Jaime de Lasuen Reischach. They had with them a Spanish passport in the name of Sanchez and an American Red Cross passport in the name of William Codo. The train arrived on schedule at Vienna Westbahnhof. As planned, Xavier and the Count melted into the crowd while Charles boarded a taxi.

He had the driver bring him to the apartment of Count Tamás Erdödy—whom we last encountered acting as a spy for Charles in Switzerland—at Landskrongasse No. 5. If one goes there today, the lobby is unchanged from that day over a century ago. Erdödy was completely unaware that Charles was coming but was overjoyed. When Charles filled him in on his plans, the count readily agreed to come with him and help accomplish them. As Elisabeth Kovács explains, On Holy Saturday, March 26, at 11:30 a.m., he and Erdödy drove in the car of Archduchess Maria Theresa's former chauffeur by way of Triester Strasse to Wiener Neustadt, and from there to Seebenstein, the Braganzas's castle. Charles's former personal chauffeur, Josef Schlederer, awaited them. The emperor was disguised as an English traveling salesman with make-up on his face. The journey went over the Austrian border near Sinnersdorf (Burgenland was still in Hungary at this point). Crossing the border had been easy, but they had to leave the car and driver behind. They then walked to Pinkafeld for a lunch break.[124] There, Charles was recognized by the owner of the restaurant. Sworn to secrecy though he was, he preserved the silverware and plates the emperor had used. These were on display at the restaurant until looted by Red Army soldiers in 1945.

The two incognito travelers traveled by way of Oberwart to Petersdorf and then to Sankt Mihali, arriving at 10 p.m. in a rubber-wheeled horse-drawn carriage in front of the baroque bishop's palace in Szombathely. In those days, Lent ended after the Holy Saturday service in the morning. Lent was taken very seriously, so Holy Saturday night was often spent "de-Lenting"—enjoying the foods and drinks one had avoided during the penitential season. The bishop, Janos Mikes, was throwing a party for that very purpose when Charles and Erdödy arrived. It so happened that the bishop had a secretary named László Almásy, whose adventurous life would inspire the novel and movie *The English Patient*. The young Almásy answered Erdödy's knock at the palace door and was told to summon the bishop.

In the emperor's own words:

> We arrived at the bishop's palace in Szombathely around 10 o'clock that evening. The bishop was having dinner, to which Minister József Vass was also invited. As soon as Tamás sent his servant to the bishop to ask for lodging for the night for himself and a gentleman, the bishop seemed rather indignant, but like a good host, he just came down to us in the great

[124] Elisabeth Kovács, *Untergang oder Rettung der Donaumonarchie?*, book 1, chapter 24.

> hall of the bishop's palace. He shook hands with both of us, which was followed by a short pause, after which Tamás asked if the bishop recognized who was accompanying him. The bishop said that he did not know this gentleman.
>
> To this, Tamás very solemnly explained that this was indeed His Apostolic Royal Highness, the Hungarian king.
>
> The bishop was startled and took me into a side room where he asked me, "Is that really you?"
>
> I answered yes.
>
> That broke the ice.[125]

Recovering his composure, the prelate led them upstairs, where the guests, including the Legitimist deputy Albin Lingauer (one of the Burgenlander leaders opposing his region's annexation by the Renner regime in Vienna) and the Minister of Culture, Msgr. Joseph Vass, were assembled. Bishop Mikes announced at the top of his lungs, "Ladies and Gentlemen, His Apostolic Majesty, the King!"[126] All of the important individuals in the neighborhood were summoned: Colonel Anton Lehár (younger brother of the famed composer, Franz) came at midnight. Almásy had been sent in the bishop's car to fetch Count Teleki, acting Hungarian Prime Minister, and Count Sigray, Government Commissioner for Western Hungary. He returned, guests in tow,

---

[125] Gordon Brook-Shepherd, *The Last Empress* (London: HarperCollins, 1991),p. 163.

[126] Gordon Brook-Shepherd, *The Last Habsburg* (New York: Weybright and Talley, 1968), p. 264.

around 3:30 a.m. from the Iváncz estate about thirty kilometers away.

That night, the assembled personages discussed Hungary's military situation vis-à-vis the Little Entente, Horthy, and the government. While Charles's return was sudden and unannounced, no one doubted Horthy's loyalty. Lehár later wrote that Charles "was so confident that he would meet no resistance and had relied so much on Horthy's loyalty that he believed his presence alone would solve the problem."[127] Horthy had to be persuaded to surrender power to the king by peaceful means. Count Teleki initially reacted negatively upon his arrival in Szombathely, saying that the king would either have to return to Switzerland at once or continue to Budapest very quickly. Teleki and Vass submitted to the king when he decided to continue on his way to Budapest. The convoy of cars set out on Easter Sunday morning (March 27). Teleki was to drive ahead with Vass and announce the king to Horthy. He started at 6.30 a.m. Charles, chauffeured by Almásy and accompanied by Count Sigray and Colonel Jarmy with a car following him, left at 3:30 a.m. One unforeseen result of this trip was that, confusing him with another branch of the family, Charles continually referred to Almásy as count. The young man would use the title ever after, although he was not entitled to it. After Lehár had all telegraph and telephone lines blocked, Charles arrived in Budapest between 1 p.m. and 2 p.m. Teleki and Vass had two mishaps: they got lost, accidentally or otherwise,

[127] As quoted in Elisabeth Kovács, *Untergang oder Rettung der Donaumonarchie?*, book 1, chapter 24. Some details of this paragraph can also be found here.

and only reached Budapest at 3 p.m. Horthy was caught off guard. When Sigray and Jarmy declared the arrival of the king, the wily admiral reacted negatively, as had Teleki. Horthy cited the Little Entente, declaring that they would mobilize and threaten Hungary when the king returned. The regent led the king into his heated study. The verbal struggle for power lasted two and a half hours.

Horthy refused point blank to make good on the oaths he swore to Charles—both as an admiral and, personally, at Schönbrunn back in 1918, declaring them to have been superseded by his oath to Parliament. Horthy said that the Little Entente would invade and that the Hungarian army could not be relied upon. Charles responded with Briand's guarantees, to which Horthy replied that he did not trust the French. So it went: back and forth. At last, Charles appealed to the shades of his ancestors, who would look down upon Horthy, but the admiral did not care. Having achieved nothing with him, Charles agreed to return to Szombathely. In order to try to win Horthy over, Charles awarded him the Grand Cross of the Maria Theresa Order when he left. Austrian historian Kovács explains that Horthy had asked for it a long time ago, but the chapter of the Order had postponed his request, so Charles, as the sovereign of the Order, now made the award. Horthy, a keen hunter of orders, titles, and decorations, happily accepted, although he did not change his mind.

Charles himself dictated his impressions of Horthy's attitude shortly after his return to Switzerland:

> Before I left the Regent's study, 1 asked whether my companion, Magashdzy, was loyal, as I thought I had heard the reverse. The Regent, however, assured me he was loyal and silent "as we all are."
>
> If Horthy should change again, I reflected that I should be in a better position to compel his surrender with the support of West Hungarian bayonets than with the best will-power and self-control alone and unarmed in the Palace at Buda.
>
> But at the close of our interview, I felt sure that he was reconciled to the idea of a restoration, and I parted with him in the hope that I should realize a complete accord with him. I naturally lost this belief entirely as soon as I learned that he had sent for the Entente ambassadors that same afternoon and broken the promise of silence he had given me.[128]

After a horrible twelve-hour drive (they had two breakdowns and a sandstorm during the night), Charles and his party arrived at the bishop's palace in Szombathely at 5:17 a.m. on Easter Monday (March 28).[129] Horthy had already telegraphed: Lehár was to immediately deport the king across the border, which the colonel was not willing to do. That same day, the representatives of England, France (who were unaware of his chief's actions), and Italy met and formulated a protest against the king's return in accordance with the prohibitions

[128] Herbert Vivian, *The Life of the Emperor Charles of Austria* (London: Grayson and Grayson, 1932), pp. 227–28.

[129] Most material in the following paragraphs are owed to Elisabeth Kovács.

of the ambassadors' conference. Horthy received these representatives and immediately betrayed his king to them, accusing him of fickleness and being untrue to his word—whereas he, Horthy, would abide by Trianon and prevent a restoration.

The French representative, Fouchet, did not report in detail to Briand until April 4. He told Briand that Horthy, in turmoil, had received him on Easter Monday afternoon. The conflict of conscience provoked by the oath he had sworn to the king and that he had sworn to his country was obvious. Well, the king had telegraphed Horthy that morning to submit to him. The regent requested that he should not reply until the afternoon. At three o'clock in the afternoon, he telegraphed that he "was prepared, under certain conditions, to hand over the government to His Majesty, but that he must reserve the right to keep the machinery in hand until then."[130] The king then thanked Horthy for his loyal attitude.

> But patriotism had won the day for Admiral Horthy and I (Fouchet) told him how much I congratulated him on having understood so well the real interests of his country. At first he asked me mainly about the statements he had received from the king. Afterwards Your Excellency personally, favoring the Habsburg Restoration in Budapest, had this told him through a third person whom he refused to name.[131]

Fouchet confirmed to the regent that the French government was strictly adhering to the decisions of the ambassadors'

---

[130] Vivian, *The Life of the Emperor Charles,* p. 230.

[131] As quoted in Elisabeth Kovács, *Untergang oder Rettung der Donaumonarchie?*, book 1, chapter 24.

conference of February 4, 1920. Horthy asked for a definitive explanation, and Fouchet promptly composed a letter that the French government identified itself with the Entente's decision against the Habsburgs taking power in Hungary. This letter, addressed to Teleki, was allegedly brought to the king by Andrássy and Bethlen in Szombathely.

Fouchet had changed Horthy's mind again; at 8 p.m., he no longer wished to hand over power to his king. The following day, Charles telegraphed Horthy to say that he wished to swear him in properly as regent, while he (Charles) would remain in the country to regain power when they both judged the time to be ripe. Horthy refused once more. Charles asked to speak to Fouchet's secretary and to send a message to Briand. Fouchet refused to answer this request. In Berne, Seeholzer reported on a French Council of Ministers meeting in Rambouillet, during which,

> President Millerand, Briand and Barthou took a very decided position in favor of King Charles, who was then staying in Szombathely. It was decided with a majority of the Council of Ministers, pro forma to recall the Entente note regarding the veto against the Habsburgs in Budapest, otherwise not to mobilize a man against Hungary and, if the little Entente should cause bloodshed, to immediately restrain its members in order to prevent this. The minority, led by Loucheur, Maginot and Maraud, opposed this decision in vain.[132]

[132] As quoted in Elisabeth Kovács, *Untergang oder Rettung der Donaumonarchie?*, book 1, chapter 24.

Alas, it was too little, too late. On Wednesday, March 30, Count Alexander Esterházy, Zita's chief steward, notified the Swiss Federal Council of the emperor's return to Hungary. The empress still had no news, and now Esterházy learned from the Swiss authorities that the Hungarian ambassador had already asked for the king's return to Switzerland. The attempt at restoration had failed.The following day, March 31, Horthy's Foreign Minister gave Charles his master's view of the matter. With the exception of the Romanians, the Little Entente were rattling their sabres; the British, French, Italians, and Americans loomed threateningly in the distance. But Charles could not believe that Horthy, ADC at his wedding to Zita in 1911, tearful oath giver in the dark days of 1918, would be untrue to his word. Himself being such a man of honor, it was always difficult for Charles to believe that those who had sworn allegiance to him would betray their trust—and experienced a deep and real heartbreak whenever they did so.

April 1, ironically the day on which Charles would die two years later, saw the Hungarian Parliament repeal the first two laws of 1920. Horthy's government from this time on spoke of "the King's putsch," and his followers in Parliament praised him for saving the country from such a danger. The nation, according to Horthy's propaganda, preferred the regent to the king. Meanwhile, in Szombathely, Charles came down with an illness—perhaps as much from heart as from body. His supporters, led by his Chamberlain, Joseph Count Hunyady, tried to organize some sort of military opposition to the regime in Budapest. But with Charles sick, his supporters divided over strategy as well as tactics, and with Horthy not only in firm control of the governmental machinery but backed by both the Little and Great Entente's threats (Briand, as promised, doing nothing for Charles in defeat), there was little to be done. Horthy's troops quickly cut the city off from the rest of the country.

Count Gratz, Horthy's foreign secretary, was in fact personally devoted to the King and was himself heartsick at the double role events had forced him to play. He convinced Charles that at this moment there was nothing to be done save to return to Switzerland. While neither the Czechoslovaks nor the Yugoslavs had yet to show any sign of carrying out their threats, Gratz assured the King it was only a matter of time.

On April 5, Charles began his departure from Hungary. As with that from Austria in 1919, it was done as a monarchical ceremony, rather than the quick flight "like a thief in the night" that Charles had instructed Strutt to avoid on that occasion. From the bishop's palace, accompanied by Bishop Mikes and Counts Hunyady, Szigray, and Széchenyi, and dressed as a Hungarian Field Marshal, Charles and his court processed to the train station. Once there, they greeted local dignitaries and the whole population of the place, who were wildly cheering, "Long live the King!" and "Farewell!" He mounted the train and reached the Austrian border at 3 p.m. This bit of recognition of the royal status of the man whom they had just robbed of his rights was explained to the National Assembly in Budapest by Count Teleki thus: "We could not allow that man whom the Hungarian nation had crowned with the crown of Saint Stephen to travel without the dignity he deserved."[133]

On April 6, the Assembly met again. Teleki declared that the king, badly informed, had left the country of his own accord under pressure from the conference of ambassadors, which was contrary to the Treaty of Trianon and the statutes of the League of Nations. Dr. Gratz, having resigned as foreign minister, rose to complain about the actions of the Little Entente: "There is no example in history of what the neighboring states did to Hungary on this occasion, namely that foreign governments, under the threat of *casus belli*, compel a state whose independence they themselves had recognized in a treaty. You force the state not only by prescribing its form of government and rulers, but also forbidding a Hungarian to live in his country, which he has the right to do."[134] Horthy, having thanked his troops publicly for their opposition to their king, was faced with the resignations of Teleki and Lehár, who were appalled at the hypocrisy of it all. Neither Cardinal Csernoch, who had crowned him, nor Archdukes Joseph and Albrecht had visited Charles in Szombathely.

There was plenty of talk by Renner's minions in the Viennese Parliament over Charles's transit through the country. Renner's foreign minister, Otto Bauer, who would fully support his chief's embracing of the Nazis in 1938, said, "The journey would actually only be possible if the Kaiser were

[133] As quoted in Elisabeth Kovács, *Untergang oder Rettung der Donaumonarchie?*, book 1, chapter 24.

[134] As quoted in Elisabeth Kovács, *Untergang oder Rettung der Donaumonarchie?*, book 1, chapter 24.

formally arrested at the border and made the journey as a prisoner. He had used false documents and was therefore guilty of misleading the authorities."[135] This was rather rich, coming from a would-be revolutionary for whom lying to the imperial authorities had been a lifestyle choice. For all of that, the journey by train through Austria on April 1 was relatively uneventful; although, at certain stations, mobs of socialists demonstrated and jeered.

At Buchs, Lieutenant-Colonel Kissling, commissioned by the Federal Council to receive the imperial party, inquired whether the kaiser was aware of Switzerland's new conditions. Boroviczény knew nothing, believing that the journey would go back to Prangins. Charles now received his provisional residence permit. He was not allowed to live in the canton of Vaud, in a border area, or in a large city (Zurich, Basel, Bern) and would have to reside in central Switzerland. The Swiss authorities were to be informed forty-eight hours before his possible departure. "Furthermore, the ex-emperor should be expressly informed that Swiss soil is no longer suitable for him for a longer stay and it would be better if he decided to seek asylum elsewhere. The ex-emperor is also to be prevented from receiving representatives of the press on the journey to his new place of residence."[136] What had happened? On April 2, Switzerland informed the Hungarian government of its tightened regulations, which it had concealed from the king. Foreign Ministry Section Chief

---

[135] As quoted in Elisabeth Kovács, *Untergang oder Rettung der Donaumonarchie?*, book 1, chapter 24.

[136] As quoted in Elisabeth Kovács, *Untergang oder Rettung der Donaumonarchie?*, book 1, chapter 24.

Kalman de Kanya, who was responsible for this while Foreign Minister Gratz was with the king in Szombathely, had passed it on incompletely and only spoke of the ban in the canton of Vaud. Under these changed conditions, the king would have stayed in Hungary or, according to Boroviczény, in Liechtenstein. Gratz had resigned from the Horthy regime, among other things, because of this underhandedness. He was replaced by the more integrity-flexible Kanya.

On arrival in Buchs, Emperor Charles made a calm but very tired impression. His face was contorted with pain when the conversation turned to the unsuccessful attempt at restoration. He accepted the new Swiss terms without further ado, bid farewell to the Entente officers, and thanked them. Lieutenant-Colonel Kissling and Captain Trüb received him on behalf of Switzerland, and Zita was waiting on the platform. Together with her lady-in-waiting Agnes Schönborn, she had left Prangins at 3 a.m. with Schonta and Charles's secretary, Karl Baron Werkmann von Hohensalzburg, and drove to meet the emperor in the car. After Charles and Zita were reunited, the train started to move. They reached Lucerne at 11:09 p.m. The imperial couple stayed at the Hotel National. The Schlosshotel Hertenstein on Lake Lucerne had offered itself as a new place to stay. Swiss Colonel Hans Pfyffer von Altishofen took over the discreet private surveillance for the Federal Council. The first visitor to the Hotel National was the Abbot of Dissentis, who was received in audience.

The whole adventure presented the Swiss government with a number of difficulties. The first question to be resolved was whether or not Charles remained King of Hungary. If he did, then he possessed legal immunity, as a foreign head of state. However, if he did not, then he would be subject to Swiss laws, which in turn would put the Swiss under enormous international pressure in dealing with him. But on April 12, a telegram came from Budapest that the government of Hungary still recognized him as their legal king; this was a parting gift from Gratz and Teleki before their resignations.

While that was some relief, the Swiss Federal Council wanted the imperial party to leave on the one hand—but wished to avoid any public distress for them. His minder, Colonel Hans Pfyffer von Altishofen, was instructed to tell him about the government's wishes discreetly and privately. According to the colonel, "The Emperor was so shaken that he wept. When he had calmed down, he told the Colonel that he fully understood the need to make up his own mind. He suggested staying until August. Before the 20th of this month [May] he would ask the Hungarian government to obtain permission from the Federal Council."[137]

Charles (ensconced with the imperial family in Hertenstein) was now faced with a great deal of pressure from several different directions. The Swiss wanted him to leave as soon as possible—but overtures for asylum to Britain, Sweden, Spain, France, and even Liechtenstein all were rejected. Finances were increasingly tight, and Briand—facing a possible change of government—once more urged him to try again in Hungary. Zita was very much in favor of action. Soon after, on July 26, an emissary arrived from

[137] As quoted in Elisabeth Kovács, *Untergang oder Rettung der Donaumonarchie?*, book 1, chapter 24.

Pope Benedict XV, assuring him of his support and bearing King Ferdinand of Romania's promise not to intervene militarily—which meant that there would only be the Czechoslovaks and Yugoslavs to deal with. Charles's chivalrous treatment of the Romanians in 1918 had not been forgotten, apparently. The pope convinced the Swiss authorities to extend their deadline by another three months. Remembering the heartwarming crowds at his departure from Szombathely, Charles resolved that he must return. Boroviczény, having left Horthy's service, was accepted as Chamberlain at the little court in Hertenstein. Throughout the rest of the summer, he helped spearhead preparations for another attempt, making contact with loyal circles in Austria, Hungary, Croatia, and Czechoslovakia. However, Charles's supporters in Hungary were not so sanguine.

At the end of September and beginning of October, various talks took place at Boroviczény's and Rákovsky's in Budapest. Those gathered there came to the decision on October 4 to legally approve the king's *coup d'*état, should it succeed, in accordance with the constitution. After Lehár explained all the plans, Gratz pointed to the likelihood of Yugoslav intervention (the Treaty of Trianon had restored Serb-held Baranya to Hungary). Lehár described the hopeless internal situation. The army, still loyal to the king, was to be reorganized, and the legitimist attitude of officers and men would then disappear. Lehár's distrust of Bethlen and Horthy was well founded. He presented the politicians (Gratz, Beniczky, and Rákovsky) with a decision: "If the Excellencies don't want to do so I will carry out the matter alone."[138] Thereupon, Beniczky called for final action, and Rákovsky followed suit. If the action succeeded, they would be at the disposal of the king. Gratz was silent for a while, then agreed to it. Lehár declared that this time, the king would come by plane, for which he had chosen the two best Hungarian pilots, Alexey and Fekete. On October 8, the courier arrived in Budapest, and Gratz gave him precise instructions.

Zita was pregnant again but insisted on accompanying her husband on the dangerous venture. Moreover, they would bring with them the statue of the Sacred Heart that had accompanied them on all their adventures. Again, one cannot help but be reminded of her ancestress the Duchess of Berry, insisting on leading a rising to her restore her son as King of France in 1832.

This time, there was only one way for the royal couple to return to Hungary—by airplane. Neither of them had flown before, and it must have been particularly frightening for Zita in her condition. But that would not stop them. Of their staff at Hertenstein, very few were informed of what was about to happen. The children and everyone else were told that they planned to celebrate their tenth wedding anniversary at Einseideln, the great Swiss Abbey; this was certainly in keeping with what everyone knew of them. The venerable Swiss monastery with its Marian shrine plays the same role in the life of Swiss Catholicism that Mariazell (where Charles had told Zita after their wedding that they

---

[138] As quoted in Elisabeth Kovács, *Untergang oder Rettung der Donaumonarchie?*, book 1, chapter 24.

must now "help each other to get to Heaven") does in that of central Europe.

Boroviczény was waiting for them at Rapperswill with a newly bought car and drove them to the airfield at Dubendorf, where a rented plane with a crew of one German and two Hungarian pilots awaited them. As Charles and Zita flew through the air, they were rewarded with what—had they known it—would be the last sight of Austria they would have together. Below them, the Alps eventually gave way to the Danube and its plains. They dipped lower over Vienna so that the couple could see Schönbrunn and the Stephansdom. At last, they landed on the western Hungarian plain at Count Joseph Csiraky's estate of Denesfa near Sopron. There was no one waiting for them, because the telegram sent to Colonel Lehár had been delayed. Once safely landed, they made contact with supporters and were taken to the nearby Castle of Sajtoskal, whose owner, Oliver von Rupprecht, gave them a place to rest.

The delay of the telegram had caused several problems. When Lehár had not received timely warning of their coming, he allowed the Ostenburg battalion to be broken up and its men redistributed by Horthy; so too, the trains that had been gathered for their transport to Budapest had to be gathered together again. The original plan to simply set off by rail with the troops would therefore not work. Charles resolved to drive to Sopron and set up his headquarters at the barracks there. Ironically, this was the very city in which the little archduke had first been commended to the prayers of what would become the Gebetsliga by Mother Vincenzia.

A quick surprise advance to Budapest was no longer possible. But worse awaited in Sopron, had Charles and Zita known—the advent into the story of General Paul Hegedus, whose treason would cost them dearly. Nevertheless, their arrival in the city went very well, as reported in the *Sopron Hírlap*. "There was already a large crowd in front of lock-up No. 48, through which it was difficult to get into the barracks. In the courtyard of the barracks, the entire garrison stood in full regalia and greeted the king with the National Anthem. After the National Anthem was sung, the king retired in front of the altar, and then Ostenburg greeted His Majesty in a speech on the occasion of his appearance. The garrison swore allegiance to the king, who during this time stood under the tree line, with a crowd of high-ranking officers behind him."[139] Charles then formed his government in the barracks: Rákovsky would be Prime Minister, with Gratz and Andrássy as Cabinet members. Lehár was named supreme commander. General Hegedus, commander of the city, swore allegiance with the rest of the troops—and, as would be seen, perjured himself in so doing; he immediately telegraphed Horthy's people in Budapest to warn them of the arrival of the king.

Although the element of surprise may have been gone, Charles and Zita's spirits were high as the three train loads of troops set out for Gyor, where Charles's uncle Franz Ferdinand had been so popular when stationed there decades before. As they found when they arrived, that love had not

[139] Pluzsik Tamás, "Our Last King," *Sopron Hírlap*, October 27, 2021, https://www.sopronitema.hu/hirek/panorama/az-utolso-kiralyunk.

been lost for the nephew. At 1 p.m., on October 22, the train arrived at its destination to a tumultuous welcome. Although the commander telegraphed Budapest ahead of their arrival, his troops immediately declared for the king. Horthy's foreign minister, Count Bánffy, reported Charles's arrival to the British High Commissioner and asked him and the other allied representatives to repeat their opposition to any Habsburg restoration.

The regent was in a bad way; he had few soldiers at his command, and at every stop along the way of Charles's railroad advance, news came of garrison after garrison going over to their king. He had the support of the Allies, but that counted for little at the moment. Sure that Charles would win and fearful of being punished for treason, Bánffy sought refuge in the French High Commissioner's house. Charles was expected to arrive by the evening of the twenty-second. Charles had been informed of the protest by the Allies at his return; but secure in Briand's support, he gave it little heed. What was Horthy to do?

Horthy ordered the tracks torn up; but Charles's troops proved adept at repairing them. Despite the delays, at 6 a.m., on October 23, the royal train arrived at Biatorbágy, very near to Budapest. Horthy's military aid, Gyula Gömbös, went to the Technical University of Budapest and told the students that their king was deluded and under the control of a band of renegade Czechs and Slovaks who were coming to pillage the city. Without even uniforms to give the hapless and deluded students, he prepared to send them into battle.

Another imposture was underway. Colonel Lehár shared his royal master's inability to understand the dishonorable.

Because General Hegedus was the higher ranking officer, Lehár insisted that Charles make him supreme commander. Charles did not trust Hegedus and preferred to retain Lehár as head of the little army. But Lehár vociferously assured him of Hegedus's loyalty, and very reluctantly, Charles acceded to the trusting old soldier's wishes. When the royal train arrived at Budaors, on the outskirts of the capital, shots rang out from the neighboring hill of Kelenfold. Hegedus said that he would reconnoiter the military situation. Having received a car for the purpose, he drove to the prime minister's residence in Budapest and met the Allied High Commissioners and Horthy there at 10:45 a.m. He informed them that he had taken no oath to Charles, had not accepted command under him, and that he wanted to avoid civil war.

Lehár, in the meantime, was both anxious for the safety of the royal couple and hesitant to attack—especially in Hegedus's absence; nor did he wish to push on to Budapest with the Kelenfold troops able to fire on the royal train. At last, he felt he could no longer wait, and he ordered an assault. But the delay had been sufficient for troops loyal to Horthy to be brought in from the eastern counties. By 2:00 p.m., these had fully occupied the position—and Hegedus, feigning loyalty, returned to say that the admiral would resist the king to the end. Artillery was brought by the Horthyites, and Charles ordered Lehár to cease fire. Hegedus negotiated a truce, which was supposedly intended to allow the troops on both sides to rest. After surveying the royal positions carefully, he revealed them to Horthy's commander on the spot and then informed Charles that since his two sons were in Horthy's forces, he would have to resign. His treason was complete.

On December 10, 1921, the traitorous general's statement was read out to the National Assembly by the deputy Stefan Somogyi: "I represented my oath of allegiance as still valid so that I might win the King's confidence at all costs, with the object of influencing his decisions in matters vital to the interests of the country, and of continuing to play the double part which I had played against the King in the interests of the country on the occasion of his sojourn at Easter."[140]

The next day, October 24, 1921, when Charles's representatives were supposed to be negotiating with Horthy's men, under the impression that the armistice was to last until 8 a.m., the Horthyites attacked. They captured the Oszterburg troops, who—trusting to Hegedus's honor—were unprepared, and they fired at the first car in the royal train. Charles was standing at the station as all of this occurred. He realized that the game was lost. He and Zita had returned to Hungary to fulfill their coronation oaths, unite their divided peoples (beginning with the Magyars), and protect them against Bolshevism, as well as help the cause of peace in Europe. But as things stood, the king understood that the regent would quite happily engage in a civil war to maintain his rule. Thinking of how all his peoples had been bled white by the World War, and how the Hungarians had then suffered under the Kun dictatorship, he could not bring himself to inflict yet more horror upon them for the sake of his crown. It was a dilemma that would also be faced by

[140] Vivian, *The Life of the Emperor Charles*, p. 259.

Kings Alphonso XIII of Spain, Umberto II of Italy, Michael of Romania, Leopold III of Belgium, and Constantine II of Greece as the twentieth century wore on. They all responded as Charles did; in perfect hindsight, it is possible to question whether the later results were worth their self-sacrifice. Certainly, there have been many bloody pages of history written since then by republican leaders determined to hold on to power at all costs.

In any case, Charles and his troops reentered the train and sped back the way they had come toward Tata, where Count and Countess Esterházy, who had accompanied them on the train, offered the royal couple refuge at their castle. Once they arrived, Charles ordered the troops to disperse, and Lehár and Ostenburg to flee. That night, six would-be assassins attempted to murder Charles and Zita, but were stopped by the Count and his servants. The next day, Horthy's troops arrived at the Esterházy Palace. Charles and Zita were now prisoners of the regent.

Since October 22, there had been a flurry of communications between the various interested parties—the Allies, the Little Entente, and the Swiss—who believed that Charles had lied to them, although he had never acceded to their orders that he cease all political activity. Once again, as he had promised he would do, Briand offered absolutely no support to the defeated monarch, who had undertaken both escapades at his urging. Of course, as that was the agreement, Charles had no recriminations against him. But the Swiss certainly had a great many for Charles. The emperor's mother and the entourage who stayed behind felt it: the Swiss decreed the expulsion of Bishop Dr. Seydl, Colonel

Count Ledochowski, Captain von Schonta, and Captain Baron von Werkmann and his wife under Article 70 of the constitution for "having brought the internal and external security of Switzerland into danger."[141] They were given six days to make arrangements. The Grand Duchy of Luxembourg declared its willingness to receive them, but the French and German Governments objected to their passage and only assented under a strict package of restrictions.

The ladies of the imperial party at Hertenstein were Charles's mother, Archduchess Maria Josefa; his grandmother, Archduchess Maria Theresa; his aunt, Archduchess Maria Annunziata; and the empress's sister, Princess Isabella of Bourbon. After some notes of annoyance, the Archduchess Maria Theresa was allowed to take the seven imperial children back to the Bourbon-Parma Castle Wartegg on the Lake of Constance. The two other Archduchesses also left: one to Germany, the other to Liechtenstein.

Although the Czechoslovaks and Yugoslavs threatened to send troops if Charles was not expelled immediately from Hungary, Romania, true to King Ferdinand's word, declared they would use only diplomacy, not military action. Italy had declared itself in solidarity with the Serbs.

When news came of Charles's capture on October 24, the Allied ambassadors met in Paris to discuss his fate. The Swiss apologized for allowing him to escape. The Czechoslovaks and Yugoslavs demanded that he be banished from Europe. Various places were discussed. It was agreed that Charles would be taken somewhere far out to sea, to be supervised

[141] Vivian, *The Life of the Emperor Charles*, 273.

by a local government—and in a place that would be fairly cheap to maintain him and his family. While he was not permitted to have access to any of his own funds, no one wished to support him financially—not the successor governments who were enjoying the revenue from his properties (a situation that persists to the present as regards his family), nor the Americans, British, French, and Italians, whose victory had put him in this precarious position.

On October 24, Horthy decided to house Charles, Zita, Andrássy, Gratz, Rákovsky, and Boroviczény at the Benedictine Monastery at Tihany, on a peninsula in Lake Balaton. The monks were delighted with their illustrious visitors, whom they greeted warmly. The quartet of advisers debated whether they should advise Charles to abdicate or to wait to be dethroned. Charles and Zita angrily refused the very notion of abdication. They had taken oaths before God at the anointing and coronation that to them were quite as sacred as the ones they took at their wedding, and only the same thing—death—could absolve the couple from them.

The royal party arrived at Tihany on October 26, to find the abbey transformed into a quasi-military installation. To show their submission to the victors, Horthy's government had Allied officers present the following day to assure their presence. Representatives from Horthy's Foreign Office arrived, expecting Charles and Zita to abdicate. They were disappointed by their reception, to say the least.

The Council of Ambassadors in Paris decreed on October 27 that the imperial couple would have to be interned. They would be taken by boat on the Danube to Constantinople, and then aboard HMS *Cardiff* to Madeira, a Portuguese island in the Atlantic (ironically, one of those places Franz Joseph's tragic spouse, Empress Elizabeth, had sought solitude in the palmy days of the nineteenth century). If the Portuguese would take them, they need not worry about expenses, since the Allies would guarantee everything.

Cardinal Csernoch came to Tihany to visit Charles and Zita, after refusing point-blank to try to persuade them to abdicate. He was impressed with the fact that they, despite having aged under the strain, were bearing up. Charles told the cardinal of his determination to defend the Holy Crown and gave him two letters: one was to the National Assembly, protesting his forthcoming deposition, and the other to Horthy's government, attacking his extradition.

On October 31, Albert Apponyi and Count Miklós Széchenyi visited the royal couple. After the touching meeting, Charles and Zita asked the abbot of Tihany to come to their room to thank him for his hospitality. Abbot Ciprián Halbik would write about this encounter to the abbot of Pannonhalma:

> After their arrival, as soon as they had lunch, they invited me to their room, received me very graciously, seated me, and immediately began the discourse. . . . When I offered our willing service to Their Majesties, they only asked for a special small Mass. They kept me with them for about 8–10 minutes.
>
> They attended Mass outside on the Sunday. On the afternoon of their departure on the 31st, they went to confession, and in the evening they performed the Itinerarium [A prayer from the Roman Breviary

> for those who are about to make a journey] with Br. Otmár, and after their dinner, they went to the chapel again, and from there they went to the cars that were already ready. I met them when leaving the chapel, and they said goodbye again with a silent but warm handshake.[142]

It was 7 p.m. when the car with the royal couple, followed by one with the lady-in-waiting, Agnes von Broviczény, the chambermaid, and their majesties' valet, drove in the dark to the railway station. The same Allied officers, Guzzoni, Hinaux, and Selby, who had accompanied the emperor from Hungary to Switzerland six months earlier, were responsible for his and his wife's safe departure from Hungary. The special train departing at around 8 p.m. left Aszófő for Baja on the banks of the Danube to meet the English river ship *Glowworm*. In the presence of Section Chief Kánya and Colonel Tihámer Simenfálvy, they handed over the prisoners to Lieutenant Johnson on November 1 at 7:30 a.m., who had to take them to Constantinople aboard the ship. On board, on behalf of Pope Benedict XV, Apostolic Nuncio Schioppa gave them the papal blessing. Their conversation lasted forty-five minutes, and the nuncio reported to Rome about the magnificent inner attitude of the royal couple. Charles affirmed that he had not abdicated. Immediately before leaving the port, the French colonel inquired about Charles's possible wishes. The emperor thanked him and said that the only thing he had asked of him beforehand was the safety of

[142] As quoted in the article "King Charles IV in Tihany," https://www.tihanyiapatsag.hu/Az_Apatsagrol/IV_Karoly_kiraly_Tihanyban.html.

their followers. Now, as the ship slowly sailed away, the three Entente officers saluted, as did the emperor. The imperial and royal couple began, what was for them, a journey into the unknown.

On November 3, the debate began in the National Assembly on the bill deposing Charles as King submitted by Horthy to that body. For three days, the debate raged. All the while that Horthy's and Charles's supporters argued, they were only too aware that the Czechoslovaks and Yugoslavs were ready to intervene—and behind them the Western Allies. For Charles's proponents, Horthy had essentially given up Hungary's independence; Horthy's allies justified their actions in terms of preserving said independence. Count Apponyi argued that appeal should be made to the League of Nations, which organization's newly minted charter forbade interference in members' internal affairs by other members. It was of course a moot point—Horthy had the power and the backing of Hungary's enemies. On November 6, Charles was deposed as King of Hungary by the National Assembly.

The Papal Nuncio took a very different view of the matter. According to him and his legal adviser in his report to Benedict XV, Horthy and his minions had so mangled Hungarian law and violated their own oaths that none of it was legal. His advice to Benedict XV was simple; in the current situation, so long as Charles refused to abdicate, he remained king.

Cardinal Csernoch, on the other hand, had a much more elastic view of things. On the day Charles was declared deposed, he declared the Church uninterested in daily politics. So long as the Church's rights and privileges were not violated, Horthy would have his full support. The Cardinal of Budapest had taken his historical place alongside his brother cardinals, Piffl, Richelieu, and Wolsey, in putting immediate political goals against both honor and the long-term interests of the Church—two things that can never be separated.

As with Renner, Czernin, and Masaryk, Horthy and his supporters achieved what they wished and got what they wanted in the immediate. Except for Renner, who would make treason a lifestyle choice, they, their people, all of Europe, and indeed, the world would pay a terrible price—one that we, their descendants, are continuing to pay.

Chapter 10

DEATH OF AN EMPEROR

"I go from a corruptible to an incorruptible crown; where no disturbance can be, no disturbance in the world."

—King Charles I, Whitehall, January 30, 1649[143]

"I die innocent of all the crimes laid to my charge;
I pardon those who have occasioned my death;
and I pray to God that the blood you are going
to shed may never be visited on France."

—King Louis XVI, Paris, January 21, 1793[144]

"I am suffering that my peoples may come back together.
. . . I can't go on much longer. . . . Thy will be done.
. . . Yes . . . Yes . . . As you will it . . . Jesus!"

—Emperor Charles I, Madeira, April 1, 1922[145]

Agnes von Boroviczény and the empress's high steward, Count Alexander Esterházy, accompanied them

[143] Liam Sims, "Charles I and the Eikon Basilike," Cambridge University Library Special Editions, January 30, 2014, https://specialcollections-blog.lib.cam.ac.uk/?p=6793.

[144] "The Execution of Louis XVI, 1793," Eye Witness to History, http://www.eyewitnesstohistory.com/louis.htm.

[145] Nathan Cochran, "Blessed Karl of Austria: A Short Biography," Gebetsliga, https://www.gebetsliga.com/english/emperor-karl/biography/.

to Galati. The commander of the Danube Flotilla, Captain Arthur Snagge, arrived on the afternoon of November 1.

Boarding the *Glowworm,* he asked the emperor, on his word of honor, not to attempt to escape. Charles did so.

Down the Danube, the voyage went very slowly; the water level was only two and a half feet in places. As darkness fell, the motor stopped. There was only one warm room on the ship, in which sat their majesties, their escort, and the captain. Vice-Admiral Arthur Snagge discussed with the British ambassador in Bucharest everything he had talked about with the imperial couple. Having neither her own clothes nor shoes, Zita was a bit annoyed about her borrowed castoffs. Charles insisted that he had not abdicated; he would never break his coronation oath. His deposition contradicted the constitution. They spoke of Charles's peace efforts, the Danube Federation, the confiscation of his private property by the Hungarian government, and the failure of his second attempt at restoration. Zita hoped that she would be allowed to take her children out of Switzerland.

Early in the morning on November 3, the *Glowworm* passed Belgrade. But the increasing shallowness of the water forced the ship to halt in Romanian waters—what there were of them anyway. King Ferdinand of Romania offered a rail journey to Galati. As he had shown during both restoration attempts, the king was still grateful for Charles's behavior toward him in 1918. Snagge initially refused because he did not trust the Romanians. The following day, three Romanian officers came aboard to recommend the special train Ferdinand had arranged for them, which was waiting at Orsova. As it turned out, one of the Romanians had been in the Austro-Hungarian army during the war and excitedly blurted out that he had seen Charles when he came to visit the front.

Since it was now apparent even to Snagge that there was no other way to send the imperial couple off, they were awoken early on November 5. Driving to Orsova, they were greeted by cheering crowds, shouting *Eljen*!—"Long live the King!"—the area being inhabited mostly by ethnic Magyars. The train brought them to Galati on Monday the sixth. They sailed from Galati to Sulina on the Romanian luxury liner *Princess Maria*. While having lunch, Charles and Zita noticed that the taste of the dishes was very familiar. The empress observed, "They might have been prepared in our own palace kitchens back in Vienna."[146] It turned out that the chef aboard the ship had indeed worked in the palace and tried to show his loyalty by making something as close to what he had done for them before as possible.

At Sulina, the imperial party boarded HMS *Cardiff*, met her captain, Lionel Maitland-Kirwan, and bid farewell to Snagge. As Maitland-Kirwan was now responsible for the prisoners, he, too, received the imperial word of honor not to attempt to escape. On November 8, the ship entered the Bosphorus, recalling to Zita and Charles their state visit in May of 1918. They lay anchor, and the captain went ashore for instructions. While there, they received a telegram from Colonel Strutt that the children were well and safe; this, the first news they had of them in eighteen days, was an enormous relief. The following

---

[146] Gordon Brook-Shepherd, *The Last Empress* (London: HarperCollins, 1991), p. 204.

day, the *Cardiff* got underway again. The captain informed Charles and Zita that they were bound for Gibraltar. The empress observed that, since they were not stopping at Malta, Madeira was indeed their final destination. Maitland-Kirwan replied that he hoped so, as Ascension was also possible, and it was not an overly pleasant place.

On November 15, they arrived at Gibraltar. The governor, the distinguished General Sir Horace Lockwood Smith-Dorrien, and his wife, Lady Olive, wished to board and pay their respects but were not permitted, nor were the Hunyadis allowed to go ashore and shop for the imperial couple—both of these slights on order from the admiral at Constantinople to whom Maitland-Kirwan was responsible. Two days later, an English priest was allowed aboard, and Charles and Zita were able to attend Mass for the first time in seventeen days. The next day, they set sail, arriving at Funchal on November 19. In the morning, the ship's officers assembled in the wardroom to bid their guests goodbye. They expressed the wish they would soon be returning to bring the imperial couple home. As the ship pulled into Funchal Harbor, Charles pointed out to his wife a church with two flat towers up on the hill above the town, saying it must be a shrine to the Blessed Virgin. "It reminds me of our churches at home. We'll visit it as soon as we can."[147] It was the church of Nossa Senhora do Monte, where he would be entombed six months later.

[147] James Bogle and Joanna Bogle, *A Heart for Europe* (Leominster: Gracewing, 2004), p. 140.

The Mayor of Funchal welcomed Charles and Zita as distinguished guests. Given that the ambassadors' conference had not decided who was financing the stay in Madeira, Charles and Zita would stay at the Villa Victoria, the annex of the Hotel Reid (now a private residence), at their own expense.

On November 25, Papal Secretary of State Cardinal Gasparri asked the Bishop of Funchal to offer the exiled couple pastoral care. Monsignor Antonio Homen de Gueiva was thus appointed as the temporary court chaplain to Charles and Zita. A private oratory was erected in the Villa Victoria, in which there was a tabernacle for the Blessed Sacrament and celebration of Holy Mass when their majesties were unable to come to the cathedral. As it turned out, this spiritual assistance would be fundamental to their survival.

Once they were settled, Zita wrote letters to friends back in Europe, assuring them of the couple's well-being. Typical of these was one such that related, "We are happy in beautiful memories. . . . All our friends were as true as gold. . . . All is well here. We have perfect weather, as warm as spring, so that the windows need never be shut and one can sit out of doors in the shade without wraps. . . . The people are friendly everywhere. . . . I wish you could be as peaceful as we are."[148]

Zita appealed to the conference of Allied ambassadors to be allowed to bring her children from Switzerland to Madeira. But the council was dragging out the decision on

[148] Herbert Vivian, *The Life of the Emperor Charles of Austria* (London: Grayson and Grayson, 1932), pp. 275–76

their financial arrangements and wanted a list of the emperor's assets. The British consul in Madeira came, according to Zita,

> The first time to announce on behalf of the conference of ambassadors, but especially of Great Britain, that, if he [Emperor Charles] abdicates now, all his confiscated goods will be returned and that he will also be provided with material supplies by Great Britain. If he did not abdicate, nothing would ever be refunded, Britain would not allow any appanage, and any donations and money transfers from other quarters would also be prevented. [Emperor Charles] replied to the consul that his crown was not for sale. The second time he came, in the name of the same client, to separate him from us and deport him further, if there was even the slightest suspicion that he was planning a new attempt at restoration (this suspicion could of course have been fabricated at any time), to hold as a threat.[149]

Finally, in mid-December, Zita received permission to bring her children from Switzerland. During her absence, Msgr. Homen tried his best to entertain and distract Charles with a three-day hunting excursion into the mountains alongside the proprietors of the Hotel Reid. Count and Countess Hunyady returned to Hungary at the end of December. But the Portuguese Count Almeida, a longtime veteran of the

[149] As quoted in Elisabeth Kovács, *Untergang oder Rettung der Donaumonarchie?*, book 1, chapter 25. https://www.elisabethkovacs.com/neue-forschungen-zu-kaiser-karl/band-i/kapitel-xxv-madeira/.

Viennese court, joined the entourage, alongside three other servants, including Maria Schmidt, a kitchen maid who brought the emperor's personal belongings with her from Switzerland.

"The New Year's Eve prayer was offered as at home, and a huge fireworks display at midnight closed the old year. On New Year's Day, the bishop paid his respects to the emperor, who returned two days later together with Almeida and Msgr. Homen. From December 30 to February 1, 1922, the emperor kept a diary to tell his wife Zita about his life during her absence in Switzerland. Archduke Robert had to have his appendix removed, and Empress Zita wanted to be in Zurich for the operation."[150] The Portuguese provided her with a passport. But she had to pass through France, and the Little Entente protested. At first, the French denied her the right of passage, but then some smart person recalled that it was only the emperor who was in detention. But the Horthy regime protested. In response, the Allies' ambassadors demanded that Switzerland accept responsibility if Zita suddenly decided to descend upon Hungary in a third coup attempt with little Otto, which is certainly a testament to their fearful respect for the empress-queen's abilities, if not to their own intelligence or compassion. The Swiss utterly refused to do so. But they finally agreed to admit her to the country under the following conditions: there was to be no male escort; the empress was to stay at the Zurich hospital; receive no visitors or relations; be kept under police

[150] Elisabeth Kovács, *Untergang oder Rettung der Donaumonarchie?*, book 1, chapter 25.

observation during her visit; and she was to depart as soon as her son was out of danger. On January 4, 1922, she traveled by way of Spain and Paris to Switzerland, where she was welcomed by the former legation counselor in Vienna, the envoy Dr. Karl Egger, who accompanied her and supervised her travel.

Meanwhile, Charles prepared a memorandum for an interview between Count Almeida and the British journalist Lethbridge. Therein he very interestingly and clearly presented the problems of the dissolution of Austria-Hungary caused by the peace treaties. The second paper from this period is the so-called "Draft Constitution, Top Secret!," which was a detailed sketch of a future Danube Federation. This would comprise four national states and four national armies, two free states, Vienna and Trieste, which would be a constitutional monarchy held together by the dynasty in the primogeniture of succession. Charles had in mind a complete revision of the political changes in Central Europe: the renewal of the Holy Roman Empire under Habsburg leadership, with the recreation of the small German kingdoms and duchies, the elimination of Prussia from Germany, and a permanent alliance of Austria with France. This plan had no chance when it was written, but even now suggested a possible way forward out of central Europe's dilemma.

"Even before the empress left, the Portuguese banker Luis Rocha Machado made his summer house on the Monte above Funchal available to the imperial couple free of charge as their domicile."[151] In the meantime, the appendix oper-

---

[151] Elisabeth Kovács, *Untergang oder Rettung der Donaumonarchie?*, book

ation in Zurich on January 14 had gone well, and young Robert was on the road to recovery. Two days later, the Little Entente began shrieking alarming rumors: Zita was already in Vienna with Otto! Despite being utterly false, the Czechs and Yugoslavs lodged complaints. The Allied ambassadors sent notes to both Charles and Zita in their respective places, threatening both of them with even remoter exile if another attempt was made upon Hungary. Dr. Egger seemed ashamed when he brought this threat to Zita at her son's bedside. Historian Elisabeth Kovács explains, Empress Zita was not allowed to go to Wartegg, and she was also informed of the threats from the ambassadors' conference in the event of a third attempt at restoration. The empress left the hospital only once to have a gynecological examination. When she met her attorney, Dr. Seeholzer, she learned that the asset manager Bruno Steiner de Valmont, with whom Charles had entrusted the family jewels while he was still in Switzerland, had disappeared with all his valuables and remaining finances and could not be found. He was expelled from the country with the other courtiers but was able to postpone his departure from Switzerland for a short time and then went to Rome. From there, his trail vanished. The imperial family had no funds, and their supporters were forbidden to send them anything.[152]

Despite her worries about Robert, once it was obvious that he was on the mend, Zita decided to cut her visit short so as to put an end to both the Allies and the Little

---

1, chapter 25

[152] Elisabeth Kovács, *Untergang oder Rettung der Donaumonarchie?*, book 1, chapter 25.

Entente's ceaseless nattering. Being emotionally and physically drained—long nights by Robert's bedside were not improved by the financial news—she asked permission to rest in Paris overnight. Not only was this refused by the French authorities, but it was ordered that she must proceed on to Geneva and Bordeaux. This, "owing to bad connections, meant thirty-six hours more *en route*, no sleeping-cars, frequent changes, and long waits at stations during the nights, not to mention extortionate Swiss charges between Zurich and Bellegarde. French officials were civil, but the Swiss were not."[153] When she arrived at the Spanish border, however, she was received by the king and queen with an honor guard and given two days to rest. In Lisbon, she was joined by her six children, their nanny, Countess Therese Schmiesing Kerssenbrok, and Countess Viktoria Mensdorff. Arriving on February 2, they found that Countess Almeida had joined her husband a week earlier. The children's teachers, Joseph Dietrich from Tyrol and the young Hungarian court chaplain Paul Zsamboki, came in mid-February, and Archduke Robert, who had recovered, with Archduchess Maria Theresa at the beginning of March.

From February 18 to the end of the month, the imperial family, suites, and staff moved to the Villa do Monte. It rained frequently, wetness penetrated through the windows, and water ran off the walls, although they tried to banish the moisture with burning lamps. Even today, at that time of year, the traveler is amazed at how abruptly the microclimate switches from the warmth of Funchal to the dripping

[153] Vivian, *The Life of the Emperor Charles*, pp. 277–78.

moisture of the Monte—a walk that may be made in the space of an hour. But there was no rent, as the owner was a great fan of the imperial family.

The house turned out to be too small, and its denizens lived in very cramped conditions, inadequately equipped. The staff had to sleep on the floor in a shed that served as a storage room. The chapel had also been set up here. The emperor, who was very concerned about peace in his surroundings, compensated for all adversity, humiliation and banishment, injustice, and lack of money with his exemplary piety. He submitted to the will of God (often saying—and telling himself—not to grumble!), remained consistently calm and kind, and filled the house with a beautiful atmosphere.

> But while Charles would not grumble, the conditions they all were living in were reported by one of the ladies-in-waiting to a friend: We have no electric light, only one lavatory for the whole house, water only on the first floor and in the kitchen. There is very little space, though servants are reduced to an absolute minimum. Our only fuel is green wood, which smokes all the time, and we have to wash in cold water. The house is so damp that it all smells of mildew and the mist penetrates everywhere. The only means of communication are ox-carts and cars, which we cannot afford, or else a mountain-railway, but that does not run every day. To go to Funchal on foot would mean all day there and back. We never have enough to eat here, and the poor Emperor has only vegetables and

> pudding for dinner. The children's teacher, a doctor, lives in a tumbledown hut in the garden. The two servants and their wives live in another rickety cottage with only one room, which is divided by a partition. . . . His Majesty has had a cold and cough for weeks. Archduke Karl Ludwig is also in bed with a cold. There are plenty of cows here, but they are all tuberculous, and the milk must be boiled.[154]

Charles remained present to his children, as much as he was able. Otto and Adelheid would recall him answering their questions and trying to explain what being members of a family like theirs and being—for young Otto's sake—a ruler under God was all about. According to Kovács,

> In the last two weeks, when he was still healthy, he took the four older children for a lot of walks, kept them busy, and studied with them. . . . The flu was rampant in Madeira, and little Archduke Karl Ludwig, born in 1918, was already infected. On March 9, Charles caught a cold without paying much attention to it. On March 14, he was absent from the Mass in the chapel and was bedridden ever after. The flu, with a high fever, developed into severe pneumonia. Three doctors from Funchal, who then rented accommodation on the Monte to be available to the patient at night, were unable to defeat the illness. They administered camphor and turpentine injections that caused abscesses on the legs, applied cupping glasses, and

[154] Vivian, *The Life of the Emperor Charles,* pp. 278–79.

> placed mustard leaves on the patient's back, which had been punctured by the hypodermic needles and which burned his skin; otherwise, they gave him oxygen in the small amounts available. Charles suffered with the utmost patience, Zita nursed him day and night, and the case histories and accounts of the last two weeks of his life are heartbreaking.[155]

Oxygen would have helped Charles, but there were only one or two cylinders on Madeira—too heavy to be dragged up the Monte—so the gas had to be conveyed in small toy balloons, resulting in very little to none being left on arrival—hence the small amounts just mentioned. Because of Karl Ludwig's illness, Zita slept on the floor between his room and his father's. Having heard of a local Poor Clare nun with a reputation for holiness (and now herself a servant of God), Mother Virginia Brites of the Passion (1860–1929), Zita asked for her prayers for the healing of her husband. The nun replied that Jesus's will was that he should die in exile in Madeira but as a natural death and not the result of an attack planned by certain Germans and Austrians.

Charles's last correspondence, from late February to early March, concerned instructions for the Viennese wealth manager Albin Schager at Eckartsau to provide the ambassadors' conference with documents for the financial support of the family because none of the successor states were willing to pay for them. There was one last letter to King Alphonso XIII, concerning the treasure of the Order of the Golden

---

[155] Elisabeth Kovács, *Untergang oder Rettung der Donaumonarchie?*, book 1, chapter 25.

Fleece. In this last, he was successful. The Order, founded by Duke Philip of Burgundy in 1429, had been headed by the Spanish Habsburgs. With the end of the War of Spanish Succession, it was divided into two branches: Spanish and Austrian, of which Alphonso XIII and Charles were respective heads. After the end of World War I, King Albert I of Belgium demanded that the dignity of grand master and the treasure of the Order be transferred to him as sovereign of the lands of Burgundy. This claim came to be seriously considered during the negotiations of the Treaty of Versailles, but it was ultimately rejected due to the intervention of Alphonso XIII, who took possession of the Order's properties on behalf of the exiled Charles.

On the evening of March 27, Fr. Zsamboki proposed giving last rites to the emperor. It was around 9:30 p.m. when he entered Charles's sick room. He described what happened then as follows: "He did everything with the greatest calm and presence of mind and after confession he shook my hand warmly, as if to thank me. He also expressly assured me that he would forgive all those who worked against him and would pray and suffer for them. Then the Empress had to read him the prayers of the Extreme Unction, to which he made the responses."[156] Finally, he ordered,

> "Get Otto, he should see how an emperor dies as a Catholic." The little one was fetched, he knelt down next to the bed, that was too far for the emperor. He said Otto should come up here, that is, come to his

[156] As quoted in Elisabeth Kovács, *Untergang oder Rettung der Donaumonarchie?*, book 1, chapter 25.

> head so that he can see everything clearly. The little one was of course shaken and shook himself from pain and from crying. Then his mother told him to hold on so he wouldn't worry his father any more. Then he pulled himself together. The sick man received the anointing with great devotion, offered his hands for the anointing himself and prayed the prayers of the priest. For him the outside world seemed to have disappeared. After the holy oil I bestowed on him the blessing of the Holy Father, whose faithful son he had always been.[157]

By midnight, Charles's fever had dropped from 104 to 98.6 degrees, and it was hoped, on the morning of April 1, that the crisis was over. But Charles's condition worsened, and the fever rose again to 104 degrees. Daily Mass was offered, there was Adoration, and Charles received Viaticum. As his pains increased, he said several times, "I am suffering that my peoples may come back together." At one point, Charles turned to Zita, and asked, "Oh, why do they not let us go home? I want so much to go home with you." He then forgave his enemies and suddenly turned to Zita and told his wife to contact the King of Spain for help when he was gone. "He is chivalrous . . . he has promised me." Charles then listed each of his children and then pointed to Zita's stomach and the as-yet-unborn Elizabeth, saying, "Protect their bodies and their souls." His agony in the arms of the empress and the agonizing suffocation lasted three hours. At

---

[157] As quoted in Elisabeth Kovács, *Untergang oder Rettung der Donaumonarchie?*, book 1, chapter 25.

noon, the crown prince was summoned. He said to Zita, "I love you so much! In the heart of Jesus, we will meet again!" and then uttered his last words on this earth, "I can't go on much longer. . . . Thy will be done. . . . Yes . . . Yes . . . As you will it . . . Jesus!" Again, in Fr. Zsamboki's words, "I began the prayers for the dead. At the moment of death, April 1, 1922, at 12:23 p.m., the sun broke through fully. I prayed in the deep silence of the death room, and then an Our Father, which the others gradually joined in." Zita blurted out, "Charles, what am I going to do on my own?" But she then pulled herself together and said, "Lord, Thy will be done."[158]

Elisabeth Kovács describes part of the funeral thusly:

> The face of the dead emperor grew younger and younger in the coffin, and the news of the death of the "holy emperor" spread like wildfire in Funchal. On the evening of April 1, the embalming took place, followed by the exposure of the dead in uniform. A neighbor described what happened next: "At the coffin we men from the area took turns as a guard of honour. There were streams of people passing the coffin. People touched the corpse with their rosaries, with little pictures. Many kissed the corpse. A large crowd also attended the funeral of the [emperor]. It must have been several thousand." The funeral took place

[158] As quoted in Nathan Cochran, "Blessed Karl of Austria: A Short Biography," Gebetsliga, https://www.gebetsliga.com/english/emperor-karl/biography/; Brook-Shepherd, *The Last Habsburg*, pp. 238–240; Elisabeth Kovács, *Untergang oder Rettung der Donaumonarchie?* , book 1, chapter 25;

> on April 4, in imperial form, in the presence of the Bishop of Funchal. The body was then buried in the side chapel of the Nossa Senhora church do Monte.[159]

An Austrian woman living in Funchal described Zita at the funeral: "This woman really is to be admired. She did not for one second lose her composure, nor did the children. I saw no tears from any of them. They only looked very pale and sad. When she came out of the Church, she greeted the people on all sides and then spoke to those who had helped with the funeral. They were all under her charm. . . . But what will now become of this poor family?"[160]

Mother Virginia claimed to Zita that the emperor had appeared to her near the altar during Charles's requiem at the church of Monte. He wanted her to send a message to his widow on his behalf: he begged Zita not to remarry so as to take better care of the children (a point of which she was already convinced). Apparitions aside, it is easy to suppose that Zita decided early on never to remarry. Because her forebear, the Duchess of Berry, had pursued her own happiness and done so, she became absolutely useless to the cause of restoring her son, Henry V, the Count de Chambord, to the throne of France. There can be little doubt that with the death of Charles, next to the salvation of her immortal soul and his, restoring her son Otto to the throne of his fathers became her paramount interest in life—supreme over every lesser consideration. Alone and pregnant, she

---

[159] As quoted in Elisabeth Kovács, *Untergang oder Rettung der Donaumonarchie?*, book 1, chapter 25.
[160] Vivian, *The Life of the Emperor Charles*, p. 283.

had nevertheless to prepare to mold her son into a worthy emperor-king and his siblings into trustworthy assistants to their brother in that holy cause. Zita's devotion to God, His Mother, and the saints was all piece-of-a-piece with her devotion to the divinely appointed mission of her son and his House. Whether the sweet and laughing bride of 1911 could have done this is another question. But the decade since that happy day of her wedding had certainly strengthened her; it would also make her harder than the most difficult of circumstances. Shortly after the emperor's death, Zita and her entourage enrolled in the fraternity of the Immaculate Heart of Mary in the São Pedro church in Funchal. This is why the emperor's coffin was placed precisely in the side chapel dedicated to the Immaculate Heart in the church of Nossa Senhora do Monte. The empress had worn black beginning about four days before her husband's death. She would never wear any other color again.

On the same April 4, the requiem for the deceased king took place in the Matthias Church—his coronation church—in Budapest. According to Apostolic Nuncio Schioppa, the mourning ceremony was "imposing, solemn and sad as never before. Everyone understood the tragic fate of the unfortunate ruler." Carlists and Charles's opponents stood around the imposing catafalque, "on which lay the four royal crowns: those of the emperor, the king of Hungary, the king of Bohemia and that of the house of Habsburg. There were also two white flower crowns, one from Governor Horthy and one from the government."[161]

[161] As quoted in Elisabeth Kovács, *Untergang oder Rettung der Donaumonarchie?*, book 1, chapter 25.

> What a picture, this crowd! On the throne the regent, representative of a king who does not exist under the law! Around the bier, officers and soldiers in 'stand by,' officers and soldiers of the same army that had fired cannons at their king four months ago; a dense group of legitimists, among them Andrássy, Rákovsky, Gratz, arrested yesterday on charges of high treason and perhaps sentenced to imprisonment tomorrow for taking part in the king's (restoration) attempt. On the left Bethlen, Bánffy, and the entire government, which had the dethronement law of the Habsburgs approved in November, and at the end one of the dethroned Habsburgs, Archduke Joseph, in a large marshal's uniform, on his own tribune.
>
> The primate, who had secretly legitimized Horthy on the day of the king's dethronement, now praised the steadfastness and trust in God of the pious king, the exemplary one who had faithfully endured all the blows of fate. He lived briefly, but a long time fulfills. Though he was crushed by the bitterness of human life, he died peacefully, leaving us wishing to have him, and even time cannot quench that wish. *Vale pia anima Martyr Regni et Coronae Sancti Stephani, vive aeternum in pace Christi.*[162]

Kovács relays, "On the same day in Prague, the emperor's former Adjutant General, Prince Zdenko Lobkowitz, had a silent Holy Mass offered at St. Kajetan's. The prince

[162] As quoted in Elisabeth Kovács, *Untergang oder Rettung der Donaumonarchie?*, book 1, chapter 25.

commented, 'It was quite well attended. That's all that could have happened for the late King of Bohemia!'"[163] It was a fitting place: just as Franz Ferdinand had bought the Basilica in Hall, secularized by Joseph II, this formerly Theatine church had undergone the same treatment. In 1869, Empress Maria Anna bought the church back for the Redemptorist Order—the same Order that, under St. Clement Maria Hofbauer, had done so much to reevangelize Vienna in the early nineteenth century.

On April 6, Cardinal Piffl celebrated the funeral service as a private service in Vienna's St. Stephen's Cathedral to the accompaniment of Mozart's Requiem. Among the mourners were Chancellor Johannes Schober (who had replaced Renner), four cabinet ministers, the President of the National Council Richard Weisskirchner, and a group of Christian Social National and Federal Councilors. Catholic journalist Friedrich Funder, who witnessed the event, described it thus:

> From the midst of the crowd surrounding the cathedral, after the end of the service, the *Gott Erhalte* [the Imperial Anthem] was intoned, the old, solemn tune that had been the expression of Austrian love of fatherland and loyalty for generations. Now it flared up once more, a blaze of enthusiasm, from the heart of the imperial city. I witnessed the scene that brought the traffic in the city center to a sudden standstill. Many people cried. Voices from the windows of the tall houses mingled with the singing, it was a waving

---

[163] As quoted in Elisabeth Kovács, *Untergang oder Rettung der Donaumonarchie?*, book 1, chapter 25.

> and greeting like a loving farewell. Vienna's face had unveiled itself once more. There was no mourning session in the National Council.[164]

On April 8 at 10 a.m. in the Deutschordenskirche in Vienna, the Knights of the Order of the Golden Fleece held a requiem for its deceased Grand Master. There was no question of bringing Charles home to any of his lands. There in Madeira, his body awaits the Resurrection and Last Judgement.

---

[164] As quoted in Elisabeth Kovács, *Untergang oder Rettung der Donaumonarchie?*, book 1, chapter 25.

Chapter 11

AN EMPRESS ALONE

"The offer was such as should come from a man of Rudolf's name, yet I trust that the Queen needs no further service than such as it is our humble duty and dear delight to render her. It is our part to strive to lighten the burden that she bears, and by our love to assuage her undying grief. For she reigns now in Ruritania alone, the last of all the Elphbergs; and her only joy is to talk of Mr. Rassendyll with those few who knew him, her only hope that she may some day be with him again."

—Anthony Hope, *Rupert of Hentzau*[165]

Pregnant, with seven young children, no money to speak of, and nothing but a burning faith and a sense of duty to sustain her, Zita faced the future. As Charles had asked her to, Zita contacted King Alphonso XIII of Spain. He sent a telegram to the newly elected Pius XI, which read,

> "In the conviction that His Holiness the Pope, as doyen of the Sovereigns, is sincerely affected by the circumstances of the ex-Emperor Charles, I beg Your Holiness to add your venerated plea to mine to the

[165] Anthony Hope, *Rupert of Hentzau* (New York: Henry Holt, 1898), p. 383.

> end that his widow and children may be provided with the necessary means of livelihood, especially in view of the Empress' present condition, for which the most elementary principles of humanity demand respect and protection. I am convinced that the Sovereigns and Heads of State of the nations which were victorious over the former Austro-Hungarian Empire will join us with their proverbial generosity."[166]

Pious as this conviction was, it was unmatched by reality. The British government was singularly unconcerned. When Col. Francis Bingham Mildmay (who would be created 1st Baron Mildmay of Flete and leave the House of Commons later in the year) demanded in a letter to know what the government was doing about the situation, he received an amazingly supercilious response from Cecil Harmsworth, the Under-Secretary of State for Foreign Affairs. The Canadian future press-lord declared that Madeira was a perfectly comfortable place, and if the family were out of money, it served them right for spending it on the two attempts to retake the throne. Nevertheless, he had claimed to have no doubt that the problem would be resolved soon.

Fortunately, in 1918, George V took a direct interest. On April 20, his equerry, Lord Stamfordham, sent Sir William Tyrrell at the Foreign Office a message containing one sentence: "The King asks whether any progress has been made in Paris about the arrangements for the ex-Empress Zita."[167]

---

[166] James Bogle and Joanna Bogle, *A Heart for Europe* (Leominster: Gracewing, 2004), p. 147.
[167] Bogle, *A Heart for Europe,* p. 149.

Tyrrell's response was that nothing could be done unless Zita promised there would be no further efforts at restoration. He quotes Masaryk as saying that Czechoslovakia would invade if the Habsburgs were restored. Of course, Harmsworth left out the fact that they had no means of doing so.

Despite Zita's refusal to make any such promises, opinion in her favor grew, and at last, the French and Italian Ambassadors gave up any objection to her going to Spain with the children. A Spanish warship picked them up and brought them back to Cadiz, whence they went by train to Madrid and met with the king, who told Zita a strange story,

> King Alfonso related to her, in the night before the death of the Emperor Charles, he was over come with a feeling that, in the event of the Emperor's death, if he, the King, would not take his widow and the children under his protection, his own wife, and his own children would suffer one day the same fate. He only found peace, after he had firmly resolved to give the bereaved family a home in Spain, as the death of the Emperor seemed to be certain. King Alfonso was not less overcome than the Empress Zita, when she then told him what the Emperor Charles had said before his death.[168]

Initially, the family was housed at the Palace of El Pardo, outside Madrid. There, Elizabeth was born on May 31, 1922. But as Zita would later tell Baron von Werkmann,

[168] Bogle, pp. 150–51.

> I have a great political problem to fulfill, and perhaps it is none other than this. I have to educate my children in the spirit inherited from the Emperor. In Otto, our firstborn, all the good qualities of spirit, character and heart must be developed. Nobody knows the future. The present can lead us to pessimism. But the history of peoples and dynasties, which is not measured by the module of human lives, but by other longer periods, allows us to trust.[169]

To be sure, Zita treasured such mementos of her husband as she had, including his heart. It may sound odd to us, but the Habsburgs had a long tradition of separating the heart from the body after death; the latter would rest in the Kaisergruft under the Capuchin church in Vienna, while the former would be entombed in the Herzgruft of the Augustinerkirche, the imperial parish church by the Hofburg. Charles was interred at Madeira, and there was no telling where Zita might be buried. Therefore, she kept his heart with her against a future time when the two hearts might be buried together. Annually, Zita observed both their wedding anniversary on October 21 and Charles's name day on November 4—the feast of St. Charles Borromeo.

After Elizabeth's birth, the family moved to the north of Spain. Although El Pardo was quite literally a palace, Zita wanted to be well away from the capital with its heat and political intrigue; moreover, she had her own plans for the education of her children. The former Austrian consul in

---

[169] Website of the Association for the Beatification of the Empress Zita (Archive).

Bilbao suggested the Uribarren Palace in Lekeitio on the Bay of Biscay—destroyed during the Spanish Civil War, the Silken Palacio Uribarren Hotel, which is currently on the site, uses the presence of Zita and the children in its advertising. Its owner had emptied it of all its furniture but was prevailed upon to rent the building. From the time they arrived on August 18, the townspeople quite literally took the imperial exiles among them to their hearts.

As the empress recalled in an interview with a local journalist decades later:

> We were exiled on the island of Madeira and my husband Charles had just died. Everything was quite dark then, but we found help in His Majesty Alfonso XIII, who sent us a frigate to be transferred to Spain. First of all, we spent two months residing in the Palacio del Pardo, where we never lacked the attention of Queen María Cristina and her son, who visited us regularly. Then we found out about the interest of Adolfo de Urquijo and Ibarra—How can we forget Urquijo Ibarra! Urquijo Ibarra!—for finding us a fixed residence in the Basque Country. We had never heard of Lekeitio and yet, years later, my children and I have evoked that day when we set foot in that beautiful town. Until that moment, the children and I had been wandering from one place to another. There we began to feel like a normal family.[170]

[170] Koldo, "Interview of Antxon Urrosolo," Wayback Machine (Archive), https://web.archive.org/web/20210618185320/https://www.lekitxo.info/index.php/es/historia/acontecimientos/la-emperatriz-zita-en-lekeitio/item/852-entrevista-de-antxon-urrosolo.

On their return to the town on June 6, 1923, all four thousand inhabitants turned out to greet them, lining the streets, waving flags, and shooting off fireworks to welcome them "home."

There, for the next six years, Zita devoted herself to raising and educating her children. As they grew, she would have them regularly photographed all in a row with Otto (the tallest) at one end and Elizabeth (the smallest) at the other. Money was tight, but they managed mainly from the income of two private properties in Hungary, 10 percent of the annual profits from the Metternich vineyards in Johannisberg, and voluntary contributions from relatives, family friends, and citizens of the former Habsburg domains. Other exiled members of the dynasty, however, claimed much of this money, and there were regular requests for help from imperial officials. Untroubled by the financial woes their mother had to contend with, the children played games, took hikes around Vizcaya, and focused on the rather strict education Zita had designed for them. Regarding the heir to the throne, Hungarian tutor Fr. Job Banhegy observed,

> Otto is nearing thirteen, though he appears to be fifteen or sixteen. As to looks, Fate has been kind to him; he is tall and well proportioned, with very dark eyes and curly brown hair that falls over a high forehead. His expression is frank and as wholesome as the color of his cheeks. I find him good-hearted and able to control himself under any circumstances. As a student he shows rare intelligence and judgment, conversing fluently in several languages and taking the keenest

> interest in literature, geography, and history. He likewise shows aptitude for scientific subjects as well as athletics. As to sports, he excels in tennis.[171]

His education, and that of his brothers and sisters, was very carefully planned. Zita fully intended that he would ascend the thrones of his fathers—and be as perfectly prepared for that moment as he could be. She consulted Baron Max Hussarek von Heinlein—who, in addition to being the one-time Austrian Minister of Culture—had been her husband's penultimate chancellor—and Baron Janos Zichy—who had been the education and religion minister in Hungary from 1910 until 1913. Otto was taught Magyar by several Benedictines from the great Abbey of Pannonhalma in Hungary. Professor Niederacher taught German, Greek, and geography; Miss Street taught English; and Miss Sepibus taught French. Count Heinrich von Degenfeld-Schonburg (1890–1978) oversaw the entire program under the empress and would be Otto's lifelong confidante and advisor. Otto recalled the regiment they established for him:

> I started at six in the morning. From six to eight I did my homework. Then, after half an hour's pause, came the sessions with tutors, which lasted till midday. After lunch came more lessons until five o'clock and then, until seven, I went on working by myself. My

171 Bertita Harding, *Imperial Twilight* (Garden City: Bobbs-Merrill, 1939), p. 297.

> sister Adelheid studied with me from the beginning; the others joined in later one by one.[172]

While looking after her children during the Spanish years, she did not neglect her own spiritual life; she would attend Mass twice a day at the Basilica of the Assumption in the town, where she had a particular veneration of the image of Our Lady of Antigua. As you may recall, she had been close to the Benedictines as a girl. She renewed these ties on May 24, 1926, when she traveled from their Spanish home to France to become a Benedictine Oblate at St. Cécile (the women's monastery where her grandmother had been abbess during her widowhood), although, her status as an oblate was linked not to Saint Cécile, but to the St. Pierre monastery at Solesmes. This ceremony took place in the presence of Dom Germain Cozien, Abbot of St. Pierre and successor of Dom Prosper Gueranger. Many members of her own family were also oblates there: her mother, Duchess Maria-Antonia of Parma; Isabella, her sister, with whom she lived for so long; and her brother Xavier, who was buried there in the monks' cemetery in 1977. Even her lady-in-waiting, Countess Kersenbrock, was an oblate at the same abbey. She was followed by her daughter, Adelheid (oblation on May 18, 1931), while Rudolph and Charlotte made their own Benedictine oblations in 1950 at the monastery of Regina Laudis in Bethlehem, Connecticut.

But Zita was also very much an empress and queen-regent, even if the realms were phantom ones, existing only

---

[172] Gordon Brook-Shepherd, *The Last Empress* (London: HarperCollins, 1991), p. 221.

in the hearts of the faithful. The monarchists were very active in both Austria, Hungary, and elsewhere in the old empire and continued to labor not simply to the keep the old memory alive but to regain the future from the Renners and the Horthys, who had so damaged the present. Zita had agents in each of her son's countries and kept in close touch with them; a steady stream of adherents also found its way to Lekeitio. However, as the 1920s progressed, the sense of urgency in monarchist circles subsided.

Another issue that plagued Zita during the Spanish years was the question of Count Czernin and his Order of the Golden Fleece. He had played a difficult part as foreign minister to Charles and attempted—even threatening suicide—to force Charles to take Czernin's blame for his part in the Sixtus affair. Shortly before leaving the Foreign Ministry, Czernin had accused Charles of lying, and Charles had given him the Order of the Golden Fleece. As earlier noted, Alphonso XIII, head of the Spanish branch of the Order, had secured the Austrian branch's treasury when the Belgians tried to claim it. To this very day, the head of the House of Habsburg—as of the writing, Archduke Karl, Charles and Zita's grandson—is the head of the Austrian branch. When Charles was dying, he told his wife that Czernin must be stripped of his membership in the Order. As regent for Otto, Zita was effectively head of the Order, but the administrator was Charles's brother, Archduke Max, who was inclined, as his nephew Otto would later recall, "to dither"[173] over the matter. But matters came to a head when the Chancellor

[173] Brook-Shepherd, *The Last Empress*, p. 227.

of the Order, Count Polzer-Holditz, resigned over Czernin's remaining a member. Czernin refused, however, to do so; this was a standoff that remained until Czernin died in 1932.

Meanwhile, Spain's political difficulties were growing. Alphonso XIII, although a great friend and protector to the family—as well as Zita's cousin—was the heir of the younger branch of the Spanish Bourbons. They had displaced the older Carlist line, the head of which was now her cousin Don Jaime, who had given her away at her wedding. The three civil wars between the adherents of the two branches, plus a revolution against Alphonso's grandmother, which brought in first a republic and then an experiment with a Savoy king, at last, led to the restoration of Alphonso's father. But, as with the Duc de Berry, Alphonso XII had died before his pregnant wife, the Habsburg Maria Christina, gave birth to his son. Before, it had been Henry V, the Count de Chambord; this time, it was Alphonso XIII. King since birth, Alphonso underwent a long regency under his mother. One of the dramatic effects of that period was the attack on Spain in 1898 by the United States and its seizure of Cuba, Puerto Rico, the Philippines, and Guam.

At any rate, the political situation in Spain became ever more fragmented and polarized with Carlists, Integrists (Carlists who accepted Alphonso but wanted a more Catholic and monarchical government), Alfonsino Conservatives, Alfonsino Liberals, Socialists, Anarchists, and Communists all jockeying for position. A series of ineffective governments attempted to deal with the situation. Finally, in 1923, General Primo de Rivera, with Alphonso's approval, overthrew the latest government in a bloodless coup. Initially, he was successful in maintaining order and economic growth, but by 1929, he had turned both the king and the army against him. In that same year, Maria Christina died. She and Zita had been quite friendly, but she had warned Zita that after she died, she did not know that her son could hold on to power. Zita began to smell the telltale stench of the coming revolution.

Beyond that, the now sixteen-year-old Otto and his siblings would soon require advanced education. But where to send them? Certainly, a Catholic university in a monarchy would be best, but Spain was too unsteady. Who knew where it would be in four years? Luxembourg, where Zita's brother was married to the reigning Grand Duchess, Charlotte, was too small. But perhaps Belgium. Since they had close relatives (including King Albert and Queen Elizabeth) in Belgium, it was decided that the older children—and most especially Otto—would go to university there at Louvain.

So, in 1929, Zita moved her children to temporary quarters in Brussels before settling at Castle Ham in Steenokkerzeel, a small Belgian town near the capital, in January of 1930. The family would spend the holidays in Wenduine. One of the first pages of the golden book of the municipality of Wenduine bears the signature of Zita and her housemates. During that period, a Capuchin friar especially stayed in the community to offer daily Mass at the home of the empress.

In their new home, the imperial family was at the crossroads of Europe at a time when restorations and other alternatives to existing governments were definitely in the air. On November 30, 1930, eighty Habsburgs, other relations, and leading monarchists from the various parts of the former monarchy were gathered at Ham Castle to witness Otto's coming-of-age ceremony on his eighteenth birthday. Dressed in black but set off by her diamond-studded insignia of the Starry Cross Order, Zita proclaimed the event and read a document, which stated,

> And so His Majesty, following the last dispositions of his father who rests in God, His Late Majesty Emperor Charles of Austria, Apostolic King Charles IV of Hungary, King of Bohemia, Croatia, Slavonia, Dalmatia, Lodomeria, and Illyria, and in accordance with the ancient family rulings of our reigning house, has achieved his majority and has become, in his own right, sovereign and head of the ruling house.[174]

Otto's supporters began to multiply as the '30s wore on, and a new verse in his honor was added by popular demand to the Kaiserhymne:[175]

In Verbannung, fern den Landen
Weilst Du, Hoffnung Österreichs.
Otto, treu in festen Banden
Steh´n zu Dir wir felsengleich.
Dir, mein Kaiser, sei beschieden
Alter Ruhm und neues Glück!
Bring den Völkern endlich Frieden,
Kehr zur Heimat bald zurück!

---

[174] Brook-Shepherd, *The Last Empress*, p. 232.

[175] "Österreichs Kaiserhymne," https://www.twschwarzer.de/ottohymne.htm.

You are in exile, far from the lands,
hope of Austria.
Otto, loyal in strong bonds,
we stand by you like a rock.
May old glory and new happiness
be granted to you, my Emperor!
Finally bring peace to the peoples,
return to your homeland soon!

But how to make those pious hopes of so many a reality in the face of "democratic" establishments? These, paradoxically, were quite effective at keeping their various exiled monarchs at bay—not just the Habsburgs but the French Bourbons and the Portuguese Braganzas were systematically banned from entering their homelands—but seemed far less effective at dealing with the Great Depression.

But one European figure had managed to spare his country most of the effects of the debacle while repressing Communism and Socialism and winning the admiration of the likes of Winston Churchill and Franklin Delano Roosevelt—parts of whose "New Deal" would be inspired by this man. Moreover, although in complete control thanks to his political party's mass organization, like Primo de Rivera, he allowed his country's king to reign alongside him. Moreover, the year the Habsburgs moved from Spain, this individual had succeeded in ending his country's decades-long battle with the Catholic Church. Who was this miracle worker? His name was Benito Mussolini.

We are used to thinking of Mussolini as Hitler's not-so-smart stooge. But it is important to remember that from

1922 until 1935, Mussolini was allied with Britain and France and was initially (as we shall see) very much an opponent of Hitler. But, like Hitler, he and his movement were of Leftist origins. His father had been a Socialist and an admirer of Juarez (hence Mussolini being named Benito and not Benedetto). He had left the Socialists because of their advocacy of neutrality during World War I, and he had also come to realize the necessity of making peace with both the monarchy and the Church if he was to run Italy. Thus, he shed his youthful republicanism and anticlericalism, and the compromises left him in complete control.

It may also be remembered that Briand, back in 1921, had not believed that the Little Entente—Poland, Romania, Czechoslovakia, and Yugoslavia—had enough strength to resist either a resurgent Germany or an expansive Soviet Union. Thus, he believed that a Habsburg restoration in the two defeated remnant states of Austria and Hungary under French sponsorship could be followed up with the Little Entente joining them in a Danubian Conederation that would be capable of both tasks. He also feared, however, that the French might simply rely on the Little Entente, leaving a future Italian Government to ally with Austria, Hungary, and, perhaps, Bulgaria to do the same thing, but under Italian rather than French influence. But Briand's great fear in 1921 was Zita's brother, Sixtus's great hope in 1930—the more so because Italy had taken up Austria's dislike and distrust of Serbia and aimed it at Yugoslavia.

In regard to why Sixtus thought a Habsburg restoration might be to Italy's and Mussolini's interest and what the likely reaction of various countries to a visit to Italy by Zita might be, he wrote a memorandum in the autumn of 1930. Zita sent Count Revertera—a former Austro-Hungarian diplomat who had undertaken several delicate missions for Charles during the war—to sound out Mussolini on her visiting Italy. On January 5, 1931, the count, fresh from a visit to the *Duce,* was able to inform her that not only was Mussolini keen on her coming to Italy—the idea being that she would visit the king and queen at their hunting lodge of San Rossore in Tuscany, after which they would visit her at Pianore—but that she should bring Otto. After praising what he had heard about the prince, Mussolini expressed a desire that he should meet the king and queen's youngest daughter. Both to Revertera and (in June, while Zita was already there) to Count Colloredo-Mannsfeld, Mussolini enlarged on his proposed marriage, which both emissaries, to their host's annoyance, downplayed. To Colloredo-Mannsfeld, he asked further what Otto's plans for the future were. He replied, "Her Majesty will not indulge in any adventures, but she regards it as her duty and that of her son to follow the call, should it come, to fill any place which is his by right."[176]

Indeed, in Austria, the cause came to life again while Hungarian monarchism seemed to slumber around the figure of the regent. In December of 1931, the Mayor and Council of Ampass in Tyrol named Otto an honorary citizen—an example to be followed by literally hundreds of other towns around the country. The Socialists had been out of power for almost a decade, and in May of 1932, Engelbert Dollfuss, the "Hero-Chancellor," came to power. Ironically, Alphonso

---

[176] Brook-Shepherd, *The Last Empress*, p. 235.

XIII had felt compelled to leave Spain in 1931 in the face of growing unrest, and the Second Spanish Republic was proclaimed.

Otto was now both of age and rather savvy politically. He had read an obscure book entitled *Mein Kampf* by one Adolf Hitler. As its author became more powerful in Germany, both Otto and Zita realized that this angry man might well play an important part in European history. It was resolved to send Otto to Berlin to find out where this man and his movement were going. So, in the winter of 1932, Otto went to Berlin to study at the Agrarian Institute of Professor Max Sering. Both Sering and Count Franz von Galen (a member of the Prussian legislature and brother of Clemens von Galen, Archbishop of Muenster) were his contacts and guides in the German capital.

Hitler had hated the Habsburgs since he was a young, disappointed artist in Vienna, and he made this clear in *Mein Kampf*; nevertheless, he attempted—much as he despised Christianity, aristocracy, and monarchy in general—to use members of these three institutions whenever he could. Thus, when Otto came to Vienna, Hitler attempted to get in touch with him. According to the Archduke's account,

> I was first approached to meet Hitler by Prince August Wilhelm, the fourth or fifth in line of the Hohenzollern brothers. I had tried, if only as a matter of courtesy, to meet all of them. One afternoon, after I had lunch with the Crown Prince, his younger brother invited me for a talk in his own house. He was not only a member of the Berlin Landtag but also an

officer of the Nazi elite corps, the *Sturmabteilung*, and he received me in his SA uniform. In our talk, he sang the praises of the party and spoke only of its "Führer," whom I always pointedly referred to as "Herr Hitler." He then came out with the invitation. His Führer had told him that he wanted to talk with me.

At that, I told the Prince that I was in Berlin to study . . . and that consequently I was avoiding political conversations. Of course, this was not true because I had already met many personalities of the Democratic Conservative Party. But it was the best reason I could give. Later on, Goering himself (who at the time was, of course, president of the Berlin Landtag) made another approach through Baron Pereira, in whose apartment I was lodging. The message was the same: the Führer wanted to meet me. I gave the same answer as before, and that was the end of it.

Prince August Wilhelm was, in my eyes, a convinced Nazi but all the Hohenzollerns shared the illusion that Hitler would reinstate the monarchy once in power. I was certain that Hitler was only using them to attract Monarchist voters. I had already seen how the Crown Prince had already supported Hitler against President Hindenburg and that fundamentally he wanted to do the same thing with me as regards the Austrian voters. I had the great advantage of having already read *Mein Kampf* from start to finish and knew what his aims were. All this only reinforced my refusal to meet him. . . . On the other hand, it would have been an

> interesting experience. In fact, this was the only interesting conversation I have ever avoided in my life.[177]

But if they never spoke, Otto did get a glimpse of the self-anointed anti-Habsburg: "I saw him once, at a large rally on Bülowplatz in Berlin. Hitler hypnotized people. When he came, everyone had the feeling that Hitler was looking at him personally. This demonic look was a great power."[178] His upbringing and knowledge of Soviet Russia and what the Communists had done in Hungary and elsewhere had early taught him the evils of Communism. Otto saw, early on, the Nazis for what they were: brown-shirted Bolsheviks—or, in the pithy words of one observer, "rival gangs, same racket."[179] The twenty-year-old understood a reality that escaped a great many of his elders on all sides of the political spectrum—and continues to do so today.

In January of 1933, he had a meeting with his parents' old nemesis, Field Marshal-turned-President Paul von Hindenburg. The old man wore an Austro-Hungarian field marshal's uniform with the decorations he had received at different times from Franz Joseph and from Otto's father. He spoke only of the old days—the Franco-Prussian War and the like. A few days later, he made Hitler chancellor,

---

[177] Gordon Brook-Shepherd, *Uncrowned Emperor: The Life and Times of Otto von Habsburg* (London: Hambledon and London, 2003), pp. 79–80.

[178] Thomas Schmid, "The Kaiser's son became a champion of Europe," Welt, April 7, 2011, https://www.welt.de/kultur/history/article13467585/Der-Kaiser-Sohn-wurde-zum-Vorkaempfer-Europas.html.

[179] Stephan Baron von Hoeller-Bertram, conversation with author.

and Otto left the country. As it happened, it was none too soon; the Gestapo raided the Munich offices of *Die Gerade Weg*, a Catholic anti-Nazi newspaper, and took its editor, Otto's friend, Fritz Gerlich, to Dachau. He would be murdered there the following year. Otto went to the top of the wanted list in the Nazi pantheon of villains. This was not—from their point of view—unwise because, from that point on, Otto and Zita put saving Austria from Hitler at the top of their priorities.

Nazi victory in Germany had its ramifications in Austria. It was not just that the Pan-Germans were rapidly going brown, but the Socialist leader and arch-opportunist Karl Renner, seeing which way the wind was blowing, was also leading his minions in that direction. As he would famously tell the incoming Nazis a few years later, "You are National Socialists, we are International Socialists; we are brothers!"[180] As it happened, in March of 1933, Renner presented Chancellor Dollfuss with a conundrum. As a result of the railway workers strike called on March 1, the Austrian Parliament had to vote on a measure in response. Renner, President (speaker) of the House, resigned to be able to cast a vote as a Parliament member. The two vice presidents, belonging to other parties, resigned to do so as well. Without a president, the Parliament could not conclude the session. Under the existing constitution, the National Council could no longer function, and Dollfuss asked President Wilhelm Miklas to dissolve it, which he did.

---

[180] http://www.dokumentationsarchiv.at/SPOE/1938_Renner_NAZI.htm.

But now Dollfuss was faced with a problem. He very much feared that if he called for new elections, the Nazis and the Socialists would join in a pro-Anschluss coalition and deliver the country into the hands of Nazi Germany—which they would indeed do, five years later, under the aegis of Karl Renner. Two years earlier, in 1931, Pope Pius XI had issued an encyclical, *Quadragesimo Anno*, which called for the reorganization of society along Christian lines. Dollfuss—as much a visionary as a practical politician—saw in the self-destruction of the Austrian Parliament a way out of the trap that majoritarian democracy seemed to have prepared for his country.

He and his advisors wrote a new constitution for a new kind of state that would be based upon Christian values, with corporate representation, and without the party system that seemed doomed to make way for the Nazis, as it had in Germany. For this, he has received all sorts of insults in subsequent media, academia, and government accounts—which is ironic since these insults have been generated primarily by Karl Renner's ideological heirs. They have dubbed the Dollfuss government as "Austrofascism," which is a splendid example of poisoning the well—the propaganda technique whereby, through labeling, the victim is dismissed before its case can be examined. But as we shall see, the years 1938–1945 in Austria might as well be dubbed "Renner-Nazism."

Meanwhile, King Alphonso XIII had gone to Paris for his exile, but in June of 1933, he visited Vienna. He returned to the French capital and had lunch with Sixtus on June 20. The following day, Sixtus wrote his sister a letter in which he recorded the Spanish king's opinion that Austria was becoming ready for restoration. The king was also present in London, and he suggested that Otto go with him to meet George V and Queen Mary. On June 26, Alphonso wrote to Zita that he had lunched at Buckingham Palace with the king and queen, and they had welcomed the idea of meeting Otto as "magnificent." But George V said that he would have to consult the Foreign Office. They vetoed the idea in no uncertain terms. George V's sad letter to Zita did contain one hint of protest against "his" government's policy in that it was addressed to "Her Imperial Majesty, the Empress Zita" and was signed "I am, Madam My Cousin, Your Imperial Majesty's Good Cousin."[181]

While it was good to know that George V at least still recognized their status, it was obvious that Britain would be no help with either resisting Hitler or bringing about a restoration—and those two causes would become increasingly linked. Dollfuss and Otto got in touch: "But I have been in contact with him a lot. Politically we probably had more of the same opinion than with Schuschnigg. I respected Dollfuss immensely. The man was brave and prepared to fight for Austria to the last possible extent. Back then I saw everything from this perspective: We have to preserve Austria."[182] The anti-Habsburg laws would be removed from the new constitution. The eagle on the flag was made two-headed

---

[181] Brook-Shepherd, *The Last Empress*, p. 242.

[182] Christian Ultsch, "Otto Habsburg: 'I knew them all,'" Die Press, July 14, 2011, https://www.diepresse.com/342228/otto-habsburg-ich-habe-sie-alle-gekannt.

once more, and the old imperial uniforms were reintroduced into the army. Dollfuss began wearing his old army uniform.

In the face of the rising German menace, a foreign ally was needed, but neither Britain nor France were really interested—but Mussolini's Italy was. Similarly, Mussolini privately signaled that he would support a restoration. Shortly before his death, Dollfuss informed Karl Ernst Winter, Deputy Mayor of Vienna, that he had decided to make Otto an offer for a restoration and to convert Austria into a constitutional monarchy. But, on July 25, 1934, a band of Nazis attacked him at the chancery; he was shot and died on a sofa.

When news of the attempted putsch arrived in Rome, Mussolini ordered his army to the Brenner Pass. Hitler was forced to back down, and Kurt von Schuschnigg, Dolfuss's second-in-command and an avowed monarchist, took over the reins. In response to the increased pressure by the Nazis, more than 1,500 communities across Austria declared Otto an honorary citizen. Monarchist organizations multiplied, but their members and their goals were divided. Despite this, in 1936, Otto would be able to found an umbrella group, the Iron Ring—headed by his cousin, Maximilian, Duke of Hohenberg, oldest son of Franz Ferdinand—to direct them all. Just as his father had given a sterling example of loyalty by loving and upholding the nephew who might be said to have usurped his son's rights, Max did the same with regard to his first cousin. But Otto was not only thinking of Austria; that same year, he joined the Paneuropa Union, headed by Richard Count Coudenhove-Kalergi.

Meanwhile, Hitler attempted a charm campaign against Vienna, dispatching the affable and clever (though in a deeper sense, not that bright) Franz von Papen to try to soften up the Austrian government's resistance to Germany. Much worse, however, was the break between Italy, on the one hand, and France and Britain, on the other, over the former's late 1935 invasion of Ethiopia. It would eventually lead to Mussolini's alliance with Hitler, which was ultimately to spell doom for Austria and, although they did not yet realize it, it would also doom Italy's other client states, Hungary and Bulgaria.

Another event that would have an impact on Zita's family was the outbreak of the Spanish Civil War in July 1936. Zita's cousin, Don Jaime, the senior member of the House of Bourbon and heir to the Carlist claims to the throne, died childless in 1931. He was succeeded in his claims to the Spanish throne by his elderly uncle, Don Alfonso Carlos. A Papal Zouave and a brave combatant during the Third Carlist War in his youth, he took advantage of Alphonso XIII's departure to reorganize the movement. During the short life of the Second Republic, he breathed new life into the cause, among other things, organizing Carlist militias—the *Requetes*. As the Second Republic veered ever more leftward and the persecution of the Church and conservatives in general began to pick up, the Carlists began to draw together with other elements of the Spanish Right around the military. When, in order to forestall a Communist coup, the army revolted, the Carlists joined them and would be a key factor in the eventual victory over the Reds.

But Don Alphonso Carlos died in September of 1936, and with him, the senior branch of the Spanish Bourbons. Normally, his heir would have been Alphonso XIII himself, but there was an old law in Spain that no branch of the royal family that had taken up arms against the king could ever succeed to the throne, so as far as the Carlists were concerned, that ruled out the *de facto* king. This left the House of Bourbon-Parma as the next senior branch of the Bourbons. Zita's half-brother Elias had no interest in Spain. Sixtus, who would probably have been keen on the idea of pursuing the Spanish throne, had died two years previously, leaving only a daughter. So, Xavier was, by Carlist reckoning, the heir—and Don Alfonso Carlos had taken him under his wing. Elias helped his elderly cousin to breathe new life into Carlism, and at his death, assumed leadership of the movement. As such, he was an essential part of the struggle until the Nationalist victory in 1939. Zita watched all of these developments with sisterly concern.

As far as Austria went, Schuschnigg was a good man but a deeply conflicted one. He wanted a Habsburg restoration for Austria, but he also hoped that it could somehow one day extend to Germany as well. He did not wish to cut Austria off from Germany entirely. He assured the Hungarians that there would be no restoration but refused to rule it out in Paris. In the end, he was unable to bring himself to do the one thing that could certainly have stiffened the resolve of his countrymen—to summon back the heir to the throne. In February of 1938, he was summoned to Berchtesgaden and subjected to the rage of Hitler. It crushed him. But Otto had other ideas:

> It was like this: I discussed with various people, especially with the State Secretary for National Defense

> (General Wilhelm Zehner), what to do if things went wrong, that is, if the German Wehrmacht attacked. It was clear to me then that a war was coming. Anyone who had read *Mein Kampf* could have no doubt that this man would lead us into a war. I believed, and I was wrong, I believed that a country that does not defend itself cannot rise again after a war. That was my credo: We have to resist. But very few people understood that.[183]

But Hitler was afraid that many Austrians would; as it was, he dubbed the invasion of Austria "Case Otto."

At the last minute, Schuschnigg found his courage again. But it was too late. The Germans were massed on the frontier, and as Dollfuss had feared, Renner's Socialists and the Austrian Nazis together made a majority. There was an argument between mother and son—Zita urging Otto to fly into Vienna to lead whatever resistance there might be or die in the attempt. Otto responded that it would be pointless, as the time for such action had come and gone in February when he offered to take over the chancellorship. When his mother pressed him further, he reminded her of the second Hungarian attempt and how it had brought about Charles's death. To his horror, his mother broke down before his eyes—the only time he would ever see her do so.

The fall of Austria was followed soon thereafter by Munich and the partial partition of Czechoslovakia. But Otto was

[183] Ultsch, Otto Habsburg: "I knew them all," https://www.diepresse.com/342228/otto-habsburg-ich-habe-sie-alle-gekannt.

not out of touch with events—especially in Germany. As he put it,

> There was no war yet, Austria had disappeared. I had many contacts with a resistance group in Germany that was still relatively important at the time. It had two elements: high-ranking officers and the Church. I got a lot of information about the Church.
>
> I would like to find out, but I haven't been able to: At that time, there was someone in the top leadership of the NSDAP who worked absolutely against Hitler. And I am a witness to this myself, and for the following reason: I was told that there was important information about the ecclesiastical resistance line that crossed Holland.
>
> I arranged the handover at the border between Germany and Belgium via the Ardennes. It was a kind of jungle right on the border. And that's where the rendezvous took place, in a house that belonged to an acquaintance who was half Belgian and half Czech. I met a young seminarian, Rudolf Graber, who later became Bishop of Regensburg. He brought me an extremely interesting document: It concerns Hitler's consultations with the leaders of the NSDAP—about the step-by-step plans that they had drawn up for the future." Otto did not keep this to himself. Instead, he "gave it to William Bullitt, the US ambassador in Paris at the time, who I was friends with. He immediately recognized the importance of this paper and sent it on to Roosevelt. Roosevelt read the plans. And

> then, as the announced events occurred from month to month, Roosevelt had the feeling that the guy knew something. He invited me back then.[184]

On March 12, 1938, Otto issued a declaration asserting Austrian independence and set up a "Free Austrian" headquarters in Paris at the Hotel Cayre, which he hoped would be the nucleus of a government-in-exile. Unfortunately, the Austrian exiles were extremely divided. There were many monarchists among them, but there were also Socialists who had broken with the policy of collaboration of their leader, Karl Renner. While refusing to join Renner's treason, however, they would not accept Otto's leadership—and neither would the exiled Communists and other republicans. Thus, his attempts to build a united front among the exiles floundered.

But his efforts were not without success, however small. Otto came to know French Premier Daladier very well and was able to persuade him to create a new category of French residency for exiled Austrians. Thus, when the German government insisted upon the return of the exiles by the French as German citizens, Daladier was legally able to refuse. Thus, Otto was directly responsible for saving the lives of some fifteen thousand Austrian Jews and a great many other Austrians who were enemies of the Nazis. Of course, he received little gratitude then or now for this act—as for his other actions, as we shall see.

[184] Ultsch, "Otto Habsburg: 'I knew them all,'" https://www.diepresse.com/342228/otto-habsburg-ich-habe-sie-alle-gekannt.

The situation in Austria was quite different. There, since the Pan-Germans, Nazis, and Socialists were active collaborators, this left the work of resistance—and the risk—to adherents of the Habsburgs, Dollfuss, and to the small minority of Communists. Thus, when the leading monarchist, Baron Hans Karl von Zeßner-Spitzenberg (of course, the use of his title and "von" had been banned under Renner's antinobility law), was sent to Dachau soon after the Anschluss and was asked why he was there, he responded, "Because I see faith in God and in a Christian Austria under the leadership of the House of Habsburg as the only salvation for the independence of my fatherland."[185] So it would be, through the dreary years of the occupation. Typical of those who carried on was Fr. Heinrich Maier, who, with his comrades in the Resistance, would fight against the Nazis throughout the war years. But, as one writer rather pithily states,

> Knowledge of Maier's resistance to the Nazi terror regime was largely suppressed in Austria after the Second World War, partly because he acted against the express instructions of his church superiors, partly because his political plans for a Habsburg constitutional monarchy in Central Europe (according to the plans of Winston Churchill) were sharply rejected by Joseph Stalin and the USSR. This anti-Habsburg course also became part of the constitution of the

[185] Manfried Welan and Peter Wiltsche, *Hans Karl Zeßner-Spitzenberg. Eine Biographie* (Plattform Johannes Martinek Verlag: Perchtoldsdorf, 2020), p. 143.

> Austrian State Treaty of 1955 over the imperative efforts of the USSR.[186]

About 4,500 monarchists would be sent to camps. Much the same could be said of innumerable other heroes of the Resistance in Austria and South Tyrol. Interestingly enough, the major umbrella group of the Resistance, founded in 1944, was called O5 (it appeared as graffiti all over Vienna, and a sample survives today, inscribed on the Stephansdom). This acronym had several interesting meanings. On the one hand, the Nazis had changed Austria's name from *Österreich*, meaning "Eastern Empire," to *Ostmark*, meaning "Eastern March." Because the letter "E" is the fifth letter of the alphabet, O5 could be a reference to the old name. Secondly, there being five vowels in the alphabet, it might also refer to AEIOU, the old Habsburg motto (variously translated to, among other things, *Alles Erdreich ist Österreich untertan* or *Austriae est imperare orbi universo*, "All the world is subject to Austria." But O5 could also refer to "Otto V," the Archduke's name and number had he been Holy Roman Emperor.

As noted, Hitler hated the Habsburgs and had put Otto at the head of his most wanted list. Unable to get his hands on him, Hitler sent his cousins, Max and Ernst von Hohenberg, to Dachau. Properties that had been returned to Otto in 1935 by the Austrian government were then seized. After the war, unlike other troves of Nazi loot that the government was forced to return to its rightful owners, the current regime in Austria has successfully held on to this property.

---

[186] "Heinrich Maier," Wikpedia, https://en.wikipedia.org/wiki/Heinrich_Maier.

It has fended off several legal challenges on the basis that, in this case, restoration of the property stolen by the Nazis to the rightful owners would endanger the constitution. One can only wonder at the value of a constitution that could be threatened by ending an injustice.

When war broke out, Otto set about trying to organize some sort of Free Austrian Legion, such as the Czechs had done in World War I, as a means of maintaining Austria's place among the Allies. These ideas floundered once more because of divisions between the refugees. Zita gave him advice—both political and familial—from Belgium. In the meantime, his brother Felix had been visiting New York's World's Fair with their uncle, Zita's brother Felix, the consort of the Grand Duchess of Luxembourg, when the Germans invaded Poland. He signed up for the United States Army in response but was not deployed. Young Felix was, however, able to prepare for a visit by Otto with Franklin Delano Roosevelt. FDR was keen on meeting with the senior archduke as a result of the intelligence he had provided Ambassador Bullitt.

At the beginning of March, Otto boarded the Pan Am clipper from Paris to New York. He then went to Washington and met the president, who was already committed to the restoration of Czechoslovakia and Beneš. Theirs was an extremely cordial meeting. As Otto later recalled, "Though there was no talk of a restoration between us, we did discuss the idea of a Danubian Federation of States as the best post-war solution in Central Europe. To begin with, he was sympathetic towards it. It was only later in the war, when the pro-Soviet lobby among his advisers grew stronger in

Washington, [that] his personal support for the idea fade."[187] The conversation was so warm that FDR offered refuge in the United States to him and his family if needed. Neither could have known how soon that would be required. Otto returned to Europe at the end of April.

On the night of May 9–10, when Otto had gone to Castle Ham for his mother's birthday party, Leopold III, King of the Belgians, called personally to say that the Germans were invading. Once again, the Habsburgs had to take to the roads. Three cars filled with seventeen people and their immediate necessities—Zita, her children (save Felix, safe in America), three of the Luxembourg children who had come for the festivities, Count Degenfeld, Countess Kerssenbrock, and four of the staff took off immediately. No sooner had they departed than a projectile launched by German bombers hit the castle directly. They stopped in Brussels, where Otto and Karl Ludwig tried to make some provision for the Austrian exiles there. At 6 p.m., they set off again, reaching Dunkirk by midnight. The next day, they arrived in Laon, staying at the Chateau Fourdrain, home of the Barons de Coppee. Their stay was merely overnight. In the morning, they headed south to the Chateau Bostz, owned by Zita's brother Xavier. In 1939, after he had protested unsuccessfully to Franco about the necessity of restoring the Carlist dynasty, he had returned to his French property. Otto went to Paris to see what could be done to rally Austrian exile support for the war effort and to try to bolster government officials he knew to resist. The government fled to Tours

[187] Brook-Shepherd, *The Last Empress*, pp. 271–72.

and, later, to Bordeaux, and Otto went with them. Zita and the rest went to the nearby Chateau Lamonzie-Montastruc outside of the town. The chateau was a possession of the Grand Duchess of Luxembourg, and she and her husband Felix were already there when Zita and the family arrived on June 16. Xavier had gone to join the Belgian Army in which he had served in World War I, and when it surrendered, he joined the Resistance—at last being captured in 1944, whence he was taken to Dachau.

When the French Parliament in Bordeaux named Marshal Petain as head of state to conclude an armistice, the Germans demanded that the Habsburgs be handed over to them. But the party of exiles had already departed. They arrived—joined by several hundred Austrian exiles—at the Spanish border on June 18. All the documents they carried were now invalid. But the commander of the Spanish frontier point had been the police chief in Lekeitio when they lived there and let them, and all their newly acquired companions, cross the border.

They traveled to Portugal, where a debate ensued amongst the family members as to what their next move should be. It was discussed whether or not they should go to England. But if they did so, they would have no money, and there was no certainty that the British could hold out. The US government granted them exit visas on July 9, and the family split up, with Otto and Karl Ludwig leaving first, followed by Zita and the rest. She and her family arrived in New York on July 16, 1940. The furthest exile of the House of Habsburg had begun; for Zita, it would last thirteen years.

Chapter 12

AN EMPRESS IN THE AMERICAS

"This war would never have come unless, under American and modernising pressure, we had driven the Habsburgs out of Austria and the Hohenzollerns out of Germany. By making these vacuums we gave the opening for the Hitlerite monster to crawl out of its sewer on to the vacant thrones. No doubt these views are very unfashionable."

—Winston Churchill, April 8, 1945[188]

"If the Allies at the peace table at Versailles had allowed a Hohenzollern, a Wittelsbach, and a Habsburg to return to their thrones, there would have been no Hitler. A democratic basis of society might have been preserved by a crowned Weimar in contact with the victorious Allies."

—Winston Churchill, April 26, 1945[189]

When Zita and Elizabeth finally arrived in New York on July 20, the empress issued a communique:

[188] Winston S. Churchill, *The Second World War* (London: Cassell, 1954), vol. VI, p. 640.
[189] Martin Gilbert, *Road to Victory: Winston S. Churchill, 1941–1945* (London: William Heinemann, 1986), p. 1314.

> The empress, who holds firmly to the cause of democracy in Europe, is convinced that freedom and Christianity will triumph over barbaric totalitarianism. Her ideas about the future of Europe are the same as those expressed by Archduke Otto. She believes that a Central European confederation of states, based on democratic principles, should be formed in the Danube area after the defeat of Nazism. Such a group could form a bulwark against any future aggression of pan-Germanism or Bolshevism.[190]

Just as Zita and Otto had seen the preservation of Austrian independence from the Nazis as the major issue in 1938, so too, they saw their defeat as the major issue now. But they were also aware of the threat Stalin posed to both their own countries and all of Europe afterward. In the immediate, there was nothing to be done about Hungary, which under Horthy had joined the Axis. But they could work for a united Austrian presence among the Allies to secure the country's existence after the war and continue to push for a postwar Danubian Confederation, along the lines originated by Franz Ferdinand, championed by Charles, and pursued by his widow and children ever since. Their allies in these quests were primarily FDR—at least in the beginning—and Churchill, as well as those Austrians and others in exile and in the Resistance at home who were loyal to them and their vision.

But their opposition, apart from Hitler, was formidable. Arrayed against them were the Austrian Socialists—both

---

[190] Gordon Brook-Shepherd, *The Last Empress* (London: HarperCollins, 1991), p. 278.

those in exile and those, like Renner, who collaborated with the Nazis at home—Stalin, of course; leftist presidential advisers like Harry Hopkins; Churchill's aide, Anthony Eden (who would prove his supreme incompetence when, at last, British Prime Minister in 1955–56); and Czech president-in-exile, Eduard Beneš. This kind of *de facto* Red-Brown alliance had, for the most part, successfully torpedoed the dynasty's efforts at improving things since 1918, and their successors have continued to do so down to the present.

As soon as they arrived, Zita and her party were driven to the home of Felix's friend, the prominent Wall Street financier Calvin Bullock, who had offered him the use of his summer home in Royalston, Massachusetts. Ominously named "La Bastille" and located at 10 The Common in the center of the small town, the ten-room house was set on twenty acres of land and boasted the Donald Ross Golf Course and a garden designed by the Arts and Crafts New York-based designer, Ellen Shipman.

> The July 25, 1940 *Orange Enterprise and Journal* described the first meeting with Empress Zita in Royalston this way: "The Empress arrives with soft smiling, velvety brown eyes contrasting to the austerity of her long black high neck long sleeved dress. The former Empress Zita of Austria was ushered into a reception room in the guest house on the Calvin Bullock estate in Royalston Monday afternoon and we stood in the presence of Royalty."

The imperial family became familiar faces at Our Lady Immaculate Catholic Church in Athol, where Zita, in her black widow's attire, attracted notice.

> *The Orange Enterprise and Journal* covered the arrival of the empress's other children as well: Archduchesses Adelaide, age 26, and Charlotte, 19, and their brothers the Archdukes Karl Ludwig, 22, and Rudolph, 21. The paper stated "they are so enthusiastic about their new surroundings that smilingly, they all speak at once in their assurances that 'it is delightful, so comfortable, the hills and the fields, the views quite beautiful!'"

Enjoyable as their surroundings were, just as in Spain, they could not be permanent, although the family would return to Royalston during the summers. Zita needed a place to complete her children's education; it must be Catholic—and in a language her younger ones could understand perfectly. The answer was Laval University in Quebec. There, they had the advantage of being French speakers (the youngest children, including Elizabeth, were not yet fluent in English). In October, they moved to Quebec, having been joined by Zita's mother, Princess Maria Antonia, and her sister, Isabella, who had learning problems. They rented the Villa Saint Joseph (before and after called "Spencer Grange") at what is now 1328 Avenue Duquet but was then 239 Chemin St. Louis in Sillery. Although it was a prestigious neighborhood, and the family was living near Spencer Wood (Bois-de-Coulonge), the residence of the king's representative in the province, they had very little money.

They did have a private chapel with the Blessed Sacrament reserved there. According to Zita, "M. l'Abbé Parent is very edified by the family life we lead at Villa St. Joseph. On Sunday afternoon all the children attend Benediction of the Most Blessed Sacrament. It is only after this exercise that we go out. After Mass—at which everyone receives Holy Communion—Father Parent is invited to lunch with the family."[191] The chapel had several elements of particularly Habsburg devotion, including a statue of the Little Infant of Prague and, above the Tabernacle, a copy of an image of *Maria mit dem geneigtem Haupt* (the "Virgin with the Inclined Head"), the original of which is in the Carmelite Monastery of Vienna. This miraculous image was discovered under the rubble in an old building by Father Dominicus, the prior of the first Carmelite monastery in Rome, in 1609. The picture was restored and went to the court of Munich and then to the emperor at Vienna. It was venerated there by the Carmelite nuns, and Emperor Ferdinand II also prayed in front of the image before the Battle of the White Mountain in 1620. Ferdinand later attributed the victory of the Catholic troops to Mary's help, which is why he built the Marian Column in Prague (pulled down in 1918 and restored in 2020). During the First World War, the image was carried in large processions through the streets of Vienna to St. Stephen's Cathedral. Thousands prayed before her for peace. Emperor Franz Joseph also trusted in Mary's help through this image and had the image brought to Schönbrunn for a

[191] Website of the Association for the Beatification of the Empress Zita (Archive).

peace prayer. There is a famous image of him venerating her that was widely circulated as a postcard.

There was also a statue of St. Anne, mother of the Virgin Mary, teaching the future Mother of God. St. Anne was a very popular saint in Quebec, and the shrine of St. Anne de Beaupre had been partly financed by Anne of Austria, wife of Louis XIII (whose own father, Henry IV, died when he was quite young), and mother of Louis XIV—the Habsburg wife of a Bourbon king. As with Zita, Anne of Austria also had to conduct her son's ship of state through very choppy waters. In addition to this home spiritual life, Zita would visit the Abbey of Sainte-Marie des Deux-Montagnes near Oka when she could.

On October 21, at the College Jesus-Marie, the family was honored by a special convocation organized by Msgr. Camille Roy, the Rector of Laval, and a number of other local notables. These assemblies of students, faculty, staff, and clergy offered their homage to Zita and closed out the evening with a rousing rendition of *Gott Erhalte*. This would set a pattern that would last until the end of her stay in Quebec; the city and the province took her very much to heart as *notre imperatrice* ("our empress").

Charles De Koninck, who had taught Otto at Louvain, would be teaching the Archdukes Karl Ludwig and Rudolf and the Archduchess Charlotte philosophy at Laval. Both intellectuals, deeply pious, and Marian devotees, De Koninck and the empress found much in common as well.

From the beginning of their stay, Zita had a very cordial relationship with her neighbor, Sir Eugene Fiset, the lieutenant governor of the province, with whom she and her children would often share a *dais*, or pew, at various functions in church during her stay there. But she was also friendly with the Earl and Countess of Athlone, Governor-General and Vicereine of Canada. The latter, Princess Alice, granddaughter of Queen Victoria, invited Zita to stay at Government House, Ottawa, in the winter of 1940. Her Royal Highness would later write of Her Imperial Majesty after paying a return visit to the Villa St. Louis,

> Zita still wore the same dress as she did when she became a widow—down to the ground, right up to her hands and up to her chin, with no earrings or any bit of jewelry.
>
> In contrast, she was very talkative, well-informed, and cultivated. . . . She had her old mother with her, who was much more worldly.
>
> We sat down to a typical German tea of *Butterbrod* and little square cakes and biscuits. Only Ariel [her lady-in-waiting] and I were allowed cups of tea—the others drank tumblers of water. . . . I thought they seemed very poor.[192]

Indeed, they were. Since the family was cut off from all European funds, Zita's financial situation was more meager than ever. There were times when Zita had to prepare salads and spinach recipes with dandelions. Things improved in 1942 when the status of Austrians-in-exile was adapted to that of "friendly aliens," which allowed some frozen assets to be retrieved.

---

[192] Brook-Shepherd, *The Last Empress*, p. 284.

For the first time, however, Zita was no longer at the center of Habsburg politics; that role had been assumed by Otto. Based now in Washington, Otto was living at the Broadmoor Apartments. The senior archduke was a parishioner at the nearby church of St. Thomas the Apostle. Nicknamed the Church of the Catacombs, it occupied what was planned to become the basis of a larger church to be built in the future. This would eventually happen in 1952, and the space where Otto had assisted at Mass became the parish hall. (In the summer of 2021, this writer would present a lecture on Otto's father in that very space!). But Otto did not spend all of his time in Washington. He went on numerous speaking tours around the country, supporting the war effort and rallying his central European countrymen and their descendants behind postwar Austrian independence and the Danubian Federation. He also spent time exploring a country that he, like his great-uncle Franz Ferdinand and his cousin—the older Ludwig Salvator, found endlessly interesting.

In 1941, Zita wrote directly to Queen Mary, the widow of George V. Her son Robert was in London as the family's representative; there, too, he found the same old problems with the Czechs and the Austrian Socialists, which derailed any kind of united action for the war effort. He did manage to forge a relationship with Churchill and convince him that Austria, too, was an occupied country. Initially, Robert was able to convince the prime minister of the need for a Free Austrian Battalion under British sponsorship, but this too was derailed by the usual Czech-Austrian Socialist opposition.

Bad as this was, in the last week of April, his apartment at 59 St. James Street was destroyed in a German air raid. This news came to the ears of Queen Mary, who wrote the young Habsburg,

> I hope you realise how much I feel for you being cut off from your family and friends at this anxious moment, and that is why I asked you whether I should call you R. and that you should call me Aunt because I should like you to feel that you have someone in England to whom you can write sometimes if you like when you feel rather lonely. I have known so many members of your family personally or by name. I have always felt very Austrian at heart because my father served in the Austrian army until he married my mother in 1866 and he had so many Austrian and Hungarian friends.[193]

Her grandmother was Countess Claudine Susanna Rhédey von Kis-Rhéde of the noted Transylvanian family. The queen mother was as good as her word, and Zita wrote to thank her, addressing her as "Chere Cousine, Sa Majeste la Reine-Mere de l'Angleterre."[194] Similarly, Zita, as Empress of Austria, kept up a stream of letters to various Allied royals. On July 6, 1942, she wired Otto that she had just been visited by King George II of Greece, who would be coming to Washington if Otto wished to meet him.

---

[193] Brook-Shepherd, *The Last Empress*, p. 286.
[194] Brook-Shepherd, *The Last Empress*, p. 287.

In addition to political correspondence and giving advice on etiquette and household matters to Otto, Felix, and Robert, Zita also received a host of letters asking for help from a number of former subjects. One of the most famous of these included the Baroness von Trapp of *Sound of Music* fame. For most, all she could offer was prayer and moral support. Occasionally, if the request was small enough, she would contribute something.

Meanwhile, her sons were still trying to rally the exiles. When they had arrived at Royalston, the family found there to be three major Austrian exile organizations in the United States: oldest was the Austro-American League with a monarchist majority, which was centered in the East but represented in Ohio, Colorado, Oregon, and California; the newly-formed Austrian Action, which was virulently anti-Habsburg, being headed by Count Czernin's son, Ferdinand; and the Austrian Labor Committee, which opposed any Habsburg-Fascist grouping. Idiotic as this last comment was, it remains typical of Austrian establishment jargon down to the present.

Undeterred, Otto and his brothers formed a new Austrian committee, which included most of the Austrians—they were even able to coax the younger Czernin into serving on the board. They were joined by such illustrious exiles as Franz Werfel and Bruno Walter. Although not intended to act as a government-in-exile, the members hoped to be an Austrian presence within the Allied war effort. Unfortunately, as Soviet influence grew in Washington after Hitler invaded the Soviet Union, so did its influence on the Austrian Labour Committee. Otto asked for FDR's help in forming a united Austrian National Committee that would include everyone, but the president replied that the Austrians would have to set their own house in order. All in all, it was a very discouraging time. But Zita tried to comfort Otto in her New Year's note for 1942:

> Don't imagine that I have no feeling for all the bitter disappointments you are going through. I know it all from my own experience and it's been no different in Vienna or Hungary or whether one sits in Switzerland, Portugal, or Belgium, the United States or Canada, not even to mention Paris or England! There is only one thing to do: fulfil one's duty to God, become a better person by it and not become depressed so that one's health suffers.[195]

Ruined in the same way and in the same manner was FDR's brainchild of a Free Austrian Battalion; it would be raised and trained at Camp Atterbury, Indiana. This was a newly-built post—construction had begun a month after Pearl Harbor and was finished on August 15. The call went out for Austrian-born volunteers for a new 101st Infantry ("Free Austria") Battalion. Karl Ludwig, Felix, and Rudolf volunteered, as did Werner von Trapp (again of *Sound of Music* fame) and some 140 others. That having failed, the War Department sent out an order: "Transfer men of Austrian birth to the 101st Infantry Battalion (Separate), Camp Atterbury, Indiana, without requisition."[196]

---

[195] Brook-Shepherd, *The Last Empress*, p. 292.

[196] Tevie Jacobs, "When the Grand Dukes Drilled in Indiana," originally published in The Indianapolis Star Sunday Magazine, August 15, 1971, http://www.indianamilitary.org/Camp%20Atterbury/Austrian%20Bn/Austrian%20BN.htm.

They reached the number of 650 men. But then, somehow, the New York papers found out the whole thing, descended upon the camp, and interviewed many of the men—many of whom were Socialists or Jews, unwillingly assigned. Not too surprisingly, these men expressed unhappiness with the situation. Brass from the War Department then descended upon the post and asked each man if he wished to stay. Those who did not were immediately reassigned, and in one day, the numbers dropped down to ninety. Karl Ludwig was informed that, for the moment, the battalion would remain, but if it had not reached one thousand volunteers within six months, it would disband. By mid-July, the three brothers were discharged, and the experiment ended.

The sad truth was that as the Soviets picked up ever more of the brunt of fighting with the Germans and began to score victory after victory, their stock rose in Washington. FDR became enamored with "Uncle Joe" Stalin—a relationship that would bear fruit at Yalta when the president signed away Eastern Europe to a mass murderer who eclipsed Hitler in body count, only to be similarly outdone by Mao. The Czech government-in-exile headed by Beneš was firmly in the Soviet Camp. Otto and Zita both wrote letters and memoranda to any public figure they could about the dangers the Soviets posed to postwar Europe, only to be increasingly ignored by the most powerful.

Nevertheless, as far as official Washington was concerned, the Habsburgs had not outlived their usefulness, as was shown by the attempts of the Hungarian government to make a separate peace through their agency. Although the beginning of Horthy's experience as an Axis partner had gone well—southern Slovakia, Transcarpathia, half of Transylvania, and Vojvodina had been returned to Hungary by their German ally—by the autumn of 1942, it was obvious that the Soviet Union would be the rock upon which the Axis would crack. The Hungarians on the Eastern Front had fought well, as was their wont, against the Soviets. But their casualties were high—and higher than they would have been had the Germans not failed to supply them properly and occasionally subjected them to friendly fire. Miklos Kallay, Horthy's new prime minister, resolved to switch sides, as the Italians would the next year.

Horthy's son Stephan, who had been voted in as deputy regent, was killed in an air crash on August 22, thus ending the admiral's hopes for a Horthy dynasty. On November 8, 1942, the Allies invaded French North Africa, then loyal to Marshal Petain. This effectively ended the chance of an Axis victory in the eyes of the Hungarian public. Kallay sent Otto a message via Andor Wodianer, the anti-Nazi Hungarian ambassador to Portugal, which asked the rightful Hungarian king "to establish contact between the Hungarian government and the government of the USA in order to prepare the way for Hungary's leaving the side of the Germans and joining that of the allies at the most appropriate moment."[197]

For the next two years, Otto and the family attempted to do just that. They were in touch with key figures in Hungary alongside Kallay. Moreover, unlike the Austrians, the Hungarians in America were united. Closest to Otto was the former Smallholders' Party president, Tibor Eckhardt.

---

[197] Brook-Shepherd, *The Last Empress*, p. 298.

Kallay sent a Portuguese emissary, Dom Jose de Saldanha, to Washington with a personal message for FDR indicating Hungary's desire to change sides as soon as the Allies entered the Balkans. Not too surprisingly, Horthy put his oar in, wanting to know what guarantees he might gain for his family, property, and pension. Otto and Eckhardt had to intercept some of these messages to keep the negotiations from breaking down.

Kallay was able to establish other lines of communication with the Allies, and at the "Quadrant" meeting in Quebec between FDR and Churchill, Hungary was discussed alongside Operation Overlord and the struggle with Japan. From these meetings came a set of conditions for help to Hungary that were conveyed by the British ambassador to Turkey to his Hungarian counterpart on the former's yacht in Istanbul.

Two weeks later, Otto was due to visit FDR's home at Hyde Park. Unfortunately, he was struck ill with influenza. His mother was completely aware of the Hungarian situation, and so FDR invited her to visit him as Otto's representative at Hyde Park on September 11. There, she was able to make a pitch for Austria's independence and a Danubian Confederation. Roosevelt surprised her by bringing up once again the idea of a Free Austrian Unit, which she felt obliged to agree with; she kept to herself her misgivings about the idea based upon past experience. But she said that some sort of political representation of Austria should come first, but the president declared himself to be under too much political pressure to do that. They then talked about postwar Europe, and FDR indicated there was a possibility Hungary could keep her gains in Transylvania if she changed sides quickly enough. On this trip, Zita made the acquaintance of Elanor Roosevelt and introduced her daughters, Charlotte and Elizabeth, to the first family.

On October 19, the Soviet, British, and American foreign ministers met in Moscow and agreed that Austria would be restored after the victory but that the Austrians had "a responsibility which they cannot evade and that in the final settlement account will inevitably be taken of the part they play in resisting the German invader."[198]

By November, when FDR met with Churchill and Stalin in Tehran, he had lost interest in a Danubian Confederation. When Churchill broached the idea, Stalin spoke out against it, and Roosevelt joined him, then giving his own idea of splitting Germany and Austria into occupation zones. Churchill argued for an Allied landing in Trieste, which would allow the Allies to surge northwards and link up with Hungary. But neither of his allies were interested in this, having already consigned Hungary and the rest of central Europe to the Soviets. Finally, on March 14, 1944, Hitler, aware of Kallay's efforts, forced Horthy to dismiss him.

September 13 to 16 featured the Second Quebec Conference. FDR was a dying man and, in his last conversation with Otto, told him that he had better discuss things with John Dewey, whom he expected—incorrectly, as it turned out—would defeat him in the upcoming election. A month later, Hitler overthrew Horthy and had him taken prisoner to Germany. He abdicated as regent, but no mention was made of the king. A puppet government took over

---

[198] Brook-Shepherd, *The Last Empress*, p. 301.

the country as the Red Army passed over its eastern border. On March 27, 1945, the Crown Guard in Budapest was able to rescue the crown jewels, including the Holy Crown, and bring them over the Austrian border, eventually surrendering their sacred charges to American forces. By April 4, 1945, Hungary was in Soviet hands.

But what of Austria? A recurring myth from that day to this is that there was no Resistance in Austria. But, as mentioned, a resistance most certainly existed. At least one hundred thousand people resisted the Nazis from 1938 to 1945, thousands of whom gave their lives.[199] But the sad truth for much of today's establishment in Austria is that, while Karl Renner and his followers were dutifully obeying the Nazis, those who resisted were primarily Catholics and monarchists. We have mentioned Fr. Heinrich Maier; but there were so many more: the Antifaschistische Freiheitsbewegung Österreichs in Carinthia, led by Fr. Anton Granig, Karl Krumpl, Eduard Pumpernig, Kapistran Pieller OFM, Angelus Steinwender OFM, Georg Kofler, Arthur Trattler, Anton Jaklitsch, Wenzel Primosch, Franz Bernthaler, Karl Wanner, Ernst Ortner, and Otto Tiefenbrunner; the Maier-Messner-Caldonazzi group in Vienna (including Fr. Maier); the Großösterreichische Freiheitsbewegung, led by Jacob Kastelic in Vienna, which had contacts with Legitimist groups in Slovenia, Croatia, and Bohemia-Moravia, and quite a few more. But all of these were betrayed sooner or later. Toward the end of the war, the Tyrolean Resistance—likewise

[199] Tim Heath, Virginia Wells, and Herti Bryan, *Resistance Heroines in Nazi and Russian Occupied Austria: Anschluss and After* (Havertown: Pen & Sword Books, 2021), p. 100.

monarchist and Catholic—began gaining strength. It was to them that Otto sent his brothers Karl Ludwig and Rudolph, who thus spent the last months of the war fighting the Nazis.

They made their way across France, Switzerland, and, at last, to Austria on foot, primarily by night. Rudolf was captured by German military police near the Austrian-Liechtenstein border but was able to escape through an open window. He hid with the Capuchins at Feldkirch until the Germans gave up the search. Both brothers were reunited and joined the Tyrolean Resistance that was operating in both North and South Tyrol. They had heard rumors that the latter was to be returned to Austria after the war and so concentrated a lot of their work in that area. Felix eventually joined them as well.

Things were different for Karl Renner. Having dutifully served his Nazi masters through the occupation, he wrote an obsequious letter offering his services to Stalin. As it happened, Stalin had already decided to use the most pliable of collaborators as chancellor in a new Austrian government. After the occupation of Vienna by the Soviets, he placed Renner in the chancery.

Otto, in the meantime, rushed to Innsbruck to set up headquarters at the Hotel Kreid, which was under French occupation, like the rest of Tyrol. From there, he contacted surviving friends from the concentration camps, such as Leopold Figl, to build up an opposition to the Socialist-Communist United Front Renner was building up in Vienna for his Soviet sponsors. Once he was sufficiently in command, however, Renner invoked his Habsburg Law of 1919 to expel Otto and his brothers from the country. The sheer injustice of this act has yet to be acknowledged by official circles in Austria.

Back in Quebec, on May 5, Zita was having her fifty-third birthday. The German surrender in Berlin that day should have been a cause for rejoicing in the Villa Saint Joseph. Unfortunately, Zita and her children all realized that the House of Habsburg and their erstwhile subjects had simply exchanged one enemy for another—Communism. Moreover, Otto's friend Coudenhove-Kalergi's prediction in 1918 that, unless Europe united, it would be occupied by the Americans and the Soviets was proved entirely true. Countering Communism and uniting what remained of Europe would become the mission of the House of Habsburg.

There was a pleasant intermission in the midst of all the dreariness in the mother continent. Zita and her family met then-Msgr. Fulton J. Sheen on November 5, 1946, at the ordination of the first-ever Coadjutor Bishop of the Ukrainian Greek Catholic Exarchate of Pittsburgh (Bishop Daniel Ivancho). Msgr. Sheen gave the homily at the ordination. As always, the Habsburgs in exile attempted to maintain a presence with their former subjects of all ethnicities in the United States.

In the immediate, Europe was a wreck. Zita embarked on the mission of collecting donations for her former central European subjects. She launched a series of fifty conferences on behalf of Catholic charitable organizations all around Canada. Since her children were now all self-sufficient, she could focus on those in her former territories to whose welfare she had sworn herself at her coronation. There were many donations that needed to be sorted, cleaned, and packed. Zita enlisted the help of her mother, Maria-Antonia, her sister Princess Isabella, her youngest daughter, Elizabeth, and the Boy Scouts for such duties. Collections gathered at the first series of conferences were given to the Archdiocese of Salzburg, then under American occupation. After the success of the first series, she organized a second round of such conferences in the United States between 1946 and 1947. The empress made the trips herself, sleeping in religious institutions and traveling second class. Spending entire days giving interviews, despite her natural reserve, she used the publicity to garner more donations to the Austrians and Hungarians. Thousands of packages were sent thanks to the CARE Foundation (Cooperative for American Remittances to Europe) as well as liturgical vessels for ruined churches. These activities lasted through 1948. By this time, the sisters from whom Zita had rented the Villa Saint Joseph needed their house back, and Zita wished to move closer to her children, who, for the most part, lived in New York state.

Calvin Bullock, who had housed the family in his Royalston estate back in 1940, suggested to the children, now all working, that they buy their mother a home in Tuxedo Park, fifty-six miles or so northwest of New York. Bought by his brother-in-law, Henry Cole, in 1945, it was and is by American standards a remarkable, historic home. At the time, it was called the Voss House, after the man who built it in 1905, and it had been rented by the famed writer Mark Twain from 1907 to 1909. Located in an exclusive and private suburb, it remains—under the name The Empress's Palace in tribute to Zita's time there—an important landmark in a community that gave its name to the American version of the dinner jacket. Every room has beautiful views of the Tuxedo Lakes and surrounding mountains. Zita moved in at Christmas time in 1948. She and those of her children who lived nearby became faithful parishioners at Our Lady of Mt. Carmel Catholic Church.

This house would be the scene of the empress's last public political service to Austria. The Marshall Plan was pumping millions of American dollars into Western Europe to rebuild the devastated continent. On the floor of the Senate in Washington, it was claimed that Austria should be excluded from this largesse, given the warm welcome Hitler received in 1938—not least by Karl Renner. But Zita discussed the question with Otto and then invited around fifty senators' wives to explain to them what had really happened with Austria then and afterward. She managed to convince them—and they, in turn, convinced their husbands. So it was that Austria was not left out. Alas, as one of the websites supporting her beatification puts it so pithily, "This was her final political act, and it was for the benefit of those who had treated her as an enemy because of her married name, and those who refused to let her back in her own country until 1982!"[200]

Meanwhile, the Gebetsliga had prayed and worked for Charles's beatification since his death in 1922. Despite the enforced hiatus in their work from 1938 to 1945, they began again after World War II ended. Finally, on July 11, 1949, the process for Charles's beatification was officially opened,

---

[200] Website of the Association for the Beatification of the Empress Zita (Archive).

and it would be successfully concluded in 2004. Vatican Radio introduced the process thus: "For the honor of God and the glory of the Church, to give in our time in the person of the Servant of God, an intercessor whose image as a Catholic father, spouse and sovereign who is aware of his responsibilities and times, would be so necessary in our time of corruption and moral destruction, and the decline of marriage and the family."[201]

Zita watched her children as each began to make his or her own way in the postwar world. Otto stayed in Europe, while Felix pursued a business career in South America, and Adelheid went to Paris to begin a career in welfare work. Zita made her first return trip to Europe since leaving in 1940. Her youngest child, Elizabeth, was the first of the eight to marry. On September 12, 1949, she married Prince Heinrich von und zu Liechtenstein at the Chateau de Lignières, which was Xavier's home in France (himself having managed to survive Dachau). The groom was the son of Prince Alfred von Liechtenstein and Princess Theresa Marie of Oettingen-Oettingen. He was also a cousin of the then sovereign Prince Franz Joseph II, Prince of Liechtenstein. The following January, the empress returned to Europe for the wedding of Karl Ludwig to Princess Yolande de Ligne at her family chateau in Beloeil, Belgium.

Of course, a major question was the marriage of Otto himself. Fortunately, a suitable bride for the heir of the eight-hundred-year-old monarchy appeared in the form of a nurse

[201] Website of the Association for the Beatification of the Empress Zita (Archive).

at a refugee camp near Bayreuth, where the senior archduke was visiting in the summer of 1950. She was Princess Regina of Saxe Meiningen, whose father, Duke George, had been taken by the Soviets and died in the Gulag.

Otto and Regina were married on May 10, 1951. Since 1911, there had been much thought as to where this first imperial wedding would be held. Obviously, it could not be in either the groom's or the bride's home country. After much consultation, it was decided to hold the ceremony at the Church of Saint-François-des-Cordeliers in Nancy, France. It will be remembered that the House of Habsburg is, in fact, the House of Habsburg-Lorraine, the husband of Maria Theresa—herself the last of the main line of the Habsburgs—having married Francis, Duke of Lorraine, who was elected Holy Roman Emperor. In 1737, he had been given the Grand Duchy of Tuscany—which is how it came into Habsburg hands—in exchange for Lorraine, which in time passed to France. But the House of Habsburg-Lorraine had never forgotten their connection to the place. Their ducal ancestors were still entombed there; Marie-Antoinette of Austria stopped there to pray on her way to Paris for her marriage to her future husband, Louis XVI; and Franz Joseph also came to pray there in 1867. During the Revolution, the ducal tombs were desecrated, and their coffins ripped open. But the gravediggers took care, when burying the bones in the Boudonville cemetery, to set them apart. During the restoration, Louis XVIII and Francis I of Austria were moved by the sad state of the round chapel. This was restored, and the ducal remains solemnly reinstalled on November 9, 1826. The expiatory ceremony took place under the direction of

Nicolas-Charles de Vincent, Lorraine nobleman and former Austrian ambassador, and Charles de Forbin-Janson, Bishop of Nancy. The Emperor of Austria created a foundation in 1826, appointing a chaplain responsible for celebrating Mass daily and ensuring a solemn funeral service in November in memory of his ancestors. This service was provided continuously until 1914.

After the First World War, a group of Lorrainers, guided by Marshal Lyautey—a royalist who had been privy to and supported Charles's peace efforts—reestablished the Solemn Mass in memory of the dukes and princes of Lorraine and Bar. This Mass, celebrated on an ongoing basis since 1934, takes place in the autumn, generally at the end of October. It is organized by the Lorraine History Society and the Lorraine Museum and offered by the priest of the Saint-Epvre parish to which the Cordeliers church belongs.

Regina's tiara had been a gift of Franz Joseph to Zita in 1911, and her veil had been worn by one of Maria Theresa's daughters at her wedding. The image of Our Lady of Mariazell was brought from that shrine where Charles and Zita had pledged to help each other get to Heaven. More than three dozen Austrian and Hungarian priests assisted Marc-Armand Lallier, Bishop of Nancy, who was the celebrant. In the congregation, there were representatives in native costume of the different parts of the empire behind the Iron Curtain, and gifts were presented from such as Queen Mary and Winston Churchill. As the happy couple left the church, the crowd cheered *Vive le duc*! ("Long live the Duke!") The newlyweds would settle after their honeymoon (which included a trip to Lekeitio) at Poecking bei Starnberg. From there until his death in 2011, Otto would continue to work for the causes—political and religious—that he believed in.

But more marriages were forthcoming in the imperial family. On November 18, 1952, Archduke Felix married Princess Anne-Eugénie of Arenberg in Beaulieu-sur-mer on the Riviera. June 22, 1953, would see Archduke Rudolf marrying Countess Xénia Tschernychev-Besobrasoff at Our Lady of Mt. Carmel in Tuxedo Park. Fulton Sheen performed the ceremony, and much was made at the time of it being the second "imperial marriage" celebrated in the United States (Napoleon Bonaparte's brother Jerome's nuptials with Baltimore heiress Elizabeth Patterson being cited as the first). Robert married Princess Margherita of Savoy-Aosta (1930–2022), first civilly, on December 28, 1953, in Bourg-en-Bresse, and then religiously, the next day, in the Royal Abbey Church of Brou. The bride belonged to the House of Savoy-Aosta, a cadet branch of the Royal House of Italy. The church had a special significance for both the bride and groom: it had been built at great expense by the very powerful Margaret of Austria, Duchess of Savoy, vicereine of the Burgundian Netherlands, godmother and aunt of Charles V, and ancestress of both Robert and Margherita.

With her children primarily settled, Zita had now to think of her mother, who had celebrated her ninetieth birthday on November 28, 1952, at Berg Castle in Luxembourg. She would leave the United States behind (although her children would own the home in Tuxedo Park until 1971) and return to the Europe she had left thirteen years before. Zita settled at Berg Castle in Luxembourg, where her mother had settled after World War II. There, where her brother Felix and sister-in-law Grand Duchess Charlotte reigned, mother and daughter passed the last few quiet years of the former's life. At last, on May 14, 1959, at age ninety-six, Maria Antonia died. Zita would now have to decide—her duties as wife, mother, and daughter in the main concluded—what she would do with the remainder of her life, be it long or short.

Chapter 13

THE LONG LONELINESS

Tomorrow [the Feast of All Saints] the Church will be so overflowing with joy that she will seem to be already in possession of eternal happiness; but today she appears in the garb of penance, confessing that she is still an exile. Let us fast and pray with her; for are not we too pilgrims and strangers in this world, where all things are fleeting and hurry on to death? Year by year, as the great solemnity comes round, it has gathered from among our former companions new saints, who bless our tears and smile upon our songs of hope. Year by year the appointed time draws nearer, when we ourselves, seated at the heavenly banquet, shall receive the homage of those who succeed us, and hold out a helping hand to draw them after us to the home of everlasting happiness. Let us learn, from this very hour, to emancipate our souls, let us keep our hearts free, in the midst of the vain solicitudes and false pleasures of a strange land: the exile has no care but his banishment, no joy but that which gives him a foretaste of his fatherland.

—Dom Prosper Gueranger[202]

During this period, Otto and his siblings had not been idle. With the expulsion of the heir and his brothers

202 "October 31—Vigil of All Saints—Dom Prosper Gueranger," Sensus Fidelium, https://sensusfidelium.com/the-liturgical-year-dom-prosper-gueranger/october/october-31-vigil-of-all-saints/.

from Austrian soil and the Soviet-American dyarchy dominating Europe, it was obvious that a Danubian Confederation—with or without a Habsburg restoration—was nowhere near in the offing. The eight children would have to find some other way to apply the education and upbringing their mother had afforded them to life as they found it—and yet, in some way, remain faithful to the traditions of their House.

While his brothers and sisters could go into business or charity work, there was no doubt, for Otto, that he could not. Somehow, he must see the Habsburg Double Eagle continue to mean something in the world of affairs. But he also had to earn an income to provide for his growing family. Fortunately, the network he had built up in the United States during the war and the one that his brother Robert had constructed in London helped a great deal in both areas.

As far as income went, for the next three decades or so, he kept a backbreaking schedule of tours in the United States, explaining European history and politics—and the threat of Communism—to Americans and maintaining touch with émigré communities, many of which had been greatly expanded by recent refugees. But he was also influential among such American conservatives as Russell Kirk, William F. Buckley, Henry Regnery, Frederick Wilhelmsen, Brent Bozell, Freidrich von Hayek, and many others. Indeed, the correspondence between such figures and the archduke often shows how much they relied upon his views and practical advice. In the case of Bozell's *Triumph Magazine*, he was relied upon so much that he might have almost been regarded as a co-founder.

As far as Europe went, Otto had already begun to shift his sights somewhat before the war, joining the Pan-European Movement in the 1930s. As one of his close political collaborators, Bernd Posselt, put it,

> For him, Pan-Europe as a strong federation of peoples and ethnic groups, states and regions, founded on democracy, the rule of law, self-determination and ethnic group rights, was the mission that he had received from two sides: from his father, Emperor Charles, the last representative of the Western imperial tradition founded by Charlemagne, and by his predecessor at the head of the Pan-European movement, Richard Coudenhove-Kalergi, the founder of the modern idea of European unification, whom he met in Paris in 1936.[203]

Certainly, in Germany, Italy, Spain, and elsewhere, there were many intellectuals thinking in similar terms. Among these was the *Neues Abendland* (New West) group around Erich von Waldburg-Zeil, which numbered West German cabinet members in its number and enjoyed the tacit support of Konrad Adenauer, longtime foe of the Nazis, who became Chancellor of West Germany after the War. At a time when the German chancellor and his Christian Democratic co-founders and colleagues, Robert Schuman of France and Alcide De Gasperi of Italy, were speaking of the Crown of Charlemagne as the premier symbol of a united,

---

[203] Bernd Posselt, "That's what Otto von Habsburg lived for," Paneuropa Enuin Deutschland e.V., March 20, 2012, https://paneuropa.org/dafuer-lebte-otto-von-habsburg_id100.

free, and Christian Europe, *Neues Abendland* and its associated organizations were more explicit. They saw such a Europe as requiring the explicit revival of the *Reichsidee* (imperial ideal) of the Habsburgs, and there was little doubt who they saw as the best candidate to wear that crown. But beginning with an article in the August 15 issue of *Der Spiegel*, these groups were subject to such an intense example of what we today would call "negative press," that all the government members broke with it. The movement then began a slide into obscurity and eventual dissolution. The message was clear: Charlemagne's crown was fine with the dominant forces in Western Europe so long as there was no suggestion that someone would actually wear it. Nothing daunted Otto, whose lack of resentment was a trait he surely inherited from his father. He continued to work for European unity through collaboration with such figures as De Gaulle and the aforementioned Christian Democrats. Certainly, Otto again proved himself his father's son in this regard when, at the dying request of Admiral Horthy, he traveled to the deathbed of the erstwhile Hungarian regent in Portugal and gave him the forgiveness he requested, despite the memory of Horthy's broken oaths. Through the *Centre européen de documentation et d'information*, based in Madrid, with branches in all the major Western European countries (which owed its origins to Otto's networking with various personalities at the Barcelona Eucharistic Congress of 1953), he worked with a number of important figures of the continent's differing right-of-center groups. Among its members were veterans of the *Neues Abendland* group, Spanish adherents of Franco working to bring Spain back from the pariah status given to it after World War II, due to the German and Italian aid Franco had received during the civil war into the European (and Western) mainstream, and Gaullists, keen on the rehabilitation and return to power of de Gaulle. What these varied groupings had in common was anti-Communism and as much European independence as could be obtained from the dyarchy.

Zita had been informed of all this activity, of course. But after her mother's death in 1959, she had to decide what to do with her remaining days. With her sister and her lady-in-waiting, Countess Kerssenbrock (who had fulfilled this task since 1917, sharing all of the family's adventures at home and in exile from that date), Zita decided to move to a religious house in Zizers, Switzerland, which had begun to take in elderly lay boarders as the number of sisters dwindled. The Johannesstift would be her home for the rest of her life.

Two years later, Otto and Regina had a son, Karl, named after his grandfather. The new heir to the Habsburg claims would be followed in 1964 by Georg. With the succession assured, Otto began contemplation of his immediate political future. The spiteful Renner's anti-Habsburg law of 1919 had had as its key element this provision: In the interests of the Republic's safety, the former wearer of the crown and all other members of the House of Habsburg-Lorraine are banned from entering the land unless they specifically renounce their membership of this House and all its associated claims of sovereignty and declare themselves loyal citizens of the Republic.[204]

[204] Gordon Brook-Shepherd, *Uncrowned Emperor: The Life and Times of Otto von Habsburg* (London, Hambledon and London, 2003), p. 181.

Of course, the sententious tone of this "law," written by a man who had repeatedly betrayed his country, was amusing in the extreme. Nevertheless, it was on the books, and the government insisted on maintaining it. As early as 1955, when the Soviets left, and Austria regained its full independence, Otto began exploring means of returning. Knowing how his mother would feel, given all that she and his father had suffered to maintain the dynastic rights, he began gingerly exploring the issue with her:

> Nothing was sprung upon my mother. The subject was first broached with her in the 1950s. I had recently visited Brittany, where I had seen a statue of the Comte de Chambord, I think the only one in France. He, of course, was my Bourbon ancestor who, in the last century, had refused French republican overtures to return from exile on the grounds that he could never ascend the throne of France under the *tricoleur*. Some of us had developed a name for this whole approach to life: "Chambordisme." By that we meant a rigid adherence to all the ideas and symbols of the past, no matter how much that tied your hands in the present. When I talked about it, my mother knew that I was becoming more pragmatic in my approach to the position of our own family. A restoration seemed to be, in my own case, for all practical purposes out of the question. I was a hundred per cent émigré and I had absolutely no ground under my feet in Vienna on which to fight. I had to appraise the situation realistically and abandon the position which could no longer be sustained and

> which did not anyway make much sense to me any more. Moreover, I felt that I could not be of any real use in the broader European field, which I was already seriously envisaging, if I went on being a pretender to one of the countries of that Europe.[205]

Despite this preparation of the ground, Zita was far from happy with Otto's decision to renounce his rights for Austria. Mother and son had not had an argument on this scale since 1938. But it should not be thought that Otto was happy about the situation an unjust law had placed him and his sons in. As he later reflected,

> There was indeed a debate with her about it, but this was nothing compared with the painful conflict going on inside me. All right, I [said] to myself, if I want to act on the European stage—and I had clearly seen that European path ahead of me since the Second World War—then I could not afford to get myself in a position of conflict as Pretender to the throne of any of those European countries which would have made it difficult for me to achieve my aims. So that is why I took the step I did, for purely practical reasons. But I must confess it wasn't easy for me, not because I harboured any illusions but because of the sheer infamy of what was being demanded. I mean, to insist that one had to resign from one's own family, that was such

---

[205] Gordon Brook-Shepherd, *The Last Empress* (London: HarperCollins, 1991), p. 318.

> a crazy idea which could only have come from the brain of some demented so and so.[206]

That brain from which the Habsburg Law—like its accompanying Nobility Law—sprang was, of course, that of Karl Renner. That such a man, even today, wields such influence from beyond the grave is a strange and bitter paradox for those who contemplate Austria from the outside with love and affection. The indignity for any Habsburg—or any decent individual, for that matter—to have to submit oneself to the order of such a person must be distasteful in the extreme.

In the end, Zita reluctantly came to accept Otto's opinion. "My final decision, which was only helped along by the birth of a male heir, did, I know, hurt her. But in her fair way, she realised that my arguments were very strong. In such a critical time, as always, she then backed me to the hilt. Many people tried to use her to influence me to change my decision, but she stood absolutely by me."[207] In any case, Otto's renunciation did not bind his sons, which doubtless made the bitter pill easier for Zita. Who knew what the future would hold? Indeed, a very different sort of Socialist from Renner—Bruno Kreisky—would begin working to allow both son and mother to return to see their homeland. In Otto's case, it would not happen until 1966.

In the meantime, Zita's other children were making lives for themselves. Adelheid worked with her brother Otto in various humanitarian pursuits, and Felix moved to Mexico.

---

[206] Brook-Shepherd, *Uncrowned Emperor*, pp. 181–82.
[207] Brook-Shepherd, *The Last Empress*, p. 319.

Rudolf and Karl Ludwig moved to Belgium, while Robert was close by his mother in Switzerland. And Otto continued his punishing touring schedule. Obviously, living in a religious house and joining her fellow tenants in the daily Mass and Rosary were a happy part of Zita's life. But there was more. The Gebetsliga, which had worked for Charles's beatification since his death, having regrouped after the war, was once again at work on its aim. Zita was, obviously, an important part of their efforts.

Her husband's cause received an important assist in the late 1960s when a Polish nun living in Brazil—Sr. Maria Zita—miraculously recovered from an incurable circulatory problem in her leg, which had left her bedridden and in great pain, progressively disabling her over the next six years. Urged to pray to Charles by one of her sisters who gave her information on the then servant of God, she initially refused. But so great was her suffering that, at last, she relented one night and did so. She was walking and able to kneel by morning after years of steady decay and months of inactivity. The miracle would be medically confirmed in 2003, but news of it reached Zita shortly after the occurrence. Upon hearing the cured sister's name, she replied, "Again, he is thinking of me!"[208]

Zita would be interviewed many times for her husband's cause, and it was the growth of interest in it that led to the building of a new chapel at the Church of Santa Maria do Monte to house Charles's coffin. To be present for the transfer of the remains, she thus returned to Madeira a second

[208] Private conversation of author with an acquaintance of the Empress.

time, with Otto and Adelheid, on January 10, 1968. It must have been an incredibly poignant journey for all three of them.

Always pious, as we have seen, Zita used the years in Zizers to become ever more devout. When driven past a church, she would cross herself, and when walking past a chapel, even with the door closed, she would genuflect as much as her age would allow. In time, when this act of respect became too much for her physical strength, she never passed a church or chapel where the Blessed Sacrament was reserved without a bow and a moment of silence. Likewise, she spent long minutes preparing for the Most Holy Mass and even more time recollecting herself in thanksgiving. Several witnesses speak of her spending approximately fifteen to thirty minutes in preparation for Mass and thirty minutes of thanksgiving afterward. According to one witness, "Her assiduity at the monastic Offices was remarkable, as was her love of the Eucharist—in the Holy Sacrifice of the Mass and in the adoration of the Blessed Sacrament."[209]

Freed from her family duties, she happily returned on an annual basis to the Abbey of St. Cécile. In particular, from 1955 to 1983, she came regularly for long stays, ranging from several weeks to several months. These were often in the summer, which allowed her to attend such major events of Benedictine life as jubilees, funerals, and openings of extensions to the buildings of St. Cecile's daughter house in Kergonan.

---

[209] Website of the Association for the Beatification of the Empress Zita (Archive).

The empress had given the Abbey of St. Cecile a truly remarkable gift back in 1939, which they keep to this day. It is a statue of the Child Jesus with neither arms nor legs. Archduchess Adelheid brought it back from Spain, where she had gone after the civil war, having wanted, since 1936, to aid the sufferers there. In a parish in the Basque Country, she was shown this same statue that Communists had taken out of the church to shoot, having torn off the Infant Jesus's arms and legs. The priest and parishioners generously offered it to the archduchess to thank her for her efforts. The half-dozen Basque lay sisters who had entered Solesmes had a particular devotion to this statue.

Attending all the Masses and the hours of the Divine Office with the sisters at St. Cécile at Zizers, Zita maintained a similar regime. The first Mass at the Johannesstift was at 7 a.m., followed by two others. So long as she was able, Zita assisted at the three Holy Masses one after the other; only then would she have breakfast. In the afternoon, she recited the Rosary at 5 p.m. with the other residents of the rest home. The empress would also pray the Rosary, following her personal recitation with the Litany of Loreto said from memory in Latin. Zita, of course, maintained all of her usual devotions to the Sacred and Immaculate Hearts, the Infant of Prague, Our Lady of Mariazell, and many others. Noticeable among these was her devotion to the Holy Cross, as epitomized by her always genuflecting in front of the large wooden crucifix hanging to the right of the entrance door to the part of the building she occupied in Zizers. This last was particularly fitting, given the role she had occupied (from

1916 until relinquishing it in 1951 to Otto's wife Regina) of High Protectress of the Order of the Starry Cross.

This position—like that of the Grand Mastership of the Order of the Golden Fleece passed down from Bl. Charles to Otto and now occupied by Archduke Karl, the current Head of the House—was and is a precious remnant of the imperial and royal days, although, as with the Golden Fleece, its religious position is more important than its historical status. The Starry Cross is that rare—but not unknown—thing: a chivalric, religious order for women. Since Empress St. Helena, mother of Constantine, found the True Cross in Palestine, and the Frankish Queen Radegonde received a large relic of it in Poitiers in 567 (for the reception of which Venantius Fortunatus composed the *Vexilla Regis*), many a female sovereign has had a deep devotion to the Holy Cross. Such devotion was also an integral part of chivalric spirituality, as well as the *Pietas Austriaca*—that particular kind of religiosity cultivated for many centuries by the House of Habsburg.

For a long time, the Habsburgs had venerated a particular relic of the True Cross. It was set in gold and worn by at least two Holy Roman Emperors, Maximilian II and Ferdinand III. The latter's last wife, Empress Eleanora, was given the relic by her stepson, Emperor Leopold I, after his father's death in 1657. On Candlemas Day, 1668, the newly built Leopoldine Tract of the Vienna Hofburg burned. The empress-mother successfully escaped the conflagration but was forced to leave her beloved relic behind. To her joy and amazement, after five days, the True Cross was found in the still-glowing rubble. The golden vessel had melted, and the rock crystal had broken, but the wood of the Holy Cross was miraculously preserved.

To commemorate this extraordinary event, the Order of the Ladies of the Starry Cross (*Sternkreuzdamen*) was founded that year by Eleonora. It takes its name from the reliquary the empress had made to hold the rescued relic. Surrounded as it is by chrysolites, garnet ribbons, and enameled flower petals, the relic is embedded in a gold-plated cross with a rock crystal cover, topped by a diamond-studded crown. The right sort of lighting off the gems gives the cross its "starry" appearance—something not usually visible to the observer viewing it today in the treasure chamber of the Hofburg. The Order was confirmed by Pope Clement IX on June 28 of that year and was placed under the spiritual direction of the Prince-Bishop of Vienna. Only noble ladies could receive the Order, including princesses, countesses, and other high nobility. Once invested, members were to "devote themselves to the service and worship of the Holy Cross, and to lead a virtuous life in the exercise of religion and works of charity."[210] Two decades later, another Eleanora—this one the wife of the first one's stepson, Leopold I—reformed the Order, making it the highest female Order in the land. The Viennese Church am Hof became, in a sense, the chapel of the Order, and the chapel of Petrus Canisius in that church had murals by Carpoforo Tencalla showing the Empress St. Helena with the Cross of Christ in her hand, depicting works of mercy, such as feeding the hungry and

---

[210] "Order of the Starry Cross," Wikipedia, https://en.wikipedia.org/wiki/Order_of_the_Starry_Cross.

freeing prisoners. The two great feasts of the Order remained the anniversary of the finding of the Cross in the ruined Hofburg on February 6, and the feast of the Finding of the Holy Cross (by St. Helena) on May 3.

As the years, decades, and finally centuries passed, the religious and charitable goals of the Order—while never entirely vanishing—took second place to its social and chivalric role. The beautiful decoration blazed upon many a beautiful dress at innumerable glittering balls and other ceremonies. Always the empress or—if she predeceased her husband—her daughter would serve as High Protectress for the Order. A noteworthy and joyful example of the Order's history was Empress Elizabeth's investing several Belgian ladies with it in 1881 after the engagement to a princess of that country by her son Rudolf. After her tragic murder in 1898, the headship of the Order went to the next senior lady of the House of Habsburg, the mother of the future Emperor Charles, Archduchess Maria Josepha. When Franz Joseph died and Charles ascended the throne, Zita, in turn, succeeded her mother-in-law and would remain High Protectress of the Order until her son Otto's wedding, as we have noted. But uneventful as her mother-in-law's incumbency had been, her own would be filled with all the challenges presented by the history we have already seen.

For one thing, as when her husband would not accept the Order of the Golden Fleece until he had read its statutes and was certain he could fulfill its requirements, Zita was determined that her position would not be purely *pro forma*. But she was greatly hindered after 1918 from governing the Order by the sad fact of exile. From the beginning, Zita worked hard to restore the religious nature of the Order, ensuring that the members recited the daily prayers from the Order's special prayer book. While the Order continued to meet in Austria to observe May 3 and other feasts under the presidency of one of Zita's two official assistants, they met with her annually to offer reports and receive instructions, while the Order's insignia were dispatched to new members by mail, rather than in investitures. The times when such insignia could be awarded began to be restricted from balls and the like to more purely religious occasions.

After Zita surrendered the leadership of the Order, its prayers and devotions continued to be a part of her daily life. Regina, in the meantime, followed her mother-in-law's lead by restricting the use of insignia to purely religious occasions; moreover, since she herself was unable to enter Austria after marrying Otto (and would continue to be until the regime relaxed its strictures in 1966), she altered the statutes to allow meetings in Germany; henceforward, she could preside at the May 3 observances to which she added a religious retreat starting on May 4 and the actual investitures of new members. Through all of this, of course, the different regional groups of the Order continued their own activities as well. In recent years, the feast of the Exaltation of the Holy Cross (September 14), Corpus Christi, and some other occasions have been added to the Order's calendar, and Archduchess Gabriela has continued her mother and grandmother's expansion of the religious role of the Order in the lives of its members.

Exile also produced another religious problem for Zita—the place where she would be buried with members of her family. As long as Austria was off-limits to her, there could be no thought of her joining her husband's family at the imperial crypt in Vienna, and her husband's grave at Madeira was well on its way to becoming a shrine. She had brought Charles's heart with her through her various places of exile, and it was an old Habsburg custom that hearts and bodies be buried separately. Where, then, could she and her children be buried?

An interesting alternative presented itself. Schloss Habsburg in Aargau, Switzerland, was the ancient seat of the family. In 1047, Radbot von Habsburg, builder of the castle, also built the monastery of Muri about thirty kilometers away. This would become the burial place of the Habsburgs and serve as their spiritual center until 1415 when the rebellious Aargau expelled the governor and joined the Swiss Confederation. But the family never forgot their roots—even as emperors. In 1562, Ferdinand I gave a coat of arms to the cloister; in 1580, Philip II, King of Spain and nephew of Ferdinand I, gave another; and in 1701, Emperor Leopold I made the Abbots of Muri prince-abbots. Driven from their home in 1841, when the monastery was seized by the Canton of Aargau, the monks moved to Gries in Tyrol four years later at the invitation of Ferdinand I. In 1941, on the centennial of the theft of the abbey, the Canton of Aargau returned the abbey to the Church, and it became the seat of the local parish.

So it was that, in 1970, Archduke Robert, on behalf of the entire family, signed a contract with the Catholic parish and the Muri community for a family crypt for Charles and Zita's immediate descendants. The crypt under the Loreto chapel of the abbey church, with space for fourteen burials, was inaugurated in the same year. The entrance is a trap door in the form of an iron grille, into which the imperial double-headed eagle with the Austrian shield is incorporated at the top, and the depiction of a rising lion from the coat of arms of the Habsburg family lies at the bottom. In front of this gate are removable floor panels with rings that make it easy to access the stairs below. The deceased rest in the level crypt space below in wooden coffins with metal inner coffins.

The first burials took place in the Loreto chapel in 1971. Charles's heart urn, which Zita had taken with her in her wanderings, was placed behind the altar grille, where it was buried in a brick stele on the back wall of the chapel. Robert's Russian wife, Xenia, who died in a car accident in Belgium in 1968, was now transferred from Bruges to Muri. Zita had spent a great deal of time with Robert and his children in the aftermath of that tragedy, creating memories that last until today for her grandchildren. Two years later, the funeral of Countess Kerssenbrock followed. She had been a faithful companion in Zita's wanderings, and the empress felt this loss very deeply. In 1975, tragedy struck Robert again when Johannes, his and Xenia's son, died and was buried here. Then, too, Zita spent several months with Robert and his surviving children.

In the meantime, the crypt at Muri remains a sacred place for the Habsburgs, who visit regularly and sponsor an annual Requiem Mass for those buried there. Rudolph organized a family meeting in Muri every May, which, in addition to the memorial Mass, also included a visit to the rectory. Zita visited the burial site annually on the anniversary of Charles's death to pray at the coffins. In September, she would attend a service commemorating her husband's death. Of her five sons, Robert, Felix, and Rudolph would ultimately find their resting place in the crypt of the Loreto chapel, while Otto and Karl Ludwig would—despite the anti-Habsburg laws—be entombed at the Capuchin crypt in Vienna. In a surprising reversal, so too would Zita.

Unfortunately, 1971 saw a great tragedy for Zita and the family—the death of her eldest daughter, Adelheid. She had worked closely with her brother Otto and lived near him at Poecking. As she had wished, Adelheid was buried in Tulfes, in Tyrol. This was to honor Tulfes's special relationship to the family: during the German occupation, Tulfes was the only municipality in Austria that did not revoke the "homeland rights" returned to the Habsburgs in 1934 during the Dollfuss government. However, because of Renner's continuing laws, Zita could not attend her daughter's funeral.

On a happier note, Zita's eightieth birthday, May 9, 1972, saw a very special guest join the family and friends gathering at Zizers: Cardinal Joszef Mindszenty, Prince-Primate of Hungary. The heroic Archbishop of Esztergom, who had left Hungary involuntarily at the command of Paul VI, had been present as a young priest at Charles and Zita's coronation. Between the wars, as a young priest and then as a bishop, Mindszenty had been a stalwart of the Monarchist cause, dedicating his first church at Zalaegerszeg to the deceased emperor in 1925 (Zita had donated the pulpit). As a rising star in the Church, he upheld the rights of the dynasty and the freedom of the people against both the Nazi-collaborating Arrow Cross and the Communists, calling for Otto's return to the throne up to the point of Soviet occupation. Afterward, he shared the suffering of his country at the hands of the Soviets and was brutally tortured and imprisoned. Released during the Hungarian uprising of 1956, he sought refuge in the American Embassy when the rebellion collapsed. There, he stood as a witness—as Prince-Primate, traditional holder of royal authority during an interregnum—to Hungary's undying nationhood during the following fifteen years. But for both Paul VI and Richard Nixon, intent on some sort of rapprochement with the Soviet Union, he had become an embarrassment. Ever-loyal Hungarian that he was, he refused to live in Rome as invited to by the pope and spent the rest of his life in Vienna's Pazmaneum, the Hungarian theological college.

This birthday visit was the first of several meetings the saintly bishop would have with his queen before he died. The pair chatted in fluent Hungarian, and the cardinal offered Mass afterwards. Mindszenty himself is now a venerable. Very fittingly, one of the Hungarian Habsburgs, Archduke Michael, is president of the board of trustees of the Mindszenty Foundation, which is overseeing his cause for beatification. When the august prelate died in 1975, he would be interred at the great shrine of Mariazell, as per his wish. After the fall of the Soviet Bloc, he would be reentombed at Esztergom, in his cathedral—a ceremony in which Otto would play a prominent part.

Enjoyable as this reunion with Mindszenty was, the death of Countess Kerssenbrock in 1973 was a great blow. Zita and her sister Isabella were then joined by the much younger Baroness Maria Plappart, whose presence made things much easier. But as the '70s went on, more of her friends and acquaintances from the various decades died, icluding Mindszenty. But at the same time, her descendants multiplied: for her ninetieth birthday on May 9, 1982, fifty of her descendants gathered at Zizers. For many of the younger generation, this would mark the first time they had met.

Tremendous as this personal gift was, later in the month, at last behaving with some decency, the government of Austria dropped all objections to her visiting her Austrian realm. On May 16, 1982, Austria's last reigning empress thus far returned, crossing the border at Feldkirch from which she had left the country sixty-three years earlier. It was a day trip to Tulfes, where she could visit Adelheid's grave.

This first visit was the prelude to a number of others. On August 17, Zita visited Schloss Waldstein, near Graz, where her youngest child, Elizabeth, now a Princess of Liechtenstein, lived. The empress spent three weeks with her daughter and family in what would become an annual custom for the remaining summers of her life. While there, she visited Mariazell on September 1, where she and Charles had prayed together at the start of their married adventures together; she also prayed at Cardinal Mindszenty's tomb. No less than eight thousand pilgrims joined her there. The following summer, she would visit Sankt Jakob im Walde, where she and Charles had gotten engaged. But during this first stay, she also gave a large number of interviews and was the subject of a great deal of media attention. A nation of orphans, at last, was able to see its mother once more.

Zita returned in October to visit her mother and brother's graves at Pucheim in Upper Austria. Here, in the castle chapel dedicated to St. George, are buried not only Maria Antonia and Prince Rene (who died in 1962) but Zita's aunt, Maria das Neves, and her husband, Alfonso Carlos (I) of Bourbon and Austria-Este, the last Carlist claimant. The castle would remain in the Bourbon-Parma family until 1993.

But the following month witnessed the greatest triumph yet of an already triumphant year: Zita's return to Vienna. On November 13, Cardinal Franz Koenig offered Mass for the empress and a congregation of ten thousand at the Stephansdom; an overflow crowd watched the proceeding outside. When she arrived at the main entrance of the cathedral, the city councilor for the First District addressed her thusly: "Your Majesty, a hearty welcome awaits you in the old Imperial Capital!"[211] As she walked through the main door, the band of the Hoch-und-Deutschmeister Regiment played the imperial anthem. It must have been a terribly bittersweet moment for this woman who had seen and endured so much. One can only wonder what went through her mind as she sat in the front pew, surrounded by grandchildren and great-grandchildren.

In March of 1983, Zita would surprise a great many by granting a series of interviews with the Viennese tabloid, the *Kronenzeitung*. The topic was the nineteenth-century version of the Kennedy Assassination, the Mayerling Affair, which, as we saw, had the effect of pushing her husband

---

[211] Leo J. Hammerschmid, *Zita: The Last Empress of Austria* (Montreal: Meridian Press, 1989), p. 244.

toward the throne. She declared that, far from being an insanity-driven suicide pact, Mayerling was, in fact, a political murder. Crown Prince Rudolf had been assassinated by foreign agents because he had uncovered an international conspiracy to overthrow his father. When asked for proof, she replied,

> Alas, all proofs, that is, documentary proofs, have either disappeared or cannot be found. . . . But the surest proof is that it would have been out of the question in those days for a suicide to be given a Christian burial, and the Vatican at first immediately forbade this. Only after a detailed telegram had been sent to the Vatican by the Emperor Francis Joseph explaining the situation was permission for the funeral given.[212]

Gordon Brook-Shepherd, her foremost English-language biographer (who had the privilege of knowing her and is usually very sympathetic), opined about this episode,

> No serious historian has ever accepted this foreign murder scenario which, indeed, caused some private embarrassment among the empress' family at the time. But her motive in putting it forward seems plain. The Mayerling affair was the darkest of all religious blots on the Habsburg family escutcheon. To wipe it clean might in some way help the last Habsburg ruler to make that escutcheon shine with sainthood.[213]

---

[212] Brook-Shepherd, *The Last Empress*, p. 321.
[213] Brook-Shepherd, *The Last Empress*, p. 321.

This would seem a logical reading of the affair, were it not for one nagging fact that was brought to this writer's attention a few years ago. The monks of Heiligenkreuz Abbey, to whom the bodies of Rudolf and his mistress were delivered after their discovery at Mayerling, maintain the tradition that the Crown Prince's fingers were all broken. This implies to them that he unsuccessfully attempted to hold the bedroom door shut—with a table, perhaps—and, in any case, rules out his committing either murder or suicide. A check of the remains in the Kaisergruft would, of course, end the question. But if the fingers were intact, it would mean both Zita and the monks were wrong; if not, it would reopen a mystery that, at this late date, has never been solved—and which would do little to help the efforts of the family in the here and now.

Zita would return to visit Vienna again the following Pentecost for an outdoor Mass on the Heldenplatz near the Hofburg. Over 130,000 people—many of them Sudeten Germans expelled from Czechia after 1945, and so sharing Zita's experience of loss and exile—joined her there. She was, moreover, only feet away from the Heldentor with its Tomb of the Unknown Austrian Soldier of World War I. This memorial is flanked by two commemorative plaques: one for Franz Ferdinand and the other for Bl. Emperor Charles—respectively, the first and last victims of the Great War.

The following year, Zita suffered another loss on July 30, when her beloved sister and housemate at Zizers, Princess Isabella of Bourbon-Parma, died at the age of eighty-six. She was laid to rest in the crypt at the castle chapel of Schloss Wartegg, where Zita and Charles had first sought refuge in exile. It was also there that Zita's mother, Isabella, and brothers, Rene, Felix, Louis, and Gaetano, lived during World War I.

On a visit with her sons Otto and Robert to the Vatican, she met with Pope John Paul II. The pope welcomed the Habsburg family very happily and approached Empress Zita. She knelt and kissed his ring. The pope then said that he ought to be kneeling, declaring that he was facing "his empress." After speaking warmly and at very great length about Emperor Charles, Pope John Paul II asked, "Do you know why my name is Karol? [Charles, in English]. Because my father was very admiring of Emperor Charles of Austria, of whom he was a soldier! So he named me Karol in honor of him."[214] The loyalty the now canonized pope felt for Zita's husband would culminate in 2004 when he personally swept away objections to Charles's beatification on the part of both political and ecclesiastical opposition from Austria.

The last few years of Zita's life settled into a regular routine with the summer visits to Waldstein and occasional trips to places like Belgium to see her children. The people with whom she interacted at Zizers came to regard her very much as their own. They remembered her as at once elegant and informal, able to set them at their ease and yet revealing little of herself.[215] Her companion, Baroness Plappart, helped her get around, and despite her failing eyesight, she continued

---

[214] Marzena Devoud, "Why John Paul II's parents chose to call him Karol," Aleteia, March 31, 2022, https://fr.aleteia.org/2022/03/31/pourquoi-les-parents-de-jean-paul-ii-ont-choisi-de-lappeler-karol/.

[215] Ursina Straub, "She was 'a woman with dignity,'" Südostschweiz, March 14, 2014, https://www.suedostschweiz.ch/zeitung/das-war-eine-frau-mit-wuerde.

to follow both family doings and political occurrences in the former empire with great interest.

Zita was certainly very proud of the first stirrings of freedom in the East. After Otto began returning regularly to Hungary in 1985, she began questioning him carefully about the living conditions of the people there. Hungary was always as close to heart as Austria; on one occasion, when being interviewed and speaking of the difficulties Hungarian politicians had presented, she stopped herself and said, "but then, I shouldn't be talking this way. I AM the Queen of Hungary!"[216]

The winter of 1988–89, however, took a hard toll on her. When it had passed, Zita stayed in her apartment at the Johannesstift. During the weeks before her death, she called each of her children to her side and told them, "I shall soon depart from this Earth."[217] She did not go over the past, nor did she give any recommendations to them for the future. In early March, the empress slipped into a coma; she would not regain consciousness. Her children and their spouses took it in turns to watch over her. It was while Otto's wife, Regina, was keeping the vigil a few minutes before 1 a.m. on March 14, 1989, that Zita breathed her last. So it was that one empress passed away under the care of another.

The following day, her body was brought to the hospital in Chur, where her heart was removed. It was then placed next to Charles's at the Loretto chapel in Muri. But whereas Zita had thought she would be buried in exile when the new

[216] Brook-Shepherd, *The Last Empress*, p. 324.
[217] Hammerschmid, *Zita: The Last Empress of Austria*, p. 245.

Habsburg crypt was fitted out, the years of her rapprochement with Austria and negotiations by Otto and his son Karl ensured a very different fate for her earthly remains. Her body was placed in a wooden coffin encased in a metal one and was indeed exposed for prayer at Muri. But on March 27, the coffin was brought over the border and exhibited in state in the Marble Hall of Austria's great Augustinian Monastery of Klosterneuburg—a longtime recipient of Habsburg favors. Despite the continuing presence of the Soviet Empire, many of the thousands who filed by to pay their respects were Hungarians, Czechs, and others from Zita's lands who made their way across the Iron Curtain to join their Austrian brethren. After three days, the coffin was brought to the Stephansdom, the site of her triumphant return seven years before. Tens of thousands of mourners filed past her coffin with its purple pall and signed the books of remembrance. While the Austrian government gave permission for the rites to be held on the soil under the regime's control, as a last indignity, it insisted that every penny of the two hundred thousand pounds the funeral would cost would have to be raised by the family itself. They did so.

On April 1, 1989, sixty-seven years after Charles's death in Madeira, the Stephansdom witnessed a Pontifical Funeral Mass for Zita, accompanied by Mozart's *Requiem*. More than a hundred flower wreaths adorned both sides of the main entrance of the cathedral. On the ribbons were the last greetings of kings, archdukes, orders of knights, political parties (including the Hungarian Independence Party, the MDF), the Czech city of Ústí nad Labem, the mayor of Vienna, and others—in all the languages of the monarchy. Cardinal Groer, the Archbishop of Vienna, was the main celebrant, assisted by the Hungarian primate and bishops from Chur, Feldkirch, Katowice, Brno, and Augsburg. The Mass was attended by the empress's children, grandchildren, and fourteen of her great-grandchildren. There were innumerable dignitaries of various kinds, among whom were royals from Luxembourg, Liechtenstein, Spain, Morocco, Belgium, Jordan, and Monaco. The ambassadors of Turkey, the United States, Belgium, the Netherlands, and Canada were given special seating as a testimony to the assistance those countries had given the empress at various times after 1918.

The first reading was given by Archduke Karl, Otto's older son and future head of the dynasty; the second was read in Hungarian by Princess Elizabeth, Zita's youngest daughter. Prayers were offered in Latin, German, Hungarian, Italian, Czech, Slovak, Serbian, and Polish for the peace of the peoples of the Danube basin and Europe, for the grace of faith, hope, and love, and for God to graciously accept the life sacrifice of Emperor and King Charles, and that Empress and Queen Zita would have peace in Heaven as well. When the Mass ended, both the imperial and Hungarian anthems were sung as Zita's coffin was slowly carried to the rear of the cathedral. Outside, it was placed on the old black hearse built for imperial funerals in 1876, which had carried the coffins of Crown Prince Rudolf, Empress Elizabeth, and at last, Franz Joseph. At Zita's funeral, six black draft horses were used, courtesy of the Federal Stud in Stadl-Paura, who also provided the coachman.

Over forty thousand people lined the streets of Vienna's city center. During this time, the bells of the churches in the city center were also rung. The funeral procession lasted around three-quarters of an hour and moved, through dark clouds and a thunderstorm, from Stephansplatz by way of Graben and Kohlmarkt to Michaelerplatz and the front gate of the Hofburg; from there, the cortege wended its way through the Stallburg by way of Josephsplatz to the Albertina. At last, the route led along Tegetthoffstrasse to the Neuer Markt and the Capuchin church. Under this building is the imperial crypt—the Kaisergruft.

In addition to the Habsburgs, numerous delegations from student associations and traditional military associations from the area of the former Austro-Hungarian monarchy took part in the funeral procession, including numerous *Landsmannschaften* (Catholic, monarchist student fraternities), around 850 riflemen from North and South Tyrol, numerous citizen guards (local ceremonial units, often with band), the *Kaiserjäger*, and the Carinthian Trabanten bodyguard from St. Veit an der Glan. Civilian associations from the territory of the Austro-Hungarian Empire were also represented in their traditional costumes, such as the Transylvanian Saxons, and a number came from Soviet-ruled areas. The procession was accompanied by a total of four music bands, and an artillery division of the Kollerschlag Citizen Guard fired a twenty-one-gun salute from the Albertina.

At last, the funeral procession stopped in front of the locked door of the crypt. The herald, Heinz Anton Hafner, knocked on the door. Father Gottfried Undesser, the custodian of the Capuchin crypt, then responded from inside, "Who wants entry?"[218]

---

[218] "Imperial Crypt," Wikipedia, https://de.wikipedia.org/wiki/Kaisergruft#Begr%C3%A4bniszeremonien.

Hafner answered, "Zita, Empress of Austria, Apostolic Queen of Hungary, Queen of Bohemia, Dalmatia, Croatia, Slavonia, Galicia, Lodomeria, and Illyria, Queen of Jerusalem, Archduchess of Austria, Grand Duchess of Tuscany and of Krakow, Duchess of Lorraine and Bar, of Salzburg, Steyer, Carinthia, Carniola and Bukovina, Grand Princess of Transylvania, Margravine of Moravia, Duchess of Upper and Lower Silesia, of Modena, Piacenza and Guastalla, of Auschwitz and of Zator, Teschen, Friuli, Ragusa and Zara, Princess Countess of Habsburg and Tyrol, of Kyburg, Görz and Gradisca, Princess of Trent and Brixen, Margravine of Upper and Lower Lusatia and Istria, Countess of Hohenems, Feldkirch, Bregenz and Sonnenberg, Mistress of Trieste, of Cattaro and the Windische March, Grand Voivode of the Serbian Voivodeship, Infanta of Spain, Princess of Portugal and of Parma!"

Fr. Undesser replied, "We don't know her!"

Hafner knocked again. Once more, the question was asked, "Who wants entry?"

This time, the herald answered, "Zita, Empress of Austria and Apostolic Queen of Hungary!"

But the answer was again, "We don't know her!"

He knocked a third time and was asked the same question. Now, Hafner responded, "Zita, a mortal and sinful woman."

Thereupon, the gate was opened with the words, "Let her come in!"[219]

After this ceremony, the coffin was taken by six Tyrolean riflemen into the monastery church. The Viennese

---

[219] "Imperial Crypt," Wikipedia, https://de.wikipedia.org/wiki/Kaisergruft#Begr%C3%A4bniszeremonien.

Capuchins formed a trellis with candles, and the Vienna Boys' Choir was housed on a tribune in the "Imperial Chapel." As part of a short service accompanied by music from the boys' choir, Cardinal Franz König gave a speech and carried out the blessing.

The coffin, accompanied by the friars of the Capuchin monastery and the rest of the clergy, was then quietly carried down the stairs from the interior of the monastery church to the Capuchin crypt by six employees of the Vienna Funeral Service. While the above-mentioned salute was fired from the Albrechtsrampe (Albertina) in honor of the deceased, her coffin, followed by numerous family members, slowly passed in silence through the rooms of the "Leopoldsgruft," "Karlsgruft," "Maria-Theresiengruft," and the "Franzensgruft," and was finally placed on the ground in front of the altar of the "Crypt Chapel" at the same time as the last of the salute shots. After the family members had gathered there, Zita's eldest son Otto, in the presence of his brothers Karl Ludwig, Rudolph, Felix, and Robert, handed over the symbolic key to the coffin to Father Undesser. He addressed those present and invited them to pray. After the common Hail Mary, Cardinal König quietly blessed the coffin with Holy Water, then spoke briefly to the members of the family. After a life spent in exile, Zita had at last come home.

Chapter 14

A SAINT AMONG SINNERS?

We cannot know how much we learn
From those who never will return,
Until a flash of unforeseen
Remembrance falls on what has been.
We've each a darkening hill to climb;
And this is why, from time to time
In Tilbury Town, we look beyond
Horizons for the man Flammonde.

—Edward Arlington Robinson,
"Flammonde"[220]

The sheer arranging of the empress's funeral had an impact of its own in central Europe. The revival of such a spectacle after so many decades and the necessary cooperation of so many to make it happen was something of a catalyst. For one thing, the reenactment and rifle units that took part had been coordinated by Alexander Sixtus von Reden, a member of one of these units and author of a book published two years previously on such formations. He was in touch with

220 "Flammonde," https://www.gutenberg.org/files/1035/1035-h/1035-h.htm.

several illegal or semilegal units in Hungary and Czechoslovakia as well. To thank all the organizers, Otto distributed certificates signed by him, 1,600 of which were given to von Reden's preparatory committee, and around 400 more were handed over, mostly to various *Landsmannschaften* (Catholic Austrian Student Organizations) as well as other smaller organizations. Baron von Reden, together with Roman Baron von Gamotha, designed the Zita Memorial Cross for participants in the funeral and used the certificates of gratitude received from Archduke Otto as certificates for this award. The date of the foundation was Empress Zita's birthday, May 9, 1989, and Otto was named the founder. The gold-colored cross of the award follows the shape of the war memorial cross that was given out by Emperor Charles in 1918 but was then no longer issued. In the middle is a coat of arms with the initial "Z" for Zita, surmounted by the Austrian imperial crown and the Hungarian royal crown. The burial date, "1st IV. 1989," is inscribed on the back of the cross. The ribbon is in the color of the empress's standard (pink) with a black-yellow-red-white-green central stripe—the colors of Austria and Hungary. In all, about 1,600 of these would be given out to various participants, the first decorations given out (other than the Orders of the Golden Fleece and the Starry Cross) by the head of the House since 1918.

On this foundation, the "Military Chancellery for Traditional Regiments, Citizens, and Rifle Corps on the Territory of the Former Austro-Hungarian Monarchy" was founded in Vienna in 1989 and constituted as an association in Regau in 1993. Named after the point of contact between the emperor and the Imperial and Royal Army leadership, the new military chancellery was created in response to the re-establishment of numerous citizen corps and traditional regiments in the successor states of the Danube monarchy after the fall of Communism. Baron von Reden was initially entrusted with its management. This organization has played a key role in the growth of such traditional units—and their coordination in various cultural events, many having to do directly with the memory of the Habsburgs.

But as the emergence of such units in Communist countries presaged, mere months after the death of Empress Zita, the Soviet Bloc's collapse—a key date in which was an event inspired by Otto, the famed Pan-European Picnic, that gathering on the Hungarian border and featured the breaking open of a small section of the Iron Curtain. This was held on the Austro-Hungarian border near Sopron, Hungary, on August 19, 1989. The border gate between Austria and Hungary was opened at this event, food was served, and East German refugees surged through. Thus began a series of events that would, in time, see Germany reunified, the Iron Curtain fall, and the Eastern Bloc disintegrate. The Communist governments and, following them, the Warsaw Pact subsequently dissolved, the Cold War ended, and as a result, the Soviet Union ultimately collapsed. A horrible burden was lifted off the shoulders of mankind. As Wordsworth wrote in a very different context, "Bliss was it in that dawn to be alive, but to be young was very Heaven!"[221] Many saw in that rapid fall the first fruits of Zita's death; some even attributed the end of the Soviet Bloc to her intercession.

---

[221] William Wordsworth, *The Prelude*, Book 11.

Moreover, as the years went by, her husband's cause came closer and closer to achieving beatification, which finally occurred at the Vatican on October 3, 2004. In his homily that day, the pope declared that,

> The decisive task of Christians consists in seeking, recognizing and following God's will in all things. The Christian statesman, Charles of Austria, confronted this challenge every day. To his eyes, war appeared as 'something appalling.' Amid the tumult of the First World War, he strove to promote the peace initiative of my Predecessor, Benedict XV. From the beginning, the Emperor Charles conceived of his office as a holy service to his people. His chief concern was to follow the Christian vocation to holiness also in his political actions. For this reason, his thoughts turned to social assistance. May he be an example for all of us, especially for those who have political responsibilities in Europe today![222]

Zita's own cause would be introduced in time. But at the moment, devotion to Bl. Charles—and so curiosity about Zita—spread wildly in Catholic circles, not least in the United States. As of this writing, there are thirty shrines in honor of Bl. Charles in the United States of America, and the branch of the Gebetsliga there is very active. Bl. Charles appeals to so many people for different reasons. As an exemplary husband, father, and son (the latter in what

[222] Pope John Paul II, Homily, *Beatification of Five Servants of God*, October 3, 2004, https://www.vatican.va/content/john-paul-ii/en/homilies/2004/documents/hf_jp-ii_hom_20041003_beatifications.html.

amounted to a broken home), he is a tremendous guide and example for people living in those situations. As a wise and just ruler, and a valiant yet humane soldier, he appeals to any with aspirations to lead—or to be led by someone with those qualities, so lacking in the world today. Indeed, the kind of self-sacrificial and Christ-like leadership he offered is rare in many corners of Church or state in our time. In a word, once one gets to really know him, the emperor-king is hard *not* to love. His effective intercession continues; since his beatification, another miracle has been approved—the curing of a then non-Catholic woman with cancer—and, at this writing, it appears as though a third miracle may be *en route* to approval.

Not too surprising, especially given the choice of his feast day, the cause for Zita's beatification was opened. As the website of the association for her beatification tells us,

> In 2008, the Congregation for the Causes of Saints at the Vatican authorized opening the process of beatification for Empress Zita in the Diocese of Le Mans. The reason for this is because from 1899 to 1989 Solesmes (in the Diocese of Le Mans) was the spiritual center for the Empress: three of her sisters were Benedictines at Sainte-Cécile Abbey where the Empress frequently stayed, remaining in contact there until the end of her life. Moreover, the Empress was an oblate of Saint-Pierre Abbey in Solesmes.[223]

[223] Website of the Association for the Beatification of the Empress Zita (Archive).

Her cited virtues were as "Wife and Mother, Faithful Widow, Simplicity, Humility, and Charity."[224] As with Bl. Charles—and in part driven by the growth of his *cultus*—interest in the Servant of God Zita has grown exponentially in the United States, where the headquarters of the cause is at Solesmes's daughter Abbey of Our Lady of Clear Creek in Hulbert, Oklahoma. At the time of this writing, her authoritative spiritual biography is being compiled, for which people who knew her are being interviewed, her letters and other writings are being examined, and in essence, her life is being examined with a fine-toothed comb. If nothing untoward emerges and the reasons for the opening of the cause appear justified by the results, then the Church will issue a decree that she lived a life of "heroic virtue," and she will, henceforth, be called "Venerable Zita." If her intercession subsequently produces at least one miracle, she shall be beatified and called "Blessed," as is her husband. At that point (unless he has been canonized in the meantime), their causes for canonization shall be united; if, as, and when the time comes that they are canonized, they shall have the approbation "Sts. Charles and Zita, Confessors," with the feast of October 21.

But we are quite a long way from that event if indeed it comes to pass. Unlike Charles, Zita lived a long time and dealt with a great many more people than her husband, and not all of those were entirely pleased with her. She was a forceful woman to be sure; one person who knew her said to

---

[224] Website of the Association for the Beatification of the Empress Zita (Archive).

me that, while on the one hand, he personally was sure that she was a saint, he would not have been surprised to find that she ate iron filings for breakfast.

But in trying to understand her, it has struck me that Zita might well have been haunted by the memory of her great-great-grandmother, the Duchess of Berry, who, as you may recall, essentially abandoned her son's cause by seeking personal happiness in a marriage (and beginning a family that still survives in Austria), thereby destroying her usefulness to that cause. Raised by a father, Robert of Parma, who, in turn, was raised by that abandoned son, Henry, Comte de Chambord, we can only imagine what effect that story had upon Zita when she found herself in the same position. What we can know is that as difficult as she may have been for those around her at times, without her, Otto and his brothers and sisters could and would not have been who they were—and that in itself is no small achievement, given how little she had to work with.

Another thing that must be borne in mind is that if she is indeed beatified, this shall raise the stock of the House of Habsburg as a whole, as did the beatification of Bl. Charles. While not a reason for beatification (and for some, a good reason *against* it), it points out another issue. For both Charles and Zita, their religion and their politics were inseparable. At the end of the day, their desire for a Danubian Confederation achieved through a Habsburg restoration—as with their son's desire for a Union of Europe—was not a question of self-aggrandizement or of simply bettering the position of the dynasty. Rather, they saw the vocation of their family as one of divine origin. In a real sense, achieving that vocation was not mere self-fulfillment but a God-given duty to their subjects, whose happiness in this life—and so, to some degree, in the next—depended upon it. It is for precisely this reason that Bl. Charles offered his death agonies "that his peoples might come back together,"[225] and that their eldest son dedicated his life—when convinced that he could not pursue precisely the same ends due to the current situation—to bringing together, in a free and Christian union, all of the European peoples, each of which various of his ancestors had reigned over. To the best of her ability, and mindful of her own dynasty with whom the history of the House of Habsburg was so intertwined, Zita did her very best to help her husband and children achieve what she saw as their God-given destinies.

Of course, we are no longer living in 1918 or even 1989. The fall of Communism and the moral collapse of the West has created an entirely new situation, where only some of the nations over which Charles and Zita once ruled seem to have any idea of a healthy alternative to either western European/American-style moral decay, or Russian-style authoritarianism. Otto saw a Habsburg Confederation of Danubian states as unattainable in his time and so chose to work for a sort of renewed Christendom. Regardless of what Europe or the world may need for political salvation, however, each of us still requires for our personal spiritual salvation precisely what Charles and Zita sought. Each of us in our daily lives faces some form of the challenges that they also faced.

[225] Nathan Cochran, "Blessed Karl of Austria: A Short Biography," Gebetsliga, https://www.gebetsliga.com/english/emperor-karl/biography/.

Quite possibly, he, as a Blessed, and she, as a Servant of God, achieved what all of us are called on to pursue.

That said, I asked a woman active in Zita's cause what attracted her most to the figure of the empress. Her response was, "I was impressed by the fact that although called on time and again to do the most difficult things imaginable, she always did so as a faithful Catholic woman. Today, that is an example that all of us women need." I could not help but think that the same was true of Bl. Charles as a paradigm for modern Catholic masculinity. In this, as in so much else, the imperial couple were very well matched.

AFTERWORD

And so, we have come at last to the end of our story. Ever since beginning the book on Bl. Charles in 2018, I have lived with the tale of the last reigning Habsburgs. Having corresponded with their son Otto from the time that I was in high school until his death (and having met him twice), I can say that he has played a large role in my own intellectual formation, and therefore, so did Charles and Zita—albeit secondhand. In the past five years, I have met a number of their descendants and relatives, visited many of the places where their drama was lived out, and traveled all over their dominions, which has strongly reinforced my affection for them both. Certainly, both research and experience have strengthened my understanding of and regard for them, and if I have been able, through either or both of these books, to pass on some of the religious, cultural, and political gifts they have given me in this fashion, then I have begun to repay the debt I owe them.

Charles A. Coulombe
Trumau, Austria
November 8, 2023
Feast of St. Michael and All the Heavenly Powers
(Byzantine Calendar)

APPENDIX I

French,

I am in the middle of you.

You opened the doors of France to me and I could not deny myself the happiness of seeing my homeland again.

But I don't want to give, by a prolonged presence, new pretexts for the agitation of minds so troubled at this moment. So I'm leaving the Chambord that you gave me and whose name I have borne with pride for forty years, on the paths of exile. By moving away from it, I want to tell you, I am not separating myself from you, France knows that I belong to her. I cannot decline that monarchical right is the patrimony of the nation, nor decline the duties which it imposes towards it. These duties, I will fulfill them, believe my word as an honest man and as a King. God helping, we will found together and when you wish, on the broad foundations of administrative decentralization and local franchises, a government in conformity with the real needs of the country. We will give as guarantees to those public liberties to which every Christian people is entitled, universal suffrage, honestly practiced, and the control of the two chambers, and we will resume by restoring its true character, the national movement of the end of the last century. A minority revolted against the wishes of the country made it the starting point of a period of demoralization by lies and disorganization by violence. Its criminal attacks imposed the revolution on a country which asked only for reforms and consequently pushed it towards the abyss where yesterday it would have perished, without the heroic effort of our army. It is the working classes, those workers in the fields and in the towns, whose fate has been the object of my keenest concerns and my dearest studies, who have suffered the most from this social disorder. But France, cruelly disillusioned by disasters without examples, will understand that one does not return to the truth by changing error, that one does not escape by expedients from eternal necessities. She will call me and I will come to her completely, with my devotion, my principle and my flag. On the occasion of this flag, I was imposed conditions that I must not undergo.

FRENCH!

I am ready to do anything to help my country rise from its ruins and regain its place in the world. The only sacrifice I cannot make to him is that of my honour. I am and I want to be of my time, I pay a sincere homage to all its greatness, and whatever the color of the flag under which our soldiers marched, I admired their heroism, and gave thanks to God for all that their bravery added to the treasure of the glories of France.

Between you and me, there must be no misunderstanding or ulterior motive. No, I won't leave, because ignorance or credulity will have spoken of privileges, absolutism, or intolerance, what else do I know? of tithes, of phantom feudal rights, which the most daring bad faith tries to resurrect in your eyes, I will not allow the standard of Henry IV to be snatched from my hands, of François I and Joan of Arc. It is with it that your fathers, led by mine, conquered this Alsace and this Lorraine whose fidelity will be the consolation in our misfortunes. It defeated barbarism on this land of Africa, witness to the first feats of arms of the princes of my family. It is what will overcome the new barbarism with which the world is threatened. I will entrust it without fear to the vigilance of our army: it has never followed, the Army knows, except the paths of honour. I received it as a sacred deposit from the old King my ancestor, dying in exile. It has always been for me inseparable from the memory of the absent fatherland, it has floated over my cradle, and I want it to shade my grave.[226]

[226] Chambord Manifesto (July 1871), https://www.demainlamonarchie.com/documents-lettres-discours-citation.

APPENDIX II

I had authentic information from the Archduke Karl, and I learned a great deal from men who worked for the Archduke Franz Ferdinand and were familiar with his political principles. There is no doubt that the Archduke had ideas about the internal constitutional structure of the Monarchy and the principles on which it should be reformed which were in sharp opposition to the principles of those in authority in Hungary. This very fact was a national crime in their eyes. None the less, although many of his political friends thought to win the favour of the Archduke by Magyarophobe memoranda, and although Tisza and all the other influential Hungarian politicians feared the heir-apparent, because they were alarmed for their own power, it does not by any means follow that the Archduke hated Hungary. That was not the case. I have a thorough knowledge of the principles which governed the Archduke's political thought. I have gradually assembled the various parts that complete the picture. Nowhere have I come across any signs of that hatred of Hungary which was and still is falsely imputed to him. The blame for spreading this legend mostly belongs to those who feared him or who far overshot the mark in their blind zeal. From my study of his personality I have emerged convinced that he would have been a great Emperor and a worthy wearer of the crown of Saint Stephen, for this crown was sacred to him, far more sacred than to those Magyars who, when he came to their country, received their King crowned with the crown of Saint Stephen with machine gun fire. It was not the Hungarians that Franz Ferdinand hated, but the selfish, chauvinistic Magyar leaders in Hungarian politics, whom he recognized as Hungary's most dangerous enemies. Them he did hate. And he hated them with the passionate determination native to him.

As these political leaders were almost the sole representatives of Hungary, it was only natural if the feelings of hatred which Franz Ferdinand felt more or less impersonally for the chauvinistic policy of Hungary, became generalized into hatred for Hungary itself. But I believe that I am not wrong in asserting that the then heir to the Throne rightly recognized that by maintaining Hungary intact he was safe-guarding the most precious jewel in his crown. For this reason he devoted special attention to Hungarian conditions. Nothing interested him more than what was happening in Hungary, nothing made him more uneasy than the short-sighted policy of the privileged leaders of Hungary, for, from the point of view of her future sovereign, he realized that this policy was bound to endanger the existence of Hungary in an extreme degree. The melancholy final phase shows how correct the Archduke's judgment was. It would, however, be a great mistake to think that the World War alone was responsible for Hungary's melancholy end. The World War merely hastened her ruin. It would have happened in any case. The national will of the non-Magyar majority of the population of Hungary would have made itself felt by revolutionary methods in any circumstances. The hate of the Archduke Franz Ferdinand, therefore, was not for Hungary and the Magyars, but for those who by their political power ruled Hungary to her detriment, and this was the reason why they and their innumerable satellites in business circles looked forward with dread to the reign of Franz Ferdinand. A well-directed bullet released them from this dread. The then Hungarian deputy, Prince Lajos Windischgraetz, who arrived in Budapest immediately after the Sarajevo murder, describes the atmosphere then prevailing in the Hungarian capital in the following words: "Political circles in Budapest were as if released from a nightmare. Undisguised joy was apparent in Tisza's party. A sigh of relief seemed to go up from the country!"[227]

[227] Polzer-Hoeditz, *The Emperor Karl*, pp. 53–54.

BIBLIOGRAPHY

Bassett, Richard. *For God and Kaiser: The Imperial Austrian Army*, 1619–1918. Yale University Press, 2015.

Becsi, Zoltan. *Forbidden Federalism: Secret Diplomacy and the Struggle for a Danubian Confederation 1918–1921*. Helena History, 2020.

Bogle, James and Joanna Bogle. *A Heart for Europe: The Lives of Emperor Charles and Empress Zita of Austria-Hungary*. Gracewing, 2000.

Brook-Shepherd, Gordon. *The Last Empress*. HarperCollins, 1991.

———. *The Last Habsburg*. Weidenfeld & Nicolson, 1968.

———. *Uncrowned Emperor: The Life and Times of Otto von Habsburg*. Bloomsbury, 2007.

Viscount Bryce, James. *The Holy Roman Empire*. MacMillan, 1871.

von Coudenhove-Kalergi, Richard. *Pan Europe*. Knopf, 1926.

Debris, Cyrille. *De choses et d'autres - Le surnaturel dans la vie de l'Impératrice Zita*. Presses de la Deliverance, 2018.

———. *Zita: Portrait intime d'une Impératrice*. CERF, 2014.

Demmerle, Eva. *Kaiser Karl, Mythos & Wirklichkeit*. Amalthea Signum Verlag, 2016.

———. *Das Haus Habsburg*. HF Ullmann Verlag, 2011 and 2014.

———. *Otto von Habsburg*. Amalthea, 2007.

———. *Der Habsburg-Faktor: Visionen* für das *neue Jahrtausend. Eva Demmerle im Gespräch mit Otto von Habsburg*. REDLINE, 2007.

———. *Kaiser Karl I. „Selig, die Frieden stiften ..."* Amalthea, 2004.

Feigl, Erich. *Kaiserin Zita: Von Oesterreich, Nach Oesterreich*. Amalthea, 1986.

Harding, Bertita. *Imperial Twilight: The Story of Karl and Zita of Hungary*. Bobbs-Merrill, 1939.

von Habsburg, Eduard. *The Habsburg Way: Seven Rules for Turbulent Times*. Sophia Institute, 2023.

von Habsburg, Otto. *Charles V*. Weidenfeld and Nicolson, 1967.

———. *Die Reichsidee. Geschichte und Zukunft einer übernationalen Ordnung*. Amalthea, 1991.

———. *The Social Order of Tomorrow: State and Society in the Atomic Age*. Newman Press, 1959.

Hammerschmid, Leo. *Zita: The Last Empress of Austria*. Meridian, 1989.

Heer, Friedrich. *The Holy Roman Empire*. Phoenix, 2002.

Holborn, Hajo. *A History of Modern Germany, 1840–1945*. Princeton University, 1982.

Judson, Pieter. *The Habsburg Empire: A New History*. Harvard University Press, 2016.

von Lichem, Heinz. *Karl I: ein Kaiser sucht den Frieden*. Tyrolia, 1996.

Longo, James. *Hitler and the Habsburgs*. Diversion Books, 2018.

Gies McGuigan, Dorothy. *The Habsburgs*. Doubleday, 1966.

Wess Mitchell, A. *The Grand Strategy of The Habsburg Empire*. Princeton University Press, 2018.

Montfort, Elizabeth. *Charles et Zita de Habsbourg: Itineraire Spirituel d'Un Couple*. Artege, 2021.

Nichols, Aidan. *Christendom Awake!* T. & T. Clark, 1999.

Count Polzer-Hoditz, Arthur. *The Emperor Karl*. Putnam, 1930.

Unowsky, Daniel L. *The Pomp and Politics of Patriotism: Imperial Celebrations in Habsburg Austria 1848–1916*. Purdue University Press, 2005.

Unterreiner, Katrin. *Emperor Franz Josef, 1830–1916: Myth and Truth*. Brandstätter Verlag, 2015.

Vivian, Herbert. *The Life of the Emperor Charles of Austria*. Grayson and Grayson, 1932.

Walsh, William S. *Curiosities of Popular Customs*. J. B. Lippincott, 1897.

Wassensteiner, Friedrich. *Franz Ferdinand – Der verhinderte Herrsher*. Verlag Kremayr & Scheriau GmbH & Co. KG, 2014.

Wiesinger, Alois. *Occult Phenomena in the Light of Theolog*. Newman, 1957.

Winkelhofer, Martina. *The Everyday Life of the Emperor: Francis Joseph and His Imperial Court*. Haymon, 2012.

Online Resources

Ballinger Fletcher, Zita. "Blessed Karl: A True Soldier." http://www.emperorcharles.org/blog/2019/6/29/blessed-karl-a-true-soldier.

Fux, Ildefons Maria. "Der selige Karl von Österreich und seine Beziehung zum Heiligsten Herzen Jesu," https://www.stjosef.at/artikel/sel_karl_v_oesterreich_herzjesu.htm.

Kovács, Elisabeth. "Kaiser Karl Research." https://www.elisabethkovacs.com/neue-forschungen-zu-kaiser-karl/.

Gebtsliga Central Site. https://www.gebetsliga.com.

Gebetsliga Worldwide. https://www.gebetsliga.com/home/wander-reliquie/weltweit/.

Gebetsliga North America. http://www.emperorcharles\.org/.

Friends of Empress Zita. http://associationimperatricezita.com/2340-2/.

Archduke Karl von Habsburg. https://www.karlvonhabsburg.at/.

Finis Austriae. https://finisaustriae.it/.

World of the Habsburgs. https://www.habsburger.net/en.

GAZETTEER

AUSTRIA

Vienna

Vienna Hofburg. http://www.burghauptmannschaft.at/php/detail.php?ukatnr=21196&parent=21187.

Michaelerkirche. https://www.michaelerkirche.at/en/.

Augustinerkirche. https://augustinerkirche.augustiner.at/.

Kapuzinerkirche. https://www.kapuziner.at/kapuziner/wo-wir-sind/wien/.

Kaisergruft. https://www.kapuzinergruft.com/site/en/home.

Stephansdom. https://www.stephanskirche.at/.

Schottenstift (Charles' School). http://www.schotten.wien/schottengymnasium/schulgeschichte/.

Teutonic Order. http://www.deutscher-orden.at/site/home.

Imperial Chancellery. https://www.bundeskanzleramt.gv.at/en/federal-chancellery/visit-us.html?lang=en.

Austrian Parliament Building. https://www.parlament.gv.at/ENGL/PERK/HIS/MON/index.shtml.

Votivkirche. https://www.votivkirche.at/.

Karlskirche. http://www.pfarre-karlskirche.at/.

Palais Augarten (Charles' childhood home). http://www.burgen-austria.com/archive.php?id=90.

Belvedere Palais (Franz Ferdinand's town house). https://www.belvedere.at/das-museum.
Schönbrunn. https://www.schoenbrunn.at/en/.
Schlosskapelle Schönbrunn. http://www.schlosskapelle.at/.
Hofmobiliendepot (Imperial Furniture Collection). https://www.hofmobiliendepot.at/en/.
Military Chancery (Headquarters for reenactment units). http://www.militaerkanzlei-wien.org/.
Schloss Hetzendorf. https://www.wien.gv.at/bildung/schulen/modeschule/schloss/architektur.html.
Schlosskirche Hetzendorf. https://www.schlosskirche.at/.
Hermesvilla. https://www.wienmuseum.at/de/standorte/hermesvilla.html.
Canisiuskirche. https://www.pfarre-canisius.at/.

Lower Austria

The Castles at Laxenburg. https://www.schloss-laxenburg.at
Kaiserhaus Baden. http://kaiserhaus-baden.at/.
Schloss Frohsdorf. http://petit-versailles.com/.
Schloss Shwarzau. https://www.justiz.gv.at/web2013/ja_schwarzau/justizanstalt-schwarzau~2c94848542ec4981014449659e7c401f.de.html.
Schloss Persenbeug. http://www.persenbeug.at/.
Villa Wartholtz. https://schloss-wartholz.at/.
Schloss Artstetten. https://www.schloss-artstetten.at/en/.
Schloss Eckartsau. https://www.schlosseckartsau.at/.

Upper Austria

Kaiservilla, Bad Ischl. https://www.kaiservilla.at/index.php/en/2-uncategorised/1-welcome-en.

Styria

Basilica of Mariazell. https://www.basilika-mariazell.at/.
Gasthaus Orthofer, Sankt Jakob in Walde. https://www.orthofer.at/.

Tyrol

Basilica of the Sacred Heart, Tyrol. https://www.herzjesukloster-hall.at/.

HUNGARY

Budapest

Royal Castle. http://budacastlebudapest.com/.
Coronation Church: https://www.matyas-templom.hu/main.php?Lang=EN.
St. Stephen's Basilica. http://en.bazilika.biz/.

Pest

Royal Castle, Gödöllő. http://www.kiralyikastely.hu/main_page.

Vas

Bishop's Palace, Szombathely. http://www.latogatokozpont.martinus.hu/angol.html.

Komárom-Esztergom

Esterházy Palace, Tata. http://www.museum.hu/museum/1634/Esterhazy_Palace/actual?f.

Esztergom Basilica. https://www.bazilika-esztergom.hu/hu/?nyelv=2&oldal=28.

Veszprém

Tihany Abbey. http://www.tihanyiapatsag.hu/Tihanyi_Bences_Apatsag.html.

Bl. Charles IV Chapel, Ajka. https://plebaniaajka.wordpress.com/miserend/boldog-iv-karoly-kapolna-csinger/.

Győr-Moson-Sopron

Pejachevich Palace, Sopron. https://sopronanno.hu/bejegyzes/a-pejacsevich-palota.

Charles IV Chapel, Denesfa. http://denesfa.hu/kiralykapolna/a-kiralykapolna.html.

Abbey of Pannonhalma. https://bences.hu/lang/en/.

CZECHIA

Prague

Prague Castle. https://www.hrad.cz/en/prague-castle-for-visitors.
St. Vitus Cathedral. https://www.katedralasvatehovita.cz/en.
Charles-Ferdinand University. https://cuni.cz/UKEN-106.html.

Central Bohemia

Chateau Brandýs nad Labem. http://www.brandyszamek.cz/.
Basilica of St. Wenceslaus, Stara Boleslav. https://www.staraboleslav.com/indexAJ.php.
Karlstejn Castle. https://www.hrad-karlstejn.cz/en.
Konopiste Castle. https://www.zamek-konopiste.cz/en.
Chlum Castle. https://www.chlumutrebone.cz/zamek.

North Bohemia

Zakupy Castle. https://www.zamek-zakupy.cz/en.

Karlovy Vary

Imperial Kurhaus, Františkovy Lázně. https://www.imperialfrantiskovylazne.cz/en.

CROATIA

Dubrovnik–Neretva

Lokrum Island. http://www.lokrum.hr/eng.

POLAND

Silesia

Habsburg Palace, Cieszyn. http://www.zamekcieszyn.pl/.

ITALY

South Tyrol

Karlspromenade, Brixen. https://www.hiwio.com/de/Artikel/Karlspromenade-bei-Brixen-114.

Hotel Elephant, Brixen. https://www.hotelelephant.com.

Friuli-Venezia Giulia

Miramare Castle, Trieste. http://www.miramare.beniculturali.it.

San Giusto Cathedral, Trieste. http://www.sangiustomartire.it/.

Tuscany

Villa Borbone, Pianore. http://www.comune.camaiore.lu.it/it/arte-cultura/villa-le-pianore.

SWITZERLAND

Aargau

Muri Monastery. https://www.murikultur.ch/habsburger.

Habsburg Castle. https://www.ag.ch/de/bks/kultur/.museen_schloesser/schloss_habsburg/schloss_habsburg.jsp.

Sankt Gallen

Schloss Wartegg. https://wartegg.ch/en/.

Geneve

Villa Prangins. https://www.golfdomaineimperial.com/en/page-history-p3.php.

Grisons

Sankt Johanns Stift, Zizers. https://www.suedostschweiz.ch/ereignisse/2019-08-30/eine-neue-schlossherrin-in-graubuenden.

FRANCE

Pays de La Loire

Abbaye Sainte Cecle de Solesmes. http://www.saintececiledesolesmes.org/.

Centre-Val de Loire

Chateau de Chambord: https://www.chambord.org/en/.

Auvergne

Chateau de Bostz: https://presence-bourbon.com/presentation-vieux-bostz/.

BELGIUM

Brabant

Castle Ter Ham, Steenokkerzeel: https://www.kasteelterham.be/en.

GERMANY

Bavaria

Kloster Zangberg: http://www.kloster-zangberg.de/.

ENGLAND

Isle of Wight

St. Cecilia's Abbey, Ryde: https://www.stceciliasabbey.org.uk/.

Nottinghamshire

Wellbeck Abbey: https://www.welbeck.co.uk/.

St. Mary's Catholic Church, Worksop: https://worksopcatholicchurches.weebly.com/st-marys-worksop.html.

SPAIN

Madrid

Palacio El Pardo: https://www.patrimonionacional.es/real-sitio/palacio-real-de-el-pardo.

Vasconadas

Uribarren Palace, Lekeitio: https://www.hoteles-silken.com/en/hotel-palacio-uribarren-lekeitio/.
Basilica, Lekeitio: http://basilicalekeitio.blogspot.com/.

MADEIRA

Funchal

Our Lady of Monte Church: https://en.wikipedia.org/wiki/Church_of_Our_Lady_of_Monte.
Reid's Palace Hotel: https://cosmopolis.ch/reids-palace/.
Quinta do Monte: https://ifcn.madeira.gov.pt/quintas-e-jardins/quintas/quinta-do-imperador.html.

UNITED STATES OF AMERICA

Massachusetts

La Bastille House, Royalston: https://www.nehomemag.com/all-is-calm/.

New York

The Empress' Palace, Tuxedo Park: http://www.tuxedoparkrealestate.com/propertydetails.aspx?propertyid=77.

CANADA

Quebec

Spencer Grange Villa, Sillery: https://www.ville.quebec.qc.ca/citoyens/patrimoine/bati/fiche.aspx?fiche=2159.